TELEVISION: THE CREATIVE EXPERIENCE

TELEVISION: THE CREATIVE EXPERIENCE

A Survey of Anglo-American Progress

Edited by A. WILLIAM BLUEM *and* ROGER MANVELL

Communication Arts Books
HASTINGS HOUSE, PUBLISHERS
New York

Library of Congress Catalog Card Number 67-15345

Printed in the United States of America

Contents

I. THE ART AND TECHNIQUE
OF TELEVISION DRAMA

After some deliberation, the editors agreed that the style established in each of the journals, Television Quarterly *and* Journal of the Society of Film and Television Arts, *from which these articles and essays are taken should be preserved. If the problems and challenges of the medium in both England and the U.S.A. are similar enough to warrant the combination of views that are presented here, the editorial styles of the two journals are different—in all matters from spelling (e.g. programme/program) to layout and editorial commentary. It seemed best, therefore, to allow the standard differences of spelling which occur in the British and American contributions to remain unchanged, more particularly as this book is intended for both the American and the British reader.*

A regular television service was initiated in Britain in 1936 by the BBC (a broadcasting corporation set up by Royal Charter for broadcasting in sound) but the service was closed down when war was declared in 1939. The BBC resumed television in 1946, gradually expanding it from the London area to achieve a national coverage.

The Television Act of 1954 authorised the establishment of the Independent Television Authority to appoint and supervise a number of commercial television companies which collectively in 1955 began to provide a competitive national service.

The BBC was authorised to initiate a second channel in 1964 on 625 lines on the UHF channels. Colour Television test transmissions by the BBC began in 1955.

Television was initiated in the U.S.A. in the 1940's by the established radio networks, such as the Columbia Broadcasting System (CBS) and the National Broadcasting Company (NBC), under the control of the Federal Communications Commission.

There are now over 700 local stations in operation; of these more than 100 are non-commercial.

The Editors wish to express their sincere appreciation to the two organizations which have supported the publications from which the selections in this book have been taken. In the U.S.A., our thanks to the Editorial Board of "Television Quarterly" and to the Trustees and members of the National Academy of Television Arts and Sciences. In Great Britain, to the "Journal of the Society of Film and Television Arts."

Introduction

TELEVISION is a medium with an immense future but almost no past As a branch of broadcasting, it could draw at first on the experience of sound radio; as a picture medium it could derive initially some pointers in technique from the cinema. But it was soon discovered that neither of these media was anything like the same as television, and that those dedicated to television had to create their own way of developing a medium which was in so many respects unique. Their main problem was they had to try out the various potentialities of television before the rapt gaze of millions, whose eager but conservative patronage only too often limited the scope of the medium before it had had any chance to expand properly and demonstrate what it could do in both entertainment and information.

On both sides of the Atlantic, executives, directors, writers, actors, and technicians have all felt the need to map the territory they were exploring and exchange ideas on the potentialities of the home screen. They have found their principal platform in two journals: in the United States it is the *Television Quarterly*, founded in 1962 and published by the National Academy of Television Arts and Sciences in co-operation with Syracuse University under the editorship of A. William Bluem; in Great Britain it is the *Journal* of the Society of Film and Television Arts, edited by Roger Manvell and founded in 1959 as the successor to the *Journal* of the British Film Academy. (The Academy amalgamated in that year with the Guild of Television Producers and Directors to form the Society of Film and Television Arts.)

This book is an anthology of essays and discussions originally published in these journals. It forms a survey which reflects the thinking in America and Britain about television by those responsible in one way or another for what has been and is being produced. The rapid developments that have taken place in a very short time are reflected in the range of these pieces. Authors have in each case been invited to add any footnotes they thought necessary in the light of their later knowledge and experience; otherwise what appears here is printed in the form in which it was first published, and the original date of publication should in each case be kept in mind.

The essays and discussions have been grouped under broad headings which reflect the various fields of television production, and as far as possible contributions on each subject included have been matched from each country. Though most of what appears in this book is the result of direct experience in production, we have included a number of essays speculating on the future and emphasising what those working in television would like to see it undertake.

What emerges from this anthology is the sheer vitality of the best in British and American television programming, its very close relationship to the public it serves, and the growing sense of responsibility that exists in many lively minds among those working for it. Complacency and apathy caused by the sheer, endless turn-over of programmes are the television programme-makers worst enemies. We hope these articles show that television has in its service many people capable of making it a medium of the first importance in our communities.

A. WILLIAM BLUEM
ROGER MANVELL

I

THE ART AND TECHNIQUE OF TELEVISION DRAMA

L'Âge d'Or

A. WILLIAM BLUEM

IT was the best and worst of times, a period of excess and excitement, fun and failure, adventure and despair. It was carried along by its own momentum for over a decade, and when America's great romance with the tube gradually turned into a comfortable *mariage de convenance* there were those who said a "Golden Age" of American television had gone by. The phrase has since found a place in all serious assessment of what TV was, is, and might become. But it has been observed that the description is vague—that it means too many things to too many people. Certainly there is some room for a not-quite-final word on what it was.

One begins, of course, by acknowledging the bitter and unrelenting few who refuse to admit that commercial television ever attained any creative mark whatever. To the grim and the dedicated, the entire period was characterized by a steady downward slide toward some kind of mass media-ocrity. It required, after all, little sensibility to see the straws in the wind, for from the outset the medium has carried a heavy payload of what might generously be described as culturally valueless and socially unredeeming. If one prefers to recall only Faye Emerson, "Uncle Miltie", Dagmar, roller derbies, *Man Against Crime* and wrestling, then the whole age was one of tarnished brass which reached its expected and inevitable end in the infamous "Quiz scandals".

Most observers, however, are inclined to regard TV's early years with enthusiasm. If there was little that was pure gold, there was a lot that glittered. Fondly remembered are *Omnibus*, Pat Weaver, a handful of fine short plays, Halley and Kefauver, *Wide Wide World*, the Army-McCarthy hearings, *Peter Pan*, *Your Show of Shows* and Murrow. There was *Project XX*, *Victory at Sea*, *Matinee Theater*. And if Hubbell Robinson's great *Playhouse* 90 seemed the end of an era to some, a post-1957 surge of actuality, documentary and public affairs programming made possible the argument that as one Golden Age died another was born. There are those who insist that the medium never really approached maturity until it finally moved to make reportage one of its prime functions.

In any general terms, then, it is difficult to locate those vague "beginnings" and "ends". The medium has grown and it has diminished. It has been adult and it has been childish. It has been magnificent and the dear Lord knows that it has been trivial. But it has been all of these from the start and only the shortest of memories would permit one to say that it has ever been all good or all bad.

Still the phase persists, and it retains a useful and precise application in the study of current medium performance because a hard core of tough, talented critics and creators have given it meaning. There *was* a Golden Age, they contend—with a real beginning and end, and a genuine and specific content.

It began with *Kraft Television Theatre* on 7th May 1947, and it closed with the final production of *Playhouse* 90 ten years later. The content was anthology drama—stories of human conflict and confrontation played with honesty and authority in living sight, sound and motion before audiences the size of which no actor, writer or director in all theatrical history would have dared to dream.

It was Hebbel who said that the theatre is "the only possible pause in a man's existence", and from the outset American television has had its share of artists and entrepreneurs who saw in this electronic marvel only those awesome possibilities for bringing multitudes into a state of engagement with themselves and their individual and collective destinies. Since Thespis committed the significant act of asking his fellow Greeks to pretend that he really *was* deity or humanity incarnate, the theatre has been that single art which carried man outside himself in order that he might better see within himself. The action, said Thespis and his descendants, is *here*—in the threshing circle, inside the proscenium arch, and within the shifting frames of the large and small screen. This was where man could see life as it is or as it ought to be. This was where he could share, through the direct and physical terms of human reenactment, that magic blend of intellectual detachment and emotional involvement which is the true *theatrical* experience.

For the "hard-line" Golden Ager this is what television is all about. It is not quite cinema and not quite the living stage. It allows for intense visual concentration, and yet at its best it is verbal. In some ways TV is the penultimate technological extension of the naturalistic drama and its rejection of romantic superficiality in favor of the vital inner revelation of human character. The entire theatrical movement toward realism in acting and staging seems to culminate upon the small screen, where it can work out its own absolutes of form and style.

Little matter that the *cinéaste* deplores the shaky lines of light upon the tiny screen. No difference that the stage-bound theorist pompously declares the medium "incapable of grandeur". Television is the medium of the mass, and here alone can the man in the living room see his private tragedy delineated with a final degree of refinement. If twentieth century man has any tragic proportion, it is observed, the events and circumstances of his time have perfectly scaled it to fit the small screen.

All of this was understood, or sensed, and so they began. Those eager Medici, networks and advertisers, were happy enough to foster their experiment. As hard and practical "communicators" they foresaw those endless hours of time stretching ahead into a limitless and profitable future, and they were astute enough to recognize that the natural *entra'cte* of the drama would provide convenient moments in which someone with something to sell might "borrow" the audience.

But in those halcyon days no one impugned anyone else's motives. Very few troubled to challenge the direct transfer of many habits and strictures from commercial radio to video. Nor, since the new medium was visual, did anyone question the justifiable and logical turn to the stage and the movies for forms of fiction, fantasy and fun.

Only later, when the medium began to dominate the time and attention of an entire population, did the regretting begin. Later, when such phenomena as "audience passivity" and "cultural democracy" began to pose hard and real dilemmas, the criticism grew shrill. Only later did the artist discover the hard fact that in an age of instantaneous mass communication he was merely another vested interest in the fight for that most precious of all commodities—the attention of an entire civilization. With that discovery, the Golden Age was over. It is a tribute to him, and to a much maligned medium, that the fight still rages. The artist's concern with quality in drama on Television is reflected in the following essays by American and British creators.

1 The TV Producer: A Dialogue*

GEORGE SCHAEFER

LEWIS FREEDMAN

INTERVIEWER: Many serious critics want to write television off as a medium in its own right; they insist it serves no serious creative purpose. We hear that television drama is a debased extension of the film, that creators are stifled by quick production techniques and working conditions that would not otherwise be tolerated. How do you feel about his?

MR. FREEDMAN: This business about being rushed—I think that's true of any art and any artist. It is certainly true of the Broadway theatre. It is true of movies. When Michaelangelo came down from the ceiling of the Sistine Chapel after nine years he probably complained about being rushed. I don't think you can create anything that deserves the name of creation; you never have enough time. You make the time you have do. Yet, my experience in television is that it is unnecessary to operate in a continual state of panic.

MR. SCHAEFER: Strangely enough, I find that I have more time in television than I had in my last theatre experience or, in a certain respect, than one has in the movies. In the ninety-minute shows I do, we rehearse for three weeks. If you balance out rehearsal hours against each minute of performance—allowing time to rework and remold—you naturally have a full, but more than adequate, schedule. In television you have that wonderful feeling that you can go back

---

* Television Quarterly, Spring, 1962.

and take a whole new approach. You say, "Gosh, why didn't we think of this? Let's go back and do the whole first act with this in mind." And you do have the time to do it.

You can't do this in the movies. The scene you shot that very first morning is what's going to be in the final screening. You can't go back. The most wonderful thoughts can conceivably develop out of your relationship with the actors by the second and third weeks of shooting, but they're worthless to you. You've got to close your mind to them because if you make that change *now* the past two weeks are dead footage. And who can afford to go back and re-do two weeks of film shooting?

So it is true, I think, that all art forms present their own limitations. Things must be done under pressure and television at its worst *is* extreme pressure, but at its best it is certainly no more rushed than other media.

MR. FREEDMAN: I've found that many of my own productions were more leisurely than they might have been in other media. When I observed the preparation of productions for Broadway they held "casting emergency" sessions in July and weren't even going into rehearsal until September! Their problem seemed as real to them as mine at this very moment—when I have to go into rehearsal on Wednesday and don't have a leading man. Yet, the leading man I will get may turn out, because of the pressure, to be more *right* than if I had him weeks ago. Perhaps that extra pressure will help me work in greater depth than I would have otherwise. Pressure doesn't have to hurt; it can help.

MR. SCHAEFER: I'm amazed, and impressed, by the procedures followed in some of the filmed series that come from the coast. The speed with which they *cast* them! Even in live television, and under pressure, you will sit down and try to figure out who might be good for this part well in advance of rehearsals. Out there I think actors must live by their telephones. The casting department or producer will throw five or six "good ideas" at you, and in forty-five minutes the deals are closed and the casting is settled. It's a different way of working.

It seems to me that the elements which contribute to panic in television are usually involved with, and stem from, the producer or director who must control time. Problems arise when a director hasn't sufficiently organized his plan of action, or when a producer delays decisions until the last possible moment and then tries to change everything a director has already done. This leads to chaos during the most precious period of rehearsal. The fine performances we see on the medium come not out of chaos but out of careful organization.

INTERVIEWER: What new problems are posed by taping? Are there some advantages? Does the "security" of taping make much difference in achieving quality in TV drama?

MR. SCHAEFER: I don't think it makes any difference. The basic problems are not helped that much by tape. Of course, if you're doing a show on tape you know that if the scenery falls on the actors, you can do the scene over again.

INTERVIEWER: Does the use of tape make any difference in scheduling? Is the schedule opened out a bit, allowing more freedom and time?

MR. FREEDMAN: No. The trap one gets into in tape—and of which we're all aware—is that people begin to use tape *like* film. They take an infinite amount of time to make an infinite number of repeats. I think this is a mistake, and I think it is bad for the performer. He knows he is going ahead ten lines, then back three, then ahead for ten more. Then you begin to get cliché performances—superficial performances. If tape is controlled, as it can be and as many of us have tried to prove, you can get the same tension, the same immediacy, which advocates of "live" TV performance say you cannot get out of an electronic or mechanical device.

INTERVIEWER: Let's turn to the question of the writer in television. Despite the critical onslaught under which the "Golden Age" has been buried by those who have started to look seriously at the "kines", we know that over three hundred original hour-long plays were written for three series during the 1950–1955 period, and that a small but significant share of them were fine, enduring works. At least there were enough of them to say, "Yes, Virginia, there *was* a 'Golden Age' in television". What is happening now? Who is writing TV drama now?

MR. SCHAEFER: There are a number of writers who would like to do nothing but original plays for television. The most obvious fact is that there is no place to use them any longer. The whole problem is complicated by the economics of the industry, combined with the degree of network and sponsor security that comes in a filmed series. These series have really taken over the hour dramatic form. I think that in all probability good authors are writing for filmed series. But with the limited time they can give to any one work it is very seldom that you will find a distinguished script.

MR. FREEDMAN: That's a problem for the producer. Five years ago a producer was deluged with scripts and ideas for TV shows because there were TV shows and series that might use them. A producer could scan the field and select material to work with. We now find that we are producing a series of dramatic shows for which all sources of supply have dried up. Too many writers have gone to the coast, where they are writing *on order*. If they have an original idea they try to turn it into a stage play and then aim it toward the films.

My job as a producer, I find, has become that of meeting as many writers as possible and trying to suggest to them that there could be a market. I'm afraid I don't make a very convincing case for it. It's a funny position to be in. I find it's forcing me closer to my concept of what a producer should really be—the man who creates. A producer is a magician. He comes out with nothing up his sleeve and five minutes later he's got a rabbit. Which is, I suppose, better than an egg.

INTERVIEWER: What conditions would have to exist to promote the development of an original anthology drama for television again?

MR. SCHAEFER: I'm not sure, but some good things are happening. This year the *Dick Powell* and *Alcoa* shows have moved into anthology writing, and some of the writing on these series has been remarkably distinguished. Of course it's all filmed, rather than "live" or taped "New York type" of production, but it's very healthy. It is *not* "writing to specifications". You know that the writer is not curbed by what has gone before. No one tells him to "do this because this is the way the characters have to behave".

The problem of the moment, I think, is to get the "live" hour and ninety-minute series *on*. As soon as there is an outlet for this kind of writing it will burst forth. The writers are still around.

MR. FREEDMAN: Yet, if you pause to consider, there is probably more fiction—that's the only word I can use—more *fiction* on television than ever before. We have fictitious characters involved in fictional situations, working out their problems. So when they talk about a "Golden Age", they are really referring to a *New York* "Golden Age" of "live" drama.

INTERVIEWER: But isn't the distinction which is pinned upon the "Golden Age" such that it offered the original, self-contained works as opposed to "writing-to-order"—to the established formats and characterizations of situation strips?

MR. FREEDMAN: Yes. The "fiction" we now talk of has moved away from a conflict of psychology or character, or a conflict of morality, to a conflict in *action*, and that's why we've had the move to film—because film is the best medium for activity. The "live" studio can't do it, with or without tape. That's why "live" TV and the theatre are better suited to a static form in which the action is *interior*. Let me ask *you* a question, George. We've both worked with stage plays, and then in TV. Do you find some in-built problems in bringing a stage play into TV?

MR. SCHAEFER: Tremendous problems. As long as they are *serious* plays—really *dramatic* vehicles—the problems are minimal, because these were originally written to have an individual, personal impact, and that's what you're dealing with in television, too. But the comedies or farces written for the theatre—those things designed to tickle the collective funnybone of a lot of people sitting together—create terrific problems in TV. You rarely sweep somebody away in television. The kind of disbelief that is needed for this broad stuff can't be found in the home. When you're in a full theatre, watching from beginning to end, you accept the silliest kinds of jokes in the third act of a good comedy. You howl at them in the theatre, but at home you'll say, "Oh, come *off it!*".

Even satire is different on television. I can only compare it with a *New Yorker* cartoon. It's very close to that. The message of a cartoon is purely personal. It hits or it doesn't. Ten people may look at the same cartoon and have quite different reactions. That's what happens with comedy on television. Those whose sense of humor matches the style of the person who makes the joke may be amused, and others just say "hmfff". And you are absolutely dead if you try to please them all. Many TV shows have been trapped in this way.

The most successful workers in TV comedy have been able to get past this block, usually with tongue in cheek. Sid Caesar at his best does it. Ernie Kovacs was brilliant at his. He would take off on an idea, often a wild one, and make it *work*. You accept the fact that people with a certain sense of humor are not going to buy this, and you still forge ahead. You must try not to lose confidence in your own sense of humor. This means disaster, because then you, and everyone else, begin to tamper with the comedy—and no one will be amused.

MR. FREEDMAN: I like Bergson's definition of laughter—a gesture from one person to another which shows how they feel about something. When you're sitting alone at home with no one there to make the gesture *to*—or with people with whom you share such identical attitudes that you don't need that kind of communication—then the idea of comedy is altered. You need the group for *funny!* The most you can aim for on TV dramatic shows is just *fun*. Chuckles and smiles. But it's too hard to get that out-loud laughter which lets people know, let's them hear you say, it's funny.

MR. SCHAEFER: While watching TV, I'm never amused by either canned laughter or "live" laughter. In fact, for me it slows it all up. If a comic is amusing me, and I have to wait for a studio audience to laugh, I get impatient. I say, "Get on with it. Be funny again." This is different from the theatre, too. There, the playing style is different, and it's geared to the audience. You don't mind the wait, you're part of it, really.

MR. FREEDMAN: The problem we've always had is the first act. That long stretch of mood-setting which you can afford when you've got people sitting in a theatre who have paid $8.80 for their seats. They're not going to get up and leave, but in TV, people will walk out.

MR. SCHAEFER: We finally decided that if they're going to watch for ninety minutes they're going to have to give us ten minutes in order to know what they're seeing. I don't think we ever lose an audience because of the necessity for exposition. It's a greater problem in the hour-long show, however. But on the very special shows, certainly on *Play of the Week*, audiences were willing to stay around and get to know what was happening.

MR. FREEDMAN: If people are really willing to wait ten or fifteen minutes while you're getting acquainted, the show has a chance to really develop and be a rock-crusher.

MR. SCHAEFER: Sometimes, after I've read the reviews, I've said to myself, "I can't believe that the critic really gave it his attention beyond the first getting-acquainted period".

MR. FREEDMAN: It's probably true that no matter how great your ending is, if the show is a slow starter a lot of people won't be there for the finish.

MR. SCHAEFER: You can *try* to use production techniques, but how far you can go before losing every bit of honesty is another matter.

INTERVIEWER: Is there something important about the continuous "live" performance of the stage, as against the rush of television or the doing it by odd-and-bits as it must be done in the film?

MR. SCHAEFER: It's an entirely different thing. When people say that television is an actor's medium in a way that films are *not*, they're completely right. A non-stop "live" TV performance has the same quality of a theatre performance simply because actors are carrying the ball. The pulse of the thing—the believability, truth, and excitement of it—are in the hands of the performer. Of course the influence of the writer and director are there too. But at the moment, the performers are telling the story and making the points. This isn't so in the movies. The tempo, the whole impact of a scene, is often set by the director and the editor when the actors are miles away doing another picture.

MR. FREEDMAN: And with tape, there's a matter of compromise. We tape an entire act at a time, and no one can stop it except the director or producer. Once the actors begin, whether it's for nine minutes or twelve minutes or forty-five minutes for a single scene, it has to *go* and nothing can stop it. Now, if the actors know this, they can give a performance. They can't *help* it, because if there's anything there at all they're caught up in it themselves, and it begins to have a cumulative thrust that you can get in theatre. There's nothing in the nature of tape which makes it impossible to get the impact and continuity of "live" performance. You go wrong only if you begin to chip away at it.

MR. SCHAEFER: It's impossible to use tape like film. Mechanically you can't edit tape that well. But something worse happens. I remember a show this season in which they just went wild. It was full of roll-overs and bursts and flashes, and I'm sure the average member of the audience didn't know what was causing it; he was probably trying to adjust his set all through the show. Ignoring mechanics, it's just foolish to attempt to do with tape what you can do with film. Film editing is a precise art in which you can deal with single frames, and all of your sound effects and dialogue and music can be added separately and with utmost control. You're working in an exact, scientific way, and it's one of the most exciting elements of film work. None of this is possible on tape.

MR. FREEDMAN: I remember that show. It was an hour-and-a-half special, and it was edited almost minute by minute. It was a brilliant editing job, but the show lost all of its lifelikeness. You could almost say it had seeped away between the splices. In between the pieces, the life just went out of it.

MR. SCHAEFER: The result is like a first rough-cut of a film. None of it is *right;* nobody's really answering anybody else. It's all wrong, and yet it's sort of all there. But in film you can spend weeks, sometimes months, picking up the beats and the breaths and the changes and the looks, and then finally you make it all of a piece. You add the sound later, and with its tremendously unifying capacity you ease over things which are still pictorially bumpy. In tape you don't have this. You just cut the tape and put a little strip behind it and hope it stays together. It goes bim, bam, bump—it just can't flow.

Certainly the best thing television can do in entertainment—not in news or public affairs, which is an exciting world to itself—is to catch actors and actresses performing in a good play at the very peak of their abilities, with the scene flowing, taking off, going back and forth, building in that wonderful interplay that great actors and actresses have. The audience is able to be on the spot and catch this in closeup, where you can almost see the actors think. The great moments of television happen then—as in *Days of Wine and Roses* and in some of the things we've been able to catch on *Hallmark*, where actors were communicating at a level of performance that you could see nowhere else *but* on television.

MR. FREEDMAN: And when television gets that good it becomes actuality. You have that kind of excitement—when top actors are *going* and they know nothing's going to stop them—which you might get at an actual event like a McCarthy trial or a parade up Broadway.

MR. SCHAEFER: And this is only possible in the theatre on different terms. There may be some *truth* taking place, but actors are trying to reach a balcony and play to thousands of people. They're projecting, talking louder, signaling to the audience with their bodies and their attitudes. Now here is something distinct that *only* television can do: to catch that glowing, growing kind of performance you might see on the stage if you were a bumblebee buzzing around everywhere you wanted to be.

This is a *distinct* contribution of television. In this unique way, the medium does something beyond the living stage and something films can't do at all.

MR. FREEDMAN: And in a way it's just beginning. We're at an historical point comparable to about 1570 in London. We sit around and say, "Do you think *The Globe* will ever come to anything, George? Will anyone really be able to write for it?"

I have a theory which is absolutely indefensible—that TV won't really reach its greatness until the generation that watches it as kids grows up and carries a belief in it. A belief such as we had for the movies, or for radio when we listened to it under the covers after the lights were out. Until that generation grows up and is really working at it, it won't be all that it can be. When I was a kid, I hid my Emerson radio under the covers and listened until midnight. I heard everything from *Little Orphan Annie* to *Fibber McGee and Molly*, and all of that was an absolutely real world for me.

MR. SCHAEFER: Yes, there was a reality about them. You believed it was really happening.

MR. FREEDMAN: There was that moment when you went into a

movie theatre and somebody took your ticket and you suddenly took a step forward into the darkness. From that moment on nothing else existed; somebody had to take your arm and pull you to a seat. You were up there *alone* with them! Until a generation grows up with *that* kind of belief, TV can go only halfway. We can't discover all of the forms for it yet.

2 TV and the Drama in Britain*

SYDNEY NEWMAN

WHATEVER dramatic egg you want, television will lay it for you. Live, I mean.†

Obviously we love being told a story—to get out of ourselves, escape—to dream of being bigger, stronger, braver, sexier—to risk life, stalk a killer, snare a "bird"—all this safely, secretly in the intimate closeness of our own television screen. If satisfying the viewer were this and no more we're not doing too badly.

Watching plays is much more than experiencing day-dreams. If nothing else, letters from viewers prove it ... "I won't let my boy go into the building trades because of last night's play." "*Martin Chuzzlewit* is great. I must read it." "When my teen-age girl proves by tonight's play that her behaviour is natural, there's something very wrong with the BBC, very wrong." "Dear Miss Blackman: sometimes at night, I get up, put on my shiny chocolate mac and go for long walks ... may we please meet. ... " (!) "The story was so true, I'll never take another drink again before driving." Thousands of letters like this come in every year, showing at least that people *believe* that plays affect manners and morals and attitudes.

---

* SFTA Journal, Spring, 1964.
† In 1964, eighteen-and-a-half weekly hours of (in alphabetical order) *Armchair Theatre, Avengers, Best of Maigret, Compact, Coronation Street, Crane, Dixon of Dock Green, Dr. Finlay's Casebook, Dr. Who, Emergency Ward 10, Festival, First Night, It's Dark Outside, The Plane Makers, Play of the Week, Sergeant Cork, Studio '64, Teletales* and last, but certainly not least, *Z Cars*. Probably each production, on average, has an audience of 12 million experience-hungry viewers.

Although the Newsom Report‡ deals with teen-age education, what it says about Drama is applicable to all. "By playing out psychologically significant situations, they (the viewer) can work out their own personal problems. Here is one way in which they can be helped to reconcile the reality of the world outside with their own private worlds." Never before in the history of man has the opportunity of rich and vicarious experience been made so graphically available to everybody for the price of a 19 in. set.

Main trouble is that too many dramas on the air today merely evoke a passive response from the audience. Too many drama programmes don't stimulate, provide and excite the imagination. Pilkington§ called them "trivial". The fault lies somewhere between the writer who won't or can't act on his awareness of his own age and society and those producing organizations who won't encourage him for reasons of ratings or in utter mistrust of the artist. We are too content with evolving a formula for a series, with two or three attractive characters dangling like carrots, leading the donkey public from week to week.

As rare exceptions some series prove the point. *Z Cars.* Years ago this programme began to howls of storm because it seemed as if the BBC was attacking the police and shattering the public's faith in the Force. But it has shown that policemen are as desperately human in enforcing the Law as we are desperately human in breaking it. More recently, *The Plane Makers*, going into the factory and the boardroom, demonstrates the drama not only of those that make a quid with their hands, but of those that manipulate a quid with their minds. *Probation Officer* was great, as is *Dr. Finlay's Casebook*. *Human Jungle*, in a syrupy way, does a job. There should be more.

At quite another level there is the straight escape stuff. *Maigret, Sergeant Cork, Avengers, Dr. Who*, relax, divert and that's useful too. But how many series just barely fill a vacuum!

What really causes the jaundiced eye today is the single play series. Speaking as a viewer, you'd think the makers of such dramas

‡ Newsom Report. The Report on the education of the 13–16 age group presented in 1963 by the Central Advisory Council for Education in England, Chairman John Newsom.

§ Pilkington. The Committee on Broadcasting (often referred to by the name of its Chairman, Sir Harry Pilkington) set up in 1960 to report to the Post-master General on the nature of broadcasting as a whole in Britain and to make recommendations about the future. Its Report was published in June 1962.

set out to illuminate the pedestrian and merely prove that it is. The loss in prestige of such programmes can be tragic for the whole development of drama in general including theatre and film. It is the single play series which unearths and gives chances to the playwrights who have power, style and an individual voice.

In the United States the anthology drama series, as it is called there, has now virtually disappeared. This has come about through the muting of the playwrights' voice by the sponsor, and through the series competing poorly with the filmed same-character-every-week series, the situation comedy and the gigantic variety "specials". The variation in week-to-week style and quality meant that the sponsor could get a better cost-per-thousand buy in another kind of show.

In England we can lay no blame at the feet of a sponsor. Here there are practically no restraints placed upon the writer (programme costs in the main are no insoluble handicap either). The fault to a large extent lies with the shortage of enough good, audience-hungry writers. More important it lies with television organizations who often discourage rather than encourage writers. Fundamental to this is the slowness of most programme companies and writers to recognize the need for the producer as distinct from the director. Even the Guild in their drama awards catagories seem to be confused in this.

I place great importance on the role of the producer who acts as a catalyst and who is the main point of trust for the writer in his connection with the director and programme team who will realize his work. Writers like Alun Owen and Clive Exton are indeed fortunate in finding Ted Kotcheff a director who understands their work and can realize it with beauty and intelligence. The same can be said for the Jack Pulman-Eric Tayler, David Mercer-Don Taylor, Alun Richards-Charles Jarrott, Bernard Kops-John Jacobs relationships. However, directors are restless people, especially the good ones, and they are continually being attracted to other media, like film and theatre. To be blunt about it, directors come and go but producers should go on for ever. And yet in England the role of the producer in the anthology series is still not an accepted position in the production fortress.

Even though plays on a week-to-week basis are totally different in terms of cast, director and story the producer's name should be the guarantee to the public of a consistency of outlook, showmanship and style. He gathers around him the writers who have something to say in an interesting way, and talented directors, designers, cameramen and so forth (or they find him). This is the basis from which a successful single play series will spring. The main thing is that the writer can trust a specific producer to do well by him. This is the new attitude I am encouraging inside the BBC Drama Group. It will take time but I am convinced it will pay off.

The writer is the man. It doesn't matter if he is a slob, a wife-beater and an uneducated oaf, if he has an ear for a line of dialogue, a feeling for characterization, and if he can, to quote the Bard, "hold as 'twere, the mirror up to nature, to show virtue her own feature, scorn her own image, and the very age and body of the time his form and pressure".

As an ordinary viewer hungry for experience I want to be entertained. I also want courage and I want hope in the future—and most single play series don't give me what I want. Not always. The good ones touch greatness, putting our younger writers alongside Ibsen, Brecht, etc.

But there aren't enough plays like Alun Owen's look into the exotic world of Welsh politics in *The Local Boy* and Bernard Kops' dive into the seedy London east-end jungle of *Stray Cats and Empty Bottles*. I liked David Turner's obsessed heroic *Bedmaker* and was charmed by Alan Sharpe's first television play, *Funny Noises with their Mouths*, and Waterhouse and Hall's TV parson confusing the new morality with the new bricks and mortar of his church. *Land of my Dreams* to the superficial eye was hardly upbeat. A sick-minded fascist, his myopic sister, a sexually frustrated wife and a sycophantic follower—the play's only characters—incredibly created with an acid pen by Clive Exton. So true was it that you *knew* that such rubbishy people existed, that they were that way for reasons of insecurity, impotence, frustration and ignorance. That they were hopelessly out-of-date, that finally the son's refusal to come home meant the world was irrevocably passing such people by. Would that James MacTaggart's BBC *First Night* could produce such plays each week, and the same goes for Eric Tayler's BBC-2 *Story Parade* of drama-tized novels. Any series that can boast of the plays I have mentioned is good. Any series that can put on such plays every week is great.

It's what we do on the in-between weeks when the play isn't so good that separates the men from the boys. Here's where casting, presentation, direction, pacing, etc., must be right on target. How often in the name of realism are we burdened with badly articulated lines, how often is life sucked out of a story because of ponderous pacing, and how often is a critical moment of change in a story thrown away in a wide, loose shot, or drowned in a welter of background noise. What is often worse is where a story point needing clarity is muddled by an obscure "artistic" camera shot or move.

The single play series has the hardest row to hoe as other safer series and programme ideas rise to the front. We must not forget the importance, the everlasting value of such a series for writers and creative directors and designers. The programme bosses, aware that the single play is the pace-setter for the entire television drama output, should help strengthen its position on the air in the way *Armchair Theatre/Studio '64* is allowed to inherit the mass following of *The Palladium Show*.

But writers must help here too. They must force themselves to regard as urgent the problems of winning and holding the big audience—to find the significant themes or old themes demonstrated in sharp contemporary terms.

God Bless Sidney Bernstein for making such a to-do about the Tennessee Williams plays. These when added to Peter Luke's BBC *Festival* series provide a real feast for the specialist theatre lover. Sartre, Becket, Chekov, Aristophanes, Frisch, writers whose work, rarely available in the theatre, is on tap every Wednesday night along with the local playwrights James Hanley, David Turner, Hugh Leonard and others. The commercial network should also provide such weekly series. At any rate BBC-2 will in Cedric Messina's *Theatre 625* series which hits off with Ken Taylor's trilogy *The Seekers* and our adult serials like *Madame Bovary*.

But series like *First Night, Armchair Theatre, Play of the Week* which reach out for new writing are, as far as I'm concerned, on the side of the angels. There are two new directions which single plays might go if they are to progress. They must add to their present reasonably realistic studio approach greater believability by getting their electronic cameras and mobile VTR units out on location, and, secondly, ridding themselves of most naturalistic trappings.

Many years ago the BBC started the "on location" move with James Brabazon's refugee play *People of Nowhere*. Joan Kemp-Welch followed with her Associated Rediffusion production. This is happening more and more frequently especially since Herbert Wise's *The Big Donkey* where our television cameras practically got the smell of a Belfast shipyard on to our screens. Naomi Capon, Alan Cooke and other directors are pushing this.

Biggest venture was, of course, our production of *Hamlet* when the entire cast was flown to Elsinore in Denmark. Two hours and fifty minutes of incredible drama where Hamlet, his mother and uncle, are no longer clever actors in a studio contrivance, but a real family in a tragic situation in their own house. No phoney papier-mâché Norman keep this but a real home of marble corridors, stairs, battlements and chapel, creatively exploited for sound and picture by Philip Saville to give a new kind of grandeur and reality to Shakespeare's old words.

So exciting are the results of our venture that it has triggered off imaginations of all, so that now we are swamped by a welter of ideas like *Henry VIII* shot in Hampton Court, right down to *The Merchant of Venice* shot you know where. I'll stop at *Oedipus Rex* in Delphi! We want some writers of today to collaborate closely with a production team to place their plays in locations where we can put our television cameras. This is a challenge of conscious artistry if we are to avoid falling into the pit of irrelevant naturalism. This will also involve getting rid of the industry-wide taboo against cutting tape. It will also mean the engineers shaking a leg and getting down to inventing a decent and economical tape editing machine.

If the above adds a greater realism to our current output of drama we must also, in desperation, move in the other direction as well. I am thinking of the totally unnaturalistic play—a dramatic shorthand. The kind of production where a good story is told in a kind of Fellini way. Maybe it will look like *Stephen D* or something we can't foresee. A story where all irrelevancies are eliminated, where we move from place to place by the simple and glorious act of the cut without the in-between fol-de-rol of getting there. To take a story and break it up in such a way that the performers don't need real rooms and real places to surround them—and I'm not referring to using the artsy-craftsy "black velours" as b.g. either. A use of music that does more than "Mickey Mouse" the action. Stills, graphics, the bold and unafraid use of "off-camera" narration—all this for a tingling kind of play where the audience is challenged to get its kicks by osmosis.

Again, to make this work, will call upon the intimate working relationship of writer, producer, director and production team.

In conclusion, we need to be aware that plays are more than trivial entertainment, that we must help our writers to have trust in their own ability to interpret their age; that those of us who produce, provide a firm and consistent environment which can amplify the writers' voices; that the single play series may founder unless it is fresh and audience winning; that if we move out of the studio for greater realism or find a new kind of dramatic communication within the studio walls, the eggs we hatch will truly be golden ones.

3   The TV Director: A Dialogue*

FIELDER COOK

FRANKLIN SCHAFFNER

INTERVIEWER: It might be profitable for our readers if we followed a step by step analysis of the reasons for your decision to work in live TV, and the relationships which the TV director holds with others within the creative complex.

First, are there certain materials which "do better" on TV than in another medium? Do you look for certain qualities within any script that make it solely television material?

MR. SCHAFFNER: All of this assumes that you *have* a script at the outset, one you have not built along with the writer. This happens rarely. Only rarely does a useable script arrive unsolicited. If you are doing an original live drama, you will start by discussing with writers the ideas they may have. You then assign the script, knowing the limitations of the medium in advance. Very rarely will an idea be broad or exciting enough, therefore, to tempt you into withholding it for development as a film or stage play.

MR. COOK: It's no more than that, I would agree. But in the larger question of why we have come back to TV, I would say that it was simply because we were given an opportunity to do what we wanted to do. Once the outline is approved by DuPont, and once they approve the general story, we have absolute control. And I think that has the greatest attraction for the director—in any medium.

---

* *Television Quarterly, Spring, 1963.*

You *control* your product. That is the director's ideal. You can get it in pictures, of course, if you have that power to finance and sell your own properties. But getting that power wears you out. The satisfactions of doing a Hollywood film are great indeed, but your control must extend beyond the hours on the studio floor—beyond your rehearsals, which are vital—and into the cutting room. You want *touch* with the final product.

In television, where this is possible, you can better practice your craft with the true consistency and productivity of the director. You make your own mistakes and you earn your own pluses, and you learn the most by doing it yourself. And while there is an awful lot of muck work one must do to make a living in any medium, television holds this final fascination.

MR. SCHAFFNER: And this works for directors or actors or writers or producers. You're productive only when you work. If you do a play or a movie a year you've spent seven months at it. What do you do for the other five months? You sit and worry about getting a bigger picture or a bigger play. In TV you're rolling 100 per cent of the time. We're practicing what we know best, which is directing and sometimes producing. And, hopefully, we're improving those skills.

There is, for one thing, a great deal more work done with actors in television. I am talking about the director-actor relationship that builds up in a rehearsal hall. There is a great deal more creative and productive exchange between these two people in television drama than is generally assumed. This doesn't exist in filmed TV at all, and exists only to a limited degree in feature-film work.

The theatre is another matter. It dumps the greatest number of exceptional, extraneous pressures on the director. You're so concerned with everyone from house manager to critic—to an actor's friend or the writer's brother—that it's almost not to be borne. They are accumulative and constant. It is very difficult, in a theatrical production, to remember what you started out to do five weeks before. There are enormous differences in your thinking over that period. I do not mean that television always gives you the chance to do the kind of work you would like to do—but it does give you the chance to be master once you are under way. Then, if you mess it up, it's your fault.

INTERVIEWER: What about relationships between the producer and director among the respective media? Do you, as directors, find that you are inhibited more in one medium than another?

MR. COOK: I think the producer has absolute control in motion pictures. The director will find that once he has shot a film—with all optimum conditions and no problems on the studio floor during his work—he gets a rough cut of the picture and that's it. The final judgment, literally, of what it will become rests with the studio and/or producer. It is not the director's film. Even when his relationship with the producer is wonderful, he still loses that final control. He can shape it—he can dictate the quality of the picture—the type of picture it will be—on the studio floor, but he may never see it again until it's scored; and then he may find that he has brought forth a comedy instead of the serious work he envisioned. But in television there are very few producers who even care to exercise this creative function. The majority would not pretend to be the creative type of producer.

INTERVIEWER: And the writer? Once you have selected your script and developed the idea with him, what is his relationship to your work?

MR. SCHAFFNER: He is the original creator. Without him nothing exists. We work with him and he works with us. I don't think there is any writer I have worked with who hasn't come out of the association with my respect. And maybe he begins to respect me. He works until his product is shown. He goes to rehearsal, and it is expected of him that he be at rehearsal all day long, every day. He is urged to be there.

I say this because, for some writers, knocking television has become a very productive pastime. Much of it starts on the coast, and it is an interesting phenomenon. I went out to the coast last year with the specific purpose of seeing ten or twelve writers who might function in some way for us on DuPont. And while there I came to understand the essential difference between an east coast and a west coast writer. An east coast writer comes in, sits down and says, "I'm a writer. I've got an idea." Then he tells you his story. A west coast writer comes in, sits down and says, "I'm a writer. What do you want me to write?" This *is* the difference, and what has caused it is filmed television. Everything that is stereotype, format, down-the-slot, unchanging, dull, useless, unchallenging, non-provocative.

MR. COOK: The writers out there do not write *drama*, they write *incident*.

MR. SCHAFFNER: Instant drama.

MR. COOK: Which may be extremely colorful—even well-written— but which eliminates the one tendon of all playwriting—a real hero. Even on a show as good as *Route 66* the heroes just barely *arrive*. They are hardly *there*. The very fact that two strangers can drive up in a sports car and become involved within five minutes cuts the tendon of playwriting. Fifty-one per cent of everything a playwright must do has already been done *for* him. We are talking about writing *character*, which is not what happens there. That's format. People expect things to be solved in five minutes.

MR. SCHAFFNER: And that creates a peculiar problem for those of us who are doing live—and there is always a connotation of "antique" in that word—drama which is original. Viewers today are so conditioned to turning on a set and seeing a formula show that they know what they are going to get the moment they turn the show on. They know the subject material, the guest star, the title, the writer—they *know* what to expect. And that's our problem. When someone has a choice between a Directors Company show and a format show the complications arise. Suppose they *do* tune us in. We have a good title. We've been well publicized. The viewer says, "What the hell. I'll take a chance this week." Now he starts to watch an original show. He watches for a minute and a half and begins to look at the clock because nobody has been killed yet. No woman is mangled. No child is in terrible danger. Then he rutches around in his seat—and all of a sudden he's not listening. And if there is any literate quality to the script he's *got* to be listening!

What this means is simply that original live drama must *persuade* an audience that television entertainment is a two-way street—must convince the viewer that he must *contribute* something, not just sit there like a dumb, soppy sponge. One of the real tragedies of television is that it has begun to lose the attention of the so-called opinion-maker in our society. The most recent study—the Steiner report—says in effect that the less educated you are, the more you watch television. I believe that one of the services we perform, and I hope this does not sound immodest, is providing the kind of material that will excite the opinion-maker and bring him back to television. Television needs the involvement of people who take time to think about what the hell is happening to us each day—not only in television, but in politics, social affairs, and other vital areas. Leo Rosten once said that the business of life was not just to enjoy yourself—but to *matter*. Good drama ought to give people both sides of the coin, and if it doesn't appear on TV what will happen to the medium? It can't survive with instant, irresponsible drama.

MR. COOK: TV drama must have the ring of life—it must display the interest of writers in the drama of life around them. We have had such contributions—last year, from writers like Rod Serling and Loring Mandel. Loring is a good example of the exception to "instant hero" because he writes about mothers and children—and involves them in human action. The best of our television writers have managed to do this. There are really too few women and children in TV drama, unless they are in those horribly emotional tragedies of incident found in the format series—and the male characters.

INTERVIEWER: May we take a moment now to review any special working relationships the director holds with actors in live TV? Do the actors really have that affinity for live TV which so many claim to have?

MR. COOK: Live drama is more fun for the actor, I'm sure.

MR. SCHAFFNER: Fun, because he can delay his commitment—the final work of his art—until it counts. He can push it back and work at it and hold it in check until *the* moment.

MR. COOK: In filmed TV it's done at once. You get to the studio, you stand up, and you commit.

MR. SCHAFFNER: That's the first and last time. You get used to it, and you do it automatically. I think it would be to the actor's advantage to save the whole force of it until it has to be laid on the line. That's doubtless why they favor live.

MR. COOK: I should think it would take an extremely strong psyche to survive four straight years of a film series performance. I would hate to direct a family-situation comedy for that long.

INTERVIEWER: Can we consider now the final editing work that a live director does? You know that you must eventually put your production before cameras, and can borrow from whatever additional cinematic strengths are available to you. Does this influence you at the outset? Do you begin to plan in terms of cameras as soon as rehearsals are under way?

MR. SCHAFFNER: No. It's a quite unconscious thing, really. As you put the set together and begin to learn the rooms, the angles you have, and then go to the general plan for staging it, you don't really concern yourself with how you're going to shoot it. You need nothing at the outset beyond your concept of telling the story.

MR. COOK: There are directors who do think camera first. They force the action by putting down camera shots before rehearsals even begin. I wait to do camera work until I am as close to the studio as possible. Sometimes not until the day before studio. You're damned lucky if you get close enough to a *performance* before then, as it takes six or seven days to see this come alive. You have to know what they are going to give on the air.

MR. SCHAFFNER: It is possible in live TV that, if you stage for the camera, you may miss the entire meaning of the play. The director's obligation is to stage the play first. When he discovers what has been done during that process, he will punctuate it visually. But I might miss the meaning of a scene if I plan for two people to play a scene "tight" for the sake of camera when the instincts as characters are to be apart—when their mere physical closeness would make them go at each other's throats. If you stage it tightly they are unable to move—to express èmotions physically by movement. You must consider the intent of the playwright, not the presence of cameras. Too much TV drama is still staged, though, with one actor way down in the foreground facing the camera and another actor way up in the background facing the camera, and how in hell they are *communicating* I don't know.

MR. COOK: There is a certain amount of preoccupation with the visually spectacular on the part of some directors. You'll see it in the extreme angles and wild productions—even when the production is not particularly wild. I think our approach has been to follow the play and let a pattern of shooting evolve out of it. The best angles I ever got, I think, have resulted when an actor has done something so absolutely brilliant that I spent three or four hours figuring out how to shoot it.

MR. SCHAFFNER: That underscores the great value of rehearsal. Simply defined, I suppose the director's function really is just staying one jump ahead of the cast. Too often a director gets great credit for "exposing what the play is about", for "interpreting" it. But it works the other way, more often than not. Again and again at rehearsals an actor does something that opens a whole new and broad horizon about what a scene should *be*. Actors, when they *are* actors, perform a marvelous function for the playwright. Just out of their own contribution before a performance is set. Just by exploring they expose an enormous amount of information. Any good actor will always bring forth the comment from a playwright that "he's putting something in I never saw before".

MR. COOK: And that goes back to the question of TV's fatal fascination. Inspiration is the product of television's approach to live drama. In the theatre it may exist for one week out of four that you have to ready a play. It does not exist in filmed TV unless you stumble on it. If you're working from instinct it might exist in motion pictures. But nowhere does it exist as deeply as in TV. Nowhere can you explore as deeply. With ten days to rehearse for a fifty-minute play you get in over 200% more time than in the theatre. It is the inspiration and what you can learn from it that makes it the best. There are playwrights at rehearsals who see something an actor shows them and rewrite for it—while you recast your thoughts. It's the inspiration and the exchange of it that show you the way toward learning—really learning—your craft.

3a Director and Performer*

PETER DEWS

CHRISTOPHER MORAHAN: a discussion with

ROGER MANVELL

MORAHAN: Casting is, of course, the first problem. You have to find the right personality for each part, the actor or actress with the talent, imagination and discipline to do the work well. There are many technical disciplines in television that are, or appear to be, frightening. And we're always up against a narrow time-schedule. Obviously the first consideration is the actor's fitness for the part, wherever he has worked or whatever he has done. But on the whole I prefer to work with people who have had some experience.

MANVELL: What sort of experience?

DEWS: Well, theatre is the most accessible form of experience for the young actor. He can begin as an amateur and learn the first disciplines in acting that way. Most young actors have never seen a television play in rehearsal, and can't therefore know the amount there is to absorb on the studio floor. All the same, I like using young actors and actresses who are new to television. Also the Regions offer one a wider choice of authentic TV performances. People with the right dialect, for example, are more available, and have been for years for sound radio plays. Indeed, experience on radio is quite an asset to the television actor. While some established theatre actors may seem at first a bit frightened of television and its technicalities, their experience and ability always tell in the end.

---

* *S F.T.A. Journal, Autumn 1961.*

MORAHAN: In any case, the business of acting is exactly the same in any medium.

DEWS: Yes. It's just a matter of applying a different technique to the same job of work. Good acting is good acting the world over. In a way television gives the actor the worst of both the worlds of film and theatre. He has the film's complications of giving his performance through a variety of shots, but, unlike films, with no pause for adjustment between them; and he has the theatre's complication of learning and giving a continuous performance, but without the theatre's essential give and take between actor and audience, night after night.

MORAHAN: But he does have the immense satisfaction of overcoming technical problems and reaching an enormous audience. And I think the opportunity to create his performance in one piece, without interruptions as in film, is a very vital one.

DEWS: The actor's job is simply to act, accepting television's limitations and challenge, and we've got to help him to develop this talent within the framework of the rules. I remember when I did my first television production. A very experienced actor, who headed the cast, gave me the most valuable advice I've ever had. I told him I was new to it—I knew he'd find out anyhow!—and he said he hated directors who told him to take no notice of the camera. I think he was right. An actor must know where his audience is, and how far away it is. He must direct his performance to where his audience is, and modify it according to the distance from which he is projecting the character. And this means realizing the technical needs of the camera. The director should bring his actors sufficiently into the technical picture to make them realize this. I let actors have camera scripts if they want them.

MORAHAN: That's all right up to a point. I think the director should only tell the actor what he's literally got to know, and tie him down as little as possible with technical considerations. I like to keep things not too clear-cut at rehearsal. What I decide to do with the cameras may be greatly modified by the way the actor shapes in rehearsal.

DEWS: Yes, I think this depends to some extent on the director's own background. The director who comes from the theatre wants to get a whole performance from everyone. Then he gathers the best moments of these performances and arranges them all pictorially, knowing what's coming from each actor: he captures a theatrical performance in television terms. The director who comes from films may tend to work out every shot in advance, planning his production rather like a film script, building up a set of shots and then getting the actors to fit their work into these shots.

MORAHAN: I must say I like to have my presentation mapped out in advance, and then discard it during rehearsal to meet the special needs and achievements of the cast. I only tell the actors what I think is essential about my ideas for presentation, and more later if particular kinds of channelling of a shot or sequence are forced on me.

DEWS: I hardly ever plan presentation in advance. There are certain shots I know I want to aim for, but generally I direct rehearsals as I would direct a theatre play. The actors must feel as near to real life as possible, and their movements must be acceptable to them. When they are happy, only then do I rough out the shots.

MORAHAN: But it is the director's job to realize on the screen the visual style and nature of the script. Every play has its own visual style and a director should be able to work in as many styles as there are plays. He does this in terms of the camera and lenses available to him, the nature of the settings and the placing of the actors within them.

DEWS: Yes, I find a play dictates its own shots. For example, I once had to produce a modern version of a Greek play, which observed like its original the classical unities. So I toyed with the idea (far from original) of using only one camera. When I aired this notion, colleagues were horrified: "What about your pace?" "What about the rhythm of your shots?" they said. I thought this nonsense. In television pace is in the script, and in the nature of the action. In the cinema, cutting can condense the action and so in itself create pace. Cutting never achieves pace on television because live action cannot be condensed.

MANVELL: What about the difference between the three-dimensional movement on the studio floor and the two-dimensional picture on the television screen?

MORAHAN: It doesn't worry me because my vision now is entirely two-dimensional. I see the actor all the time in these terms in a picture frame. But making "pretty pictures" should never become more important than the play, or the performances. I don't mean, of course, that one should forget the pictures and their composition altogether. Depth matters; the pictorial relationship of actor to actor; the relation of one shot to another. But the play and the performances come first.

DEWS: Long shots with great depth are absolutely right on television, in spite of what everyone says. What matters is that you don't give the actor in the far distance any detailed action to perform. But depth of shot has great dramatic value on television.

MORAHAN: You can show so well pictorially the relationship of the actor to his environment. But you have to suit the nature of the action to the distance of the actor from his audience.

DEWS: In spite of all this complication, a play is much easier to direct for television than in the theatre. In the theatre the attracting of the audience's attention to essential details by lighting, grouping and so on is far from simple. On television you do it by close-ups. But the relationship of the director to the actor is just the same in both media. You've got to get your actors to create what the author intends in terms of laughter, tears or tension. I think the important thing is to offer them the "emotional geography" of a scene. The actors must create the mood, the feeling of the lines. Having go their agreement to this shaping of a scene, one can then consider the technical points. I think, too, that television has a special capacity for observing the delicate, the shy, the sensitive. Good for the *pointilliste*.

MORAHAN: Yes, plays that investigate character are the best for television. This is what the television dramatists have developed best.

DEWS: And this has influenced writing in the theatre. Or is it that the new British playwrights, the Osbornes, the Weskers and the Delaneys have influenced TV drama? It's like the chicken-or-the-egg conundrum. At all events, the older drama of action has been temporarily ousted. And in a way, as television acting is the art of the microphone and stage acting that of the megaphone, TV is the more suitable medium for these performances.

MORAHAN: But whichever medium you're in, the challenge remains the same—to help the actor to flower within the true framework of that medium, to put over what the drama needs.

DEWS: And I must say that in both the theatre and on television, a lack of acting ability immediately shows up. In the cinema it can to some extent be disguised, witness the excellent performances that small children and even dogs can appear to give.

MANVELL: What about training for acting on television?

DEWS: I don't think any specific training is needed for television acting. Training is best for the theatre, so that the actor can be helped to develop his talent for working with an audience. The schools exist to discover talent and extend an actor's capacity to use the instruments of voice and body. But once the actor comes to television, he must learn to work without an audience, while at the same time realizing what has to be done for the audience that isn't there! This is particularly difficult, for example, in farce, where the actor is used to working from laugh to laugh. For television the laughter is imaginary, and the actor has to be prepared to get on with the action and not wait for his laughs.

MORAHAN: In theatre training it's important an actor gets the chance to work on as wide a range of parts as possible so as to find his strength and his limitations as an actor. There's a tendency now for young actors who are successful to become established through far too narrow a range of parts—if they don't start in repertory, that is. And repertory is dying, which is a great pity.

DEWS: Also there's the very strong influence of the Royal Court.* This has almost made a virtue of newness—seeking the unknown writer, the unknown actor. To be unknown has become all of a sudden a special kind of recommendation. And this has certainly extended the whole field of acting.

MORAHAN: It helps us find new actors all the time for television. Just as we're looking for new script-writers. So television is all the while

---

* Royal Court. The theatre in London leased by the English Stage Company in 1956 as a centre for the production of work by such new dramatists as John Osborne, John Arden, Ann Jellicoe, and N. F. Simpson, as well as the plays, first produced elsewhere, of other British dramatists of the new school, such as Harold Pinter, Arnold Wesker and Shelagh Delaney.

creating new jobs for actors, even if at the same time its influence is losing them the chance to get jobs in repertory. And good actors can take to it quite naturally, almost in no time, in a single production. If you sense with any actor that he is finding the technical side of the medium a special strain, then you can help him by working on his imagination, helping him create a sense of spontaneity and actuality, making it "real" for him, all the time troubling him as little as possible with the technical details.

DEWS: All actors are to some degree nervous, and the director can help them to overcome this by creating the right kind of environment to work in, so that they know where they are with the medium, come to working terms with it.

MORAHAN: Yes, the director must create the right climate for the actor. An actor has got to trust his director, and sense the unity of purpose that lies behind the production. This is particularly true in the production of plays in series, for which you build up a group of actors and actresses who must work together over a period of time, though it is equally desirable to generate this feeling in the short rehearsal period of a single play.

DEWS: There's always the danger that a director will cast an actor he knows well, with whom he is in sympathy, even though he may not be quite right for the part. Equally, you can easily drift into the other danger of excessive typecasting. Then there's the pressure you get to use contract artists with a quota of appearances to fulfil; on the other hand, the director may hesitate to use an actor who is too well-known for a particular kind of part, even though you know he has it in him to give you what the play needs, because the public accepts only this popular image. None of these dangers makes casting easy.

MORAHAN: And, finally, I'd like to say this about the director's work: it's his first impression on reading a new play that is all-important, because this in all probability is the impression the audience should get from the production. After he and the actors have gone through all the technical hoops, it's the strong first impression which must come over, as freshly as possible.

4 Television and the Writer*

LEWIS GREIFER

DAVID MERCER

ARTHUR SWINSON

SWINSON: The outstanding point about television drama in Britain
is that it has all happened in such a short time. It has, of course, no
written history. The dramatist working in the theatre has a tradition
that he can write to. This lack of history means that the people
coming into television begin as they come through the door. What
has been achieved so far since the war seems to me to break down
into three main phases. The first of these was from 1946 to 1955,
when there was only one producing organization—the BBC—with
the only organized television drama department in the world. This
was run by Michael Barry, who was a man of the theatre, and his
policy tended to look towards the stage for material.

Up to 1951 you could say that television drama here lacked
mobility; it originated from small studios at Alexandra Palace; it
was viewed through three cameras, each of which had only one lens.
The actors moved to the cameras not the cameras to the actors. The
result was a kind of imitation theatre.

But two important things did happen during this period. The
first was the development of dramatized documentary of the kind
associated principally with writers such as Robert Barr and Duncan
Ross, who aimed at breaking up the action into many scenes helped
by the introduction of film sequences. The second thing was the crime
serial of the kind originated by Francis Durbridge. So, by the early

---

* S.F.T.A. Journal, Autumn 1963.

nineteen-fifties, dramatized documentary and crime serials were setting the pace, and moved across the screen with more authority than the television drama of the period.

There was also the work of Nigel Kneale and Iain MacCormick, whose plays had a considerable influence. Kneale's *Quatermass* serials—full of original characterization, thought and movement—and his play *The Creature* (based on the search for the abominable snowman), helped television drama out of the rut of interiors, of rooms and offices. *1984* had a tremendous social impact, shaking the whole nation. MacCormick's *The Liberators*, the first of a series of plays, though still theatre-looking in style, was strong and effective writing.

The second phase, coming after 1955 and the arrival of commercial television, opened up the studios to floods of new writers, most of whom established themselves through a straight, realistic style of writing under the influence of Paddy Chayefsky in the States. But although this realism was healthy in its way, it put television drama into chains. It was not until 1960 or thereabouts that the third phase, the present one, started. Writers succeeded in breaking the chains of realism with such plays as Bill Naughton's *June Evening*, John Mortimer's *David and Broccoli*, John Arden's *Soldier, Soldier*, and Alun Owen's *The Ruffians*. These writers brought a new poetry into television.

So, from my point of view, 1960 became the turning-point for television drama.

MERCER: I think television's an existentialist kind of art form. It hasn't got a history. But can you really analyse it apart from the theatre and cinema as a whole?

SWINSON: Well, of course, events in the theatre are related to those in television drama. Many of our modern theatre dramatists started in television. Shaeffer, Pinter—

MERCER: Yes, everyone, no doubt, except Osborne and Wesker. But surely television drama's justification is social rather than artistic. I can't think of anything I've done which couldn't have been presented more effectively in the cinema or theatre. People may think plays like mine are successful; and it's true that *A Suitable Case for Treatment* is to be made into a film. But so far television is surely more restricted as a medium for presenting drama than either the theatre or the cinema. What emerged as important about television was that it could fulfil itself more fully than the other media. It could be prolific in production and it could reach enormous audiences. It had, therefore, social rather than artistic validity and vitality.

SWINSON: But surely it's penetrated far beyond what either the theatre or the cinema were in a position to do. Few films could look at life in the realistic way that so many television plays have done.

MERCER: If you've got a courageous producer behind you, it's true you can get things on to the screen that the cinema could never touch. Commercially, that is. The strange, the offbeat, the unusual can be got through by the stronger personalities.

GREIFER: Just because there is still no crystallized pattern of television drama it presents greater opportunities and a greater challenge than other media. Although it is a medium of mass entertainment serious writers have exploited the overwhelming need for material to get their work shown with the result that—perhaps without meaning to—television has tapped a potential of important new talent.

These new writers are bound to influence drama as a whole and the artistic tastes of British audiences. In my opinion, British television drama, although still in its infancy, has already become the best, most exciting in the world.

There are no David Mercers working in American television because there are more opportunities here for original thinking and personal styles. In America, the need is currently for large numbers of highly professional writers who can identify themselves with the multiple-series dramas, who write vividly and efficiently to a formula. We can't get writers to do this on any scale. For instance, we have not yet been able to produce anything as consistently good as *The Defenders* in this country—yet a dozen writers in the States could step in and maintain the high standard of that series.

There is no corpus of high-level professional formula writers in this country. Our writers prefer to concentrate on drama anthologies, and because demand is so great, experiment is still possible. The social need has created new artistic opportunities. It may or may not be a pure art form but it most certainly is a significant cultural phenomenon.

SWINSON: Except that many script editors get ideas above their station and over-influence writers as to the nature of the plays they should write. Like the present fashion for having plays without a plot. There's too much vague talk about art and too little about entertainment.

GREIFER: On the contrary. My brief as a script consultant is to find plays that have a beginning, middle and end. In general, it's the writers who create fashions with script departments trying to control the flood. Television drama is constantly opening up new frontiers, placing emphasis on personal relationships explored in greater depth and from fresh angles. The pure professionalism and craft of the stage dramatist is not enough for television. As soon as it gets on the screen theatrical structure and dialogue as such seems artificial and bogus. What gives television drama its unique quality and impact is truth. Simple truth is essentially good television drama. Relatively, insight is more meaningful than intellectuality.

Theatre audiences are more sophisticated and demanding of artistic merit, perhaps, but the television audience must not be thought uncouth or uncritical. They look for plays that show this essential sense of truth-to-life.

I think it was ABC in their *Armchair Theatre* rather than the BBC that took real television drama the farthest step forward.

SWINSON: I wouldn't agree with that. *Armchair Theatre* came after the main developments I've outlined at the BBC. After Ted Willis's plays like *Woman in a Dressing Gown*. After Chayefsky.

GREIFER: Well, *Armchair Theatre* moulded a group of dramatists. They brought together a whole new group of writers who turned aside from the old concepts of drama and worked specifically for television. The significance of this we are only discovering now.

MERCER: The reason I seem to be knocking television drama is that if I go on doing what I really want to do—like *A Suitable Case for Treatment*—I find I'm writing plays people wouldn't go to the theatre or the cinema to see anyway, and that are not in the end what the greater part of the television audience wants.

GREIFER: Nevertheless, you at least get the plays you want to write exposed through television.

MERCER: Yes, but if I write plays that less and less people want to see on television then I'm not fulfilling what television itself is after. I think this is a social problem—possibly a matter of the general level of our education. You find the ratings tend to fall the nearer you get to what you want to write. I only write plays to find out for myself what they're about. Initially I don't care about what the audience wants. I write the plays my way and then let them reach their audience.

SWINSON: Well, however you set about writing, it's the communication business you're in. I'm not saying anything against the theatre. Some writers will always be happier there. It's just that there are certain things television can do better, things that belong essentially to it only.

GREIFER: But David Mercer is precisely the kind of writer that television serves well. He writes intelligently and honestly about significant things. And whatever he says about his ratings he still gets a bigger audience than Shakespeare ever had. There is an unfortunate tendency among some writers and even more some critics to patronize the viewers. But who are the viewers? Effectively, the entire British people, no less. It's not only intellectual arrogance to look down on them, it's a form of paranoia. Every writer must surely welcome the opportunity television gives him of speaking directly and privately to a mass audience. It's his responsibility to treat them respectfully and honestly. The old pretentious stuff written for so-called theatrical effect is no longer fashionable. A teaspoonful of sincerity is more effective, I think, than a basinful of clever tricks.

SWINSON: Yes, the dialogue of the successful film still lacks the quality of the best television writing. Films depend so much on visual excitement. If you examine the best television drama, the quality of the dialogue is richer and fuller, and it has to be—the play depends so much on it.

GREIFER: When you consider the whole era of British films, they have collectively made far less impact on our mass culture than television has done in five years. The sheer prodigality of material has meant that original ideas and attitudes and sentiments have been given a hearing. I'm not pretending there isn't a mass of banality; but the good stuff is there, too. And it stands out. No wonder so many of our best dramatists, as well as some that are not so good, are writing for television.

MERCER: I think a good television play is just a good play that happens to be transmitted by television. Before the modern mechanical media came in, one already had a conception of what a good play was. But as soon as the technical media became available, they were discovered to be hybrids, as far as the original conception of the good play was concerned. The point now is to make these mechanical media give us their own natural authority.

SWINSON: That brings us to the point whether television drama can give us anything really new. Personally I think it's enabled us to take a closer, more honest look at the characters, thoughts and aspirations of small groups of people. Compared to it the film (which is longer) seems to need a highly organized plot with an easily recognized climax.

MERCER: Why has it got to be like that? What about Eisenstein's films, or Truffaut's? Or *Twelve Angry Men*, that surely had no plot?

GREIFER: I think the point here is that films have tended to make a god out of movement; they worship the idol of movement and sacrifice character to it. It's a cliché. Television drama styles change too frequently for clichés to gell. I think what television does best is to bring small experiences into sharp focus, seeing them in depth. Film and theatre prefer their experiences to be larger and more exceptional. Television drama at its best favours original perception; illuminating in a fresh way familiar circumstances, characters and relationships. Audiences that only too often find stage plays esoteric find their dramatic needs fulfilled on television. The cinema, in this country, at any rate, is generally too hog-tied to both the box office and its own conventions to do this kind of thing either well enough or often enough.

MERCER: But is all this really essential to television?

SWINSON: Yes, I think it is. Writers of television drama are taking a closer, more intense look at small groups of characters in a real situation. Films over and over again are unreal, unreal emotionally and unreal socially. Television, on the other hand, needs this reality. But television must not forget that it's got above everything to entertain—it can entertain and stimulate, or entertain and inform, or educate—but it must entertain.

MERCER: Well—a writer just writes, taking the medium into account, of course, but still primarily concerned with writing as he thinks he should.

SWINSON: In conventional cinema that is seldom done. But now it can be, through television.

MERCER: A writer only has in him the plays that evolve naturally from him. It's a problem—this business of supplying entertainment. I began writing in a social-realist way. Where I come from the society was made up of miners, and they understood this. But the more I go on writing in the way I like, the less I find they appreciate it back home.

GREIFER: But take your play, *A Suitable Case for Treatment*. I thought that essentially a television piece. It told us a great deal about a man put wholly in television terms—terms that wouldn't work well in either theatre or film. It had just the right canvas as you wrote it for television. Now you say it's to become a film. But how can you translate this into film without changing its scope in the process?

SWINSON: You can only too easily lose control of your subject the moment it gets into the film studios.

GREIFER: I wonder what the quality is, exactly, that enables some plays to transfer easily from the stage to television? Take Robert Bolt's *The Flowering Cherry*. That could have been written for television in the first place.

SWINSON: Is it the quality of honesty?

GREIFER: Or some kind of intimacy?

MERCER: Or the proximity of the characters to each other? An intimate engagement between the characters.

SWINSON: Shakespeare transfers, and Wilde does not.

MERCER: This discussion really reflects the social system we live in. If you've been to grammar school or university your level of acceptance and appreciation is different from what it would be if you've only been to a secondary school.

SWINSON: The really outstanding work surely offers various levels of appeal all at once.

GREIFER: The moguls have naturally stressed the fact that television is essentially an entertainment medium but, in practice, writers have resisted the pressures. The only way to maintain genuine progress in television drama is to give writers a relatively free rein. When you think of the number of important writers who cut their teeth in television it seems obvious that not only must television continue to present opportunities for new writers but it needs to extend these opportunities further. We should welcome writers which the other, more conformist media reject.

5   A Writers' Symposium*

RAY BRADBURY

DAVID CHANDLER

PAUL MONASH

BARRY TRIVERS

MR. CHANDLER: We are here today to talk about whether writers can do anything to improve the level and content of American television. We might begin with a simple question. Are we pursuing a will o' the wisp? Is it possible that writers *can* do anything to improve the content of television?

MR. MONASH: Well, a writer proposes and the network disposes. Within the framework of existing programs, the writer can obviously only write as well as he can—and leave his work to the mercies of producers, directors, actors, and so on. Sometimes, these mercies *are* merciful. In terms of program content, however, writers can propose a new, original, exciting program format, but this is about all they can do at the moment.

MR. TRIVERS: I think that the fault—the crime if you wish—of bad television had its roots on that tragic day when the writer abdicated his rights; the day when, for whatever good and sufficient reason, the Writers Guild entered into an agreement by which management became not only the owner, but the author, of material. The man who is the author of material is therefore the man who controls. He controls theme. He controls direction. He controls the integrity or artistry without which no writer can begin, much less complete, his work. I think that the series of rebuffs—the series of disembowel-

* *Television Quarterly, Spring 1963.*

ments—which take place on scripts succeeds in doing only one thing: it moves the writer out of TV into other areas.

MR. CHANDLER: Then you would lick the problem simply by abdicating? By saying it's hopeless and finding another area in which the writer can work? I don't think I could accept that.

MR. TRIVERS: Not abdication. I think *recognition* is a better word. We are part and parcel of what has been described as the world's largest medicine-man's wagon. It stretches from New York to California. We provide the banjo solo designed to attract the audience, after which the medicine is sold. We're not abdicating our rights when we recognize the medium for what it is: a commercial form of advertising, verbally articulated rather than printed. And with a great deal more influence than the newspaper.

Can you possibly conceive a newspaper being told what advertising it can carry, or what it can print, by the manufacturers of automobiles, deodorants, and toilet tissue?

MR. CHANDLER: An eloquent diagnosis—and yet you said that the way writers can improve upon this is to stop writing for TV. I don't think this a concrete proposal. What can writers *do* to improve upon it? *Now.* In the present moment.

MR. BRADBURY: One could write a book. The reasons for writing a novel are multifold. The trouble with TV writers is that they are vulnerable. So many of them have come into the field with so little experience in other forms—the short story, novel, or stage play— and this means they are dependent on a single field. If we, as a group of writers, could convince ourselves that each of us is capable of moving into other fields, then we could come back to TV with greater power. The experience one can accumulate in writing a novel, short story or one-act play will put him in a far better position to make demands upon TV. And in the process you accrue to yourself a certain reputation which will in turn produce a certain amount of constructive fear of you.

Then a producer or director may stand somewhat in awe of you. But if the writer has not cushioned himself—spread out and grown, actually—he has no defenses. The more you learn about each medium the stronger you are when you come back to the original form. So Barry's advice is sound. You return to TV and you say,

"Look, I am now *more* qualified than I have ever been to write about human beings—so shut up!" And if this happens often enough, then the Writers Guild can make its long overdue stand and take back those rights it lost. It can then say, "If you want a script you'll have no say over the major points of the script. Once you accept the idea itself, then the writer must be left alone. No cutting without his permission." We can do that only when we gain the power.

MR. TRIVERS: That is valid. I noticed a newspaper article recently about a planned rehearsal for *Little Me*. It dealt with Sid Caesar, and the headline read: *This Caesar has to take orders—Dramatists Guild has the last word. Comedian is told of clause that says author's prose can't be changed.* Now if you are looking for the line of demarcation between TV and theatre—for the root of the problem—here it is. Not only was he not permitted to make changes, but he was not permitted to *sulk* about it.

MR. CHANDLER: I wonder if you are not trying to apply a Dramatist Guild rule too mechanically. You know what happens when a play goes on. Of course the writer is the final arbiter of what has to be said and done but, as a matter of practical fact, doesn't a great deal of conferring take place? Re-writes are often made to please the star—to make him more comfortable, and so on.

MR. TRIVERS: Of course. But the key word in your statement is *writer*. The writer is consulted by the director, by the producer, by the actors. The writer—not someone else. Not the sponsor, the agency man, or the man from the network.

MR. MONASH: Let me turn to this matter of the writer's contribution to TV. Of course it's vital. We know that. Yet there is a tendency among writers to feel—and it's expressed in sessions like this—that somehow their work is necessarily spoiled by producers, directors, actors. This is not really so. I would say that it is *generally* not so. We work in a field where we have certain rigid limitations. In the NBC format, with which I am familiar, we must have exactly 48 minutes and 26 seconds of film. Would you suggest that, if we had shot 55 or 56 minutes of film, the writer be called in to sit with film editors in order to see what should be cut, what should be left in, and what should be emphasized? Because this is where a great deal of change, realignment, even distortion, takes place. I can think of very few writers who would go through this tedious process. It would be economically unfeasible for them.

MR. TRIVERS: No. You have either misinterpreted my contention or I did not make it clear. There is no medium which doesn't establish its own limitations, and a craftsman in that medium is aware of them and functions well within them. I had reference to something else— something deeper and much more vital to what we are talking about. I am talking about the *perversion*, not the alteration, of a concept, an attitude, a posture, a *theme*.

I may do a script in which I have certain things to say. I know it may be long and need cutting, and that certain parts must be made more comfortable for certain actors or actresses. But I do not recognize that condition in which I wanted to say "black is black" and came in with a "black is black" story, and they bought a "black is black" story but saw in it an opportunity to say "black is white"— and still leave my name on it. This is a perversion of my contention— the kind of alteration, of power to rewrite—that I resent.

MR. BRADBURY: And one resents the lack of honesty in people— with those who look you in the eye and say that nothing will be changed. I did a *Twilight Zone* script earlier this year—the story of a mechanical grandmother of the future. An electronic grandma who is brought in to raise children when their mother died. My idea was to create a humanistic grandmother which embodied the best principles of humanity. I thought this was fascinating. How could you build such a robot, one that would raise children with equal shares of love—distributing them equally as a robot could do? This idea was at the center of the script, and in one page I had the grandmother deliver an explanation to the family of how she came to be— telling them that mankind needed heroes to worship, and teachers and rabbis and priests—and why a robot might serve better on occasion because it couldn't die.

Well, in the middle of production they called and said it was long and they wanted to cut. With my heart sinking I asked which page; they named the page, and sure enough it was the explanation of the entire show. So I said cut here, cut there, cut anywhere but "the moment of truth". They promised; and on the strength of that I invited friends to see the show at my home. They cut it after all.

so the show was meaningless. It is this kind of dishonesty in responsible people that must end.

MR. TRIVERS: I might be able to understand it if they bought a synopsis or an idea which didn't turn out the way they expected, but the same thing will happen to a full script, seen in advance.

I sold a script which had won an early award in the contest for the lamented *Writers' Guild Show* we had once planned. It was bought for the *Lloyd Bridges Show*. It was a complete entity when they bought it, and it simply said that a man can be a hero despite his sense of opportunism. It dealt with the first six men to land on a planet, along with a rather cynical member of the crew. On this planet they found a diamond cross 12 feet high and six feet wide, and the question became how much of the cross can we take home and whom do we leave behind? I played *The Treasure of Sierra Madre* on a planet. There was a conflict and a struggle. One of the men dies, and the Commander stays behind to bury him. And in the process he discovers that the entire planet is solid diamond. Anything they picked up would have enriched them. It naturally provided for discussions of morality, in which they first asked if they had a right even to take the cross which might have been the symbol of a great civilization which had perished. With these elements to be handled it was natural that, to make it work, we had to incorporate in the men a certain sense of opportunism. Something no stronger or different than the matter of our own astronauts selling their life stories for a great deal of money and yet still being legitimate heroes. It took nothing away from the fact that they were still heroes.

This is the story they bought. And, without notifying me, they completely twisted it around and took the extra dimension out of these men. The commander ended up as insufferably noble, prating about being "missionaries in a new world" until I was embarrassed to view it, more so because another man was on it with a shared writing credit.

MR. MONASH: I'd like to turn from that for a moment and return to the question of what the writer can do for TV. Obviously writers feel abused by it, and obviously they remain in it. When I was writing I had some bad experiences, although offhand I can't really recall them. But as a producer I must feel a bit embarrassed about these sins of commission, or omission. Nevertheless, we ought to examine the whole question carefully. It would be interesting to have the producer of the *Lloyd Bridges Show* here to explain why he did what he did. Why he made the changes in Barry's script. I am sure he is not obtuse. I am sure he had what, to him, were very valid reasons. I don't know why the change was made in the grandmother script, or in the edited film. They may have shot it, and then taken it out. It may not have "worked" for someone. Perhaps they didn't even get the idea that Ray was striving for. Perhaps the audience would not have gotten it. I don't know.

But you are looking on your work as a personal possession when, unfortunately, you do place it in the hands of others. Here we ought to elaborate upon this question of the writer having more experience in order that he can gain the power to negotiate—individually at first and later through the Guild. Because it is an unfortunate fact that too many people come naked into TV—without any experience. And they are not going to get the experience after having been spoiled by TV. They are not going to work in TV, earn a great deal of money as most writers do, and then go out searching for experience. The experience should be gotten while you're young—when you are more receptive to experience.

When I was starting out, not in radio or TV, I used to feel that a writer had to be a truck driver or soldier first. All the book blurbs said it. "Mr. So-and-so has been a foreign correspondent—a sandhog." Yes, let's not leave out the fruit-pickers. These were campaign ribbons a writer wore on his uniform. You couldn't write without them.

MR. CHANDLER: You are not saying that if a writer came in with these—"I've been a longshoreman, I was wounded at Guadalcanal"—that producers would think he was a competent writer?

MR. MONASH: I am saying that he *might* be a more competent writer, because what most television writers are necessarily doing today is writing in synthetic terms about a life they have not experienced.

MR. CHANDLER: You are implying that the others wrote in non-synthetic terms to get their message across?

MR. MONASH: That is a different contention again. I'm simply extrapolating on what Ray Bradbury said.

MR. BRADBURY: And I respond to this, and would carry on this idea. Not what TV can do for us—but what we can do for TV. We can bring TV a gift of our individual selves. This is what we want to give. But only by bringing a rich self to TV can you improve the medium. I lecture to a number of college students, and I say "Stay out of television at first. Learn the other textures, the thicker ones, first. Then learn how to compact those textures—boil them down to the kind of thing that you must do for TV and the motion picture." Because you *can* be spoiled by television. You can learn what appears to be a spread-out texture in TV, and still not be a rich writer. A beginner could make a thousand dollars a month in TV. That's good pay. No one is going to start a novel for the comparatively small advances he would get against that kind of pay.

MR. MONASH: Consider the comparative skills of the average television writer and the genius exhibited by some writers of novels who remain virtually unrecognized and have to settle for associate professorships in obscure colleges.

MR. BRADBURY: And it is equally sad when anyone who makes a thousand dollars a month does not take the time to study the medium itself—to develop relationships with those who are producing and would be willing to have them observe during production. All TV shows afford this opportunity, and writers who don't take advantage of it are damned fools who don't deserve to survive in the medium.

MR. MONASH: You're simply talking about doing your present job better—as a craftsman. That goes along with the more important job of enriching yourself as an individual.

MR. CHANDLER: Both approaches are sound, and yet I have been obsessed with the feeling that television doesn't employ the writers it *has* to maximum ability. The writers, I contend, can write better than the public has seen on the screen. Why is it that what quality there is doesn't get on the screen? Why do most shows look alike? Why do they impress us as animated cartoon strips?

MR. TRIVERS: I should say that I did not for a moment intend to dwell upon the most hated failures—to create the wrong image of my relationship to television. The fact that the writer has abdicated his rights in his material does not mean that I believe the writer must surrender. He must still fight. And I think anyone worthy of the name *writer* is fighting a gallant battle. It is gallant because it is being conducted in full awareness of the odds against him.

MR. CHANDLER: I'd like Paul to consider my observation that writers can do better than they are permitted to do. Is that so?

MR. MONASH: Just the other evening I was watching a show about a rodeo rider. There was a scene that was extremely well-written as a scene—which led to another scene that was extremely well-written, as a scene. Yet the form and material was familiar as a story, and I felt no desire to keep on watching. No matter how well it was written or directed or produced or played.

I think the writers are working quite well within the limitations of the medium. If you compare the writing on TV today—and this includes comedy, which we are not discussing—I think it compares favorably with motion pictures. More than favorably. And it compares favorably with popular magazine fiction. But not Broadway. But there, you see, Barry Trivers has just declared that he wrote eight hour-dramas in the last *year*. If you compare that to the year or two years one devotes to a single Broadway play, you realize that he could not have enough time to pour himself completely into the project.

And yet, what the writer struggles against are the stricture of format. It is very difficult to write good drama when your hero is a repetitious man who does not develop, in terms of himself, over the course of 30 hours in a year. Someone like Stoney Burke or Ben Casey or Jim Kildare does not develop. The stories revolve around him, but he must remain a constant within it. What the writer can do about this—except somehow and somewhere get the best ideas to network heads and production company heads—I don't know. And those ideas must be so startling, so original, so valid, that they will enforce themselves upon the medium. They must be able to break apart the thinking of creative executives—which tends to run in analogues.

MR. TRIVERS: But this is an infringement upon their concept of what their series represents. You see, it's an environment. It must not be tampered with. "We're doing fine," they say, "so let's not fool around with this." Within that framework you can't come in with a fresh or original and vital approach. Format is the enemy of the writer.

MR. MONASH: I won't argue about the conditions. They exist. The question is what can the writer *do* about it?

MR. TRIVERS: I have one suggestion. I've been asked, on a number of occasions, about the success of *Naked City*. I have often been asked to "do a *Naked City* script" for another series, by which I *think* they meant that the approach should be in depth, and deal with character, theme, problem and personality with an extra dimension. And when they ask what the secret is, I say it is Burt Leonard, the producer. He is not the only man in this business who recognizes fine material, but I must say he is one of the rare men in this business who distinguishes the industry. I have heard him invite a sponsor to remove a commercial if he didn't like the story. I have heard him tell a network that if they did not like the theme of a show he would take it to another network. For this kind of producer the writer will kill himself, because he knows he will be defended. The writer cannot do it alone. He may make the initial contribution, although it may not always be the major one. But all the other contributions are vital too, and the writer is generally asked to solve an *assembled* problem. He cannot do it alone. We need more people who will defend fine work.

MR. BRADBURY: The shocking thing is that TV doesn't really want fine material. Something that is missing across our entire culture— not just in television—is an understanding of just what *creativity* really is. When I address intellectual or semi-intellectual groups I am constantly asked to define it. "What are the fundamentals of creativity? How do you create?"

What can I say? You create out of excitement. Out of vitality. Enthusiasm. Out of love—out of hate. Now the sponsors, just growing up with this, only know the primal benevolent or non-benevolent self-aggrandizement of it. The producers certainly do not know much about this because they haven't done it. They don't know what the creative act is. But it is simple. You just get mad as hell and you write. You get happy as hell and you write. You love life very much one day and you write an ode to it. One day you don't like it, and you say I don't like the way things are going and this is what I put down.

Not to recognize this is to stand in the way of the writer. If I were made a producer tomorrow I would line up a group of writers and ask: "What's exciting you know? What's bothering you about the world? What would you like to attack or what would you like to praise? Go home and write it, out of love, and bring it in and we'll find out what's wrong, or inadequate, or not quite correct. We'll see if it's done in the right way and if it will work." But only from that point of view. Not criticizing the basic idea, or changing it. It may run a little long and needs cutting. Or it may need to be built up slightly to put over your love or your hate. That's all.

But it is the complete misunderstanding of creativity in our entire society that plagues me, and I don't know what we in TV, or anywhere else, can do about it. We've got to find more ways to talk as we are talking now. We can write more articles. We can pin down more producers and say, "Look—this is life!" We must tell them we are not making it up. We must tell them there is a common need—that we are trying to stay sane! *All art is man's attempt to remain sane in a very difficult situation.* The world doesn't want us here and we are trying to face this chaos, whether it is inside or outside of us. This is what we are trying to arrive at, I think.

MR. CHANDLER: What is cynical and what is realistic? An advertising executive, a very fine man, told me that we were at cross-purposes. He said I was interested in a good play and he was interested in the sale of a product. If the plays are too good, he believed, the people would not listen to his message. What does one think of that?

MR. TRIVERS: I think this man was trying to oversimplify a responsibility that he has. I may seem to be switching hats, but I have always recognized that the people with whom I deal across a desk are like an iceberg, only part of which is visible to me. Behind them, or below them, if you like, there are forces more powerful—forces to which they must answer, as they execute their responsibilities.

MR. MONASH: This is not correct. You *are* seeing the major part of that iceberg. A great deal of it may have melted as it drifted down to more temperate climes where you are working. But the producer of a show is not subject to quite as much influence as you think. I had very few strictures from the network. Very little pressure and none at all from sponsors. I'm talking about *Cain's Hundred*. Once it was agreed that this show was to be done, certain basic decisions had already been made. The basic area of TV is programming, not what happens to programs once they are on the air.

And I would grow a bit more harsh in an attack upon writers. I see presentations every day from members of the Writers Guild. Presumably, these are programs they would like to write. They are terrible for the most part. Derivative. Puny. Even unintelligent. This year I have not seen a single original and arresting idea.

MR. CHANDLER: I think this is unfair. I don't want to defend the whole membership, but *Cain's Hundred* was simply *The Untouchables* reincarnate. Another network said, "Gee, they're doing so well, we'll shoot another crime show like it. Paul Monash originated it—let's let him go with it." They didn't bother you in *Cain's Hundred* because they knew you *had* all the answers of the gun, the arrest, and the incarceration. How does this relate to the kind of creativity Ray Bradbury is talking about?

MR. MONASH: I hope we are not talking about trying to do the *present* programs in a better way! They are being done rather well. What we are talking about is getting into *new* areas of programming. This year I had a strong desire to do a series based on *The Young Lions*. I looked upon it as a vast novel on film, beginning with New Year's Eve, 1939, and proceeding through the war. I was going to take the liberty of keeping the basic characters alive into the post-war era and exploring their problems. Everyone thought it was a good idea. It died, however, because of the thinking in analogues which is such a part of TV. Someone said, "Well, let's see what happens to *The Gallant Men* and *Combat*." Not someone. *Everyone*. Well, I tried to point out that this was not analagous to those shows, but I didn't penetrate the wall of thinking. All the shows projected for next year are derivative of current shows. The problem for the writer is to foster shows which are *not* derivative. I am not saying that if he solves the problem the network will solve it in the same way. The fact that *Playhouse* 90 did not come back had little to do with whether writers wanted it back or not. It had to do with network economics.

MR. TRIVERS: You accused the material now being brought in as derivative. If it is, I believe it is because of the unrelenting demands put upon writers for derivative material. I have watched show after show become another *Route* 66 or *Naked City*, another something else. Do you honestly think the writer would not want to be associated with something new and fresh? Or has he simply been rebuffed time after time, and learned that his only means of survival is to bring in the slightly altered carbon copy?

MR. MONASH: I'm not sure. I'm not sure that writers haven't taken the easy way out. I wonder if they have been pounded into submission.

MR. BRADBURY: You have stunned me without knowing it. First of all, our own Guild held a competition a few years back for our own series. The initial scripts were turned in, and I took ten of them home to read, and they were the worst bilge I ever had to wade through. I assume my ten scripts were a cross-section. This goes back to the original point I made, and indirectly supports you, Paul. Too many writers come raw into television without education in any other field. They are vulnerable, and all you can tell them is to go out and learn something in the other arts and *then* come back and kick producers in the knees.

MR. CHANDLER: Could we turn back, perhaps, to our original discussion of what the writer can do for television? We might write, each in turn, an epilogue of our own to this discussion. Barry?

MR. TRIVERS: Whatever else has been said, it goes back to our desire to improve it. *Caring* is the thing that drives me. I think man is involved in a struggle for survival at a number of levels— primarily at a physical level now, when the shadow of the bomb falls over Pomona and makes us uneasy. But there are the emotional and spiritual areas of survival too. Am I right? Man is looking, as Faulkner said, not only to *survive* but to *prevail*. This is my concern. I think the possession of certain crafts or skills are gifts which are placed in my custody to be used not only to live well, but be made some use of. To add to the sum total of human experience and throw a little light in some corner. So it matters very deeply to me when work in which I involve myself—and I can do no other kind—is mishandled or mistreated. I have not quit. Obviously I am continuing to work. I believe in television, and I know some day I will manage to overcome the resistance to my ideas. I intend to keep on fighting, and I urge all other members of the Guild to keep on fighting.

MR. MONASH: Briefly, and adhering in self-defence to the original topic—what can writers do to enhance television? Barry said it, among other things. They can keep on caring about what they do. This is not easy, because I think most writers feel that there exists a vast conspiracy to blunt their feelings. I would not call it a conspiracy. Let's say there is a *concentration* against what they want to do—*exactly* what they want to do. They do not work in a free, or even a liberal, medium. To maintain a feeling of caring, to stop worrying about what money is coming in, what the residuals are, what their status is—this is their objective. To gain this and remain a creative writer is going to be very difficult. Yet it must happen. For as the creative writers leave television, and some of them seem to be, the medium will be further downgraded. But beyond this, I'm afraid, there is very little a writer can do.

MR. CHANDLER: I'd like to save the final word for Ray Bradbury. But might I say that though we have heard a good deal about the writer's shortcomings here, I still feel the basic *malaise* comes from the other side. The writer's talent simply isn't being permitted to come through—by network or sponsor timidity as has been suggested here, by advertising agencies which don't care about content, as has also been said, and perhaps by outdated Guild rules regarding submission of material and ancient prejudices now being invoked by many producers who were former writers. All these things and many more militate against good writing getting through. I hope we as writers continue our responsible search for means to get our best work before the public.

MR. BRADBURY: I got into a cab about six months ago and as I was riding along I asked the driver if he had seen anything good on TV lately. He said "Yes. What I really like is *Twilight Zone*." I asked why and he said, "Because, when it's all over, it makes you think." This was not a well-educated cab-driver. His grammar was not perfect. But that stuck with me. The show is one of the few that tries to do something like this, and from this I conclude that we're not really feeling what the public wants and could digest. We haven't begun to do this.

Finally I would say this to writers, producers, sponsors—to everyone in television . . . all of us must do this together. . . . Go out and look at the young generation. Go to the high schools. Go to the colleges. See the immense *need*, the immense *excitement of ideas*. Then go away rejuvenated, and improve our medium.

6 A Creative Climate for TV Writers*

ANTONY KEAREY

TELEVISION is most effective when it is dealing with strongly-marked kinds of personality, either real people or fictional characters. Yet, on the other hand, the whole bias of television drama lies mostly in repetition and sameness. Drama is dominated by the sheer turn-over of the series programmes and the serials, and almost all of the main characters in these tend to be relatively obvious types of people, easily recognizable and readily acceptable—one decent, ordinary chap or decent, ordinary woman re-appearing time and again as the nurse, the housewife, the executive, the policeman, the welfare-worker, the old familiars of the screen.

It is obviously of the greatest importance for us who work in

---

* *S.F.T.A. Journal*, *Spring 1962*.

Antony Kearey writes (1965): How quickly styles change in television. In three years my points have been answered.

1. Thanks primarily to *Z Cars*, leading characters in series can be as difficult and rough-edged as the writer chooses. These policemen were not cosy father-figures, but real men, as awkward in their individualism as the criminals.

2. The anthology series has been developed with great success, *Love Story*, *Blackmail*, and now *Knock on Any Door* are prime examples, all relying on a highly original approach from writers.

3. The blurring of the line between drama and documentary helped to weaken the position of the individual play during those years. It has been productions such as *Crime and Punishment*, *Malatesta* and *Luther*—all highly individual, larger-than-life and removed from contemporary realism—that are winning viewers back again to the individual play.

4. Unfortunately the weak point remains; and a fundamental one—the position with regard to writers. It has improved but not enough.

television to try to break through this sameness and introduce as much individuality of character and presentation as we can, even in the series programmes. We should, of course, understand the reason for the popularity of ordinariness both with the public and the writer. For the home audience the people on the screen become like friends whose re-appearance they can welcome week by week; if these screen personalities were edgy, difficult, awkward, off-beat or in any way outstanding for their differences or strangeness of character, they would not seem like friends, but more like characters in dramas outside the family's normal experience.

For the writer it is far easier to measure up to a subject in a dependable, professional way in script after script if he chooses a good basic idea from the real world and then rings the changes on it in a series that goes on drawing from the infinite well of stories available in, say, such centres of activity as a newspaper office or a police court. Once a subject of this kind is set up, there is no re-alignment to be achieved, either by the creative team or by the public.

But a future that is based on the acceptability of subjects in terms of their fruitfulness in repetition seems bound in the end to choke itself with over-familiarity. For how long in any entertainment medium can you continue to exist by repeating yourself, with minor variations in dress and accent, using roughly the same theme with roughly the same restricted range of characters? Surely the object of the writer-director team should be to create as far as possible drama that has a new edge to it and characters that are newly-discovered and freshly observed.

Armchair Theatre is an interesting case of this search for freshness. As a regular production event it has set out deliberately to achieve an original approach. Maybe sometimes the originality has been overdone, attempting to give too great a "significance" through technical experiment to subjects that did not always gain from this special kind of treatment. But in general I have always felt that the plays in the *Armchair Theatre* series have been chosen to allow for an original approach in production, and that directors working in the team have been genuinely encouraged to develop originality in their productions.

We certainly have writers of originality, such as Ken Hughes, John Mortimer, Arnold Wesker, Harold Pinter and Alun Owen. But Hughes and Mortimer have not contributed recently to television, and other significant writers such as Robert Bolt and N. F. Simpson have not written directly for television at all. Unless television is content to lose all its best writers to films or the theatre, it must pay them more, make it worth while for the playwright to contribute. Through its absorption with repetition of the commonplace, television has a habit of discovering and discarding writers almost in the same moment. But we cannot afford to discard or ignore these writers so casually.

I think the main hope lies in developing subjects that enable the minds and imaginations of writers really to work, whilst at the same time allowing them the maximum freedom in technical expression. Programmes that are linked by a general theme rather than by the same subject and by the same characters.

Personally I like writers to work strange and unusual sorts of characters into their plays. These characters give directors a chance to widen their range of casting and employ new or lesser-known actors—to cast as widely as possible; and naturally the actors themselves have a chance to give a special edge to their characterization of such people. The success of the *Maigret* series illustrates this point. This is not due to the stories, which are often circuitous and obscure, but to the highly original characters that are introduced during the course of the investigations and their peculiar relationship with one another. We come back to fundamentals—the strength of television lies in the portrayal of character.

Obviously, when colour arrives, it is going to affect our work considerably. It has many advantages to offer—to the designer pre-eminently and of course to the educational and factual programmes, where producers with an eye for tone, texture, grouping and colour will be able to give inanimate subjects a dramatic, personal emphasis that they have hitherto lacked on the screen. But I do not think it will add greatly to the potentiality of drama; it may indeed bring us more production problems than it solves. In terms of the individual personality, the man and woman in close-up, it will not add a great deal to characterization; it has not done so in the cinema. Indeed, characters often come through more strongly in the black-and-white image than they do in colour.

One final point. We tend to produce to a considerable extent now what has come to be called the "dramatized documentary", and this presents certain dangers. People have television turned on in their homes so continuously that they can quite easily come to confuse fiction with fact—they have come to look so alike. I think it is very necessary for writers and directors not to blur the public's sense of what is true and untrue, real and unreal, even what is right and wrong. When people go to a theatre or a cinema they know that they are being presented with a form of life that is *fictional*, however realistic the production may be. But it is easy enough for the audience at home to become confused between the alternating flow of actuality and fiction in the ceaseless continuity of the evening's television programmes. Those of us who work in television drama should, in my view, try to pitch the fictional drama above the ordinary, so that it can never be confused with actuality. Originality for me consists in giving our work a special quality in human observation, a particular kind of vision that raises it out of the ordinary.

7 The Individual Approach: TV Drama*

DON TAYLOR

To talk of individuality in terms of television, is to make a direct challenge to the system. We are all as individual as we are allowed to be. The Corporation and the Programme Companies have made their decisions about what the public wants—as if that matters in dramatic art—and they define our individuality for us; which can be as wide as *The Age of Kings*, or as narrow as *Coronation Street*. I am, in a sense, the last one to complain: most of the plays I have done have been plays I wanted very much to do, and have reflected a personal taste, even a personal political attitude. But this freedom is the freedom of a prisoner in a large and comfortable cell. All our greatest hopes and deepest interests lie outside the walls. True individuality means room for experiment, and that barely exists in British television.

Individuality presupposes a goal, and a goal implies some sort of definition. TV drama's function is threefold as I see it: to entertain, to create a new and genuine television drama, and to re-interpret the classics in terms of television.

Of television drama as entertainment I want to say little, as British television consists of little else, and we have heard and seen

* S.F.T.A. Journal, Spring 1962.
Don Taylor writes: Since 1962 Television has changed in a basic organization way, in my opinion for the worse. The critical comments in this article are, I feel, even more relevant now than they were then, and the hopes expressed are further from being realized than ever.

enough. We must accept that much television exists merely to pass the time of day for people tired after eight hours work. But even here, at its lowest, television is a great influencer, and we ought to be aware of our responsibilities. We help to shape the patterns and values of the age, and our standards at this level should be as high as for Ibsen. We should lead the minds whose time we occupy towards a greater degree of consciousness. At present much of what is transmitted in the name of entertainment tramples those minds in the mud.

Of original television drama, the truest thing to say is that it barely exists. Few new plays are worth the viewing, for a man who looks for anything beyond a story line, and almost none repay reading or study. Since television began, no style has developed, only a bastardization of film and stage; and thought, logic and poetry have all been sacrificed to the cult of story. On this evidence posterity, if it bothers, will dismiss us as a superficial lot, with no taste beyond curiosity.

Why this sad state of things? Because plays survive through having memorable words, and words are discounted on television. We think of pictures, and stories and characters, but never words. We are sculptors who care nothing for stone, painters with heads full of images, but without the first idea how to mix paint. At the lowest dramatic level, of photographic realism, we often excel. Once in a blue moon we find realistic writers who have something to say, but by accident, not design. But the genuine dramatic language of compressed statement is unknown on television. Worse, it is unwanted. Anything that doesn't sound like the language of the street corner, or conventional theatre speech, is dismissed as false, and the result is ninety per cent emptiness. The creation of its own form of poetic— i.e. compressed, not ornamental—drama is television's highest goal. But to begin at all demands time and money for experiment. And even if the will is there, which is doubtful, in the competitive world we live in, the time and money and audacity are not. So we continue to plough a narrow furrow of worthwhile social realism across a field of nonsense. The challenging problems remain, not only unsolved but unrecognized.

My own principal interest lies in the re-interpretation of the renaissance classics for television. Possibilities are endless here, as the ground is almost untrod. The challenge is made the greater by the fact that Shakespeare in the theatre is almost dead. His meaning gets lost in a fossilized ritual of operatic acting, and obscured by gimmicky, non-academic production. But television is already doing its work. It imposed a style of acting on *An Age of Kings* not seen before in the Histories. The simple use of close-ups in *Henry VI* brought the various Lords to life in a way the stage can never do at a distance of fifty feet or more, and the direction was always slanted towards meaning, shunning the vague emotionalism which television so easily exposes. If we can now make the last step, and take poetic plays more completely out of sets and put them in the open studio, we will have done a more creative thing than television has ever achieved yet. My personal dream is of a classic television theatre, regular, once a month at least, where styles of tragedy, comedy, Restoration wit and Machiavellian villainy could be remodelled and reborn for the small screen, with the picture itself the most potent reinforcer of the poet's images. Till original television drama comes of age, such a scheme would happily employ the bulk of my time.

But in this sense individuality is a dream, an impossible chimera hardly worth the chasing, while half the nation's television is in the hands of commercial speculators and the other half has all but one finger tied. When commercial and aesthetic values come into conflict, commerce always wins, and this is what has happened, and is happening now. We are naked before the degrading forces of the profit motive. Our only weapon is our own sense of the truth, and that we must hang on to for dear life. Till the disastrous Television Act is repealed or drastically amended, our individuality exists within rigidly defined limits, and consists mainly of underpropping tottering standards. The exciting country beyond the walls at the moment remains a dream.

8   The TV Actor:
A Dialogue*

E. G. MARSHALL

GEORGE C. SCOTT

INTERVIEWER: We might begin by reflecting upon some of Tyrone Guthrie's opinions about acting for television, made originally in *The Eighth Art* and reprinted in an earlier issue of the *Quarterly.* "As to acting", he wrote:

> When, in order to protect the right image on TV, every politician is taking lessons in make-up; every ecclesiastic practicing saintly faces before the looking glass when royalty, presidents and multi-millionaires bone up on folksy ways and nice homely expressions so as to woo the Common Man by creating themselves anew in his image; when everyone, literally everyone, believes that by adding a cubit to his stature he can become a television personality, what, you may ask, is a poor actor to do? If he has a real talent for acting and takes enough trouble to develop a technique, there will always be a demand for his services. But not in TV; in the theatre. More and more, television acting will be reserved for the amateurs—queens being crowned, cardinals losing their specs and politicians wooing the electorate in Nebraska.

How does that strike you, gentlemen?

MR. MARSHALL: I would say, first of all, that when you put the work of any actor into thirty million homes, you are also adding a cubit

---

* *Television Quarterly, Winter 1964.*

to *his* stature. I don't think I'm being deprived of an opportunity to act by not being on Broadway.

I would agree with Mr. Guthrie to a point. The immediate reality of life is the most interesting aspect of television. A little girl falls from a bicycle or a President is assassinated, and the immediate quality of it is what television carries. I have great admiration for Mr. Guthrie. He's the finest director we have, but he has never done anything in the medium, and cannot appreciate the fact of it moving into the home. It is not a theatre, not a stage, but it is still a natural home for the actor.

MR. SCOTT: You have to define the kind of acting you're talking about. It's a diversified thing and matters of technique are varied. They vary for the motion picture, vary for television, and vary within the contexts of television. The actor on a series faces distinct problems from the actor in a single production.

MR. MARSHALL: On the stage you must say, as a performer, "Here I am. Now watch *me*." In television you don't have to do that, because if the director is alert he knows where the story is being told.

MR. SCOTT: It is a medium in which, like motion pictures, the actor is least in command. Someone may have decided to put the camera elsewhere at the moment an actor decided to command attention.

MR. MARSHALL: And the actor must follow the writer, in some ways. Some of the things I have seen brought from the stage to TV have been marred by an artificial quality in the writing. It may have worked for the stage, but in TV it seemed unrelated.

INTERVIEWER: Is this a reflection of what Guthrie has suggested? The two series in which you appear are literally chained to the everyday circumstances of reality. Isn't the essential theatricality of it missing?

MR. MARSHALL: Perhaps. Acting is supposed to be the recreating of life, and I don't know whether we can really recreate life unless we are involved in a total documentary style.

INTERVIEWER: Are *The Defenders* and *East Side/West Side* closer to documentary than to drama? In the sense that they deal with real social issues, and—in the larger sense, for the actor—that Robert

Shayon suggested when he pointed out that it is difficult to see a social worker passing through the irreversible crises of true drama?

MR. MARSHALL: That's what we are trying to do, I think, whether we admit it or not.

MR. SCOTT: I don't think so. E. G. may know the pitfalls better than I do, because he's been with it longer. But we're still trying to create a theatrical situation—sometimes against overwhelming odds. Perhaps this is faulty. But to duplicate reportage or documentary is not my work at all. If I were to do that I would go to work for CBS News, and learn Walter Cronkite's profession.

MR. MARSHALL: Of course we're still actors. But something has changed. In the "Golden Age" we were trying to put on plays, and I think that what we're trying to do now is put life itself on the screen. We work with things that have really occurred. We heighten, we accent and underline them, but we're no longer trying to do Ibsen. When we do Ibsen, it's a special event, but when we do "Who Do You Kill?" this is something that is happening. It's not life, but it's a terribly close reflection of life.

MR. SCOTT: To me, it goes without saying that the very thing we must not do is try to recreate a photographic image. We can't do what is done on the evening news program, because it's done so much better there. They do it in the proximity of time.

MR. MARSHALL: They can't do what we do because they cannot follow a person from breakfast to dinner. They can only say what *happened* this morning and what *happened* at dinner, but we hold the mirror to life.

MR. SCOTT: And to do it we must employ the devices of the acting profession. We are in a theatrical—I return to that word—a *theatrical* process which cannot be denied, no matter how involved it is with the life around us.

MR. MARSHALL: Yes, I see that. We're involved in art, but an editorial is also artificial in that sense. It's not reportage—it's art. In the "small a" of art, perhaps we're closer to the editorial than the reporting of events. Was it Otto Preminger who said that all of the elements of high drama were present when Ruby shot Oswald?

MR. SCOTT: But to make a drama of it, you would have to find an actor to play each of them. They would have two points of view about their roles, and all of the things that structure life into dramatic art. And the minute you did that you would be in the theatrical art. That's why the whole thing in the Dallas jail looked like a badly-staged *Circle Theatre*.

INTERVIEWER: Can we turn from the relationships between the actor and the real person and consider your attitudes toward working in a series? Many critics and practitioners would say that this is the least satisfying kind of drama. Writers, directors, and actors have protested the limitations of it. As performers, do you find the routine difficult? Are you restricted in what you can bring to a character in terms of growth and new insights?

MR. MARSHALL: Not at all. I'm not certain that characters do grow, in that sense. You can see new things that you want to reveal, as I do in the law. You get wrapped up in the subject, but not the character, and a little knowledge is a helpful thing. But you're only bringing yourself to it. How much can a man really develop in six months or a year? He may give up smoking, or learn to dance, but essentially he changes very little, and therefore there is not that much development in a series character. You don't deepen as you would in *Hamlet*, where the lightning flash may strike and you see new things suddenly. The only deepening that happens in a series is that your knowledge of the subject—whether it be law or social work or anything else—becomes broader.

MR. SCOTT: I agree that it has never been done properly in a series. But I think it can be done, and—he said shyly—this is what we are intending to do.

MR. MARSHALL: I'll await with great interest to see what happens to the character of Brock. But I think you'll stay the same. How are you going to change?

MR. SCOTT: It takes a lot of jockeying with people who make it their business to stand in your way. But it can, and should, be done.

MR. MARSHALL: Let's reduce it to a simple—maybe absurd—level. You're playing a mechanic, and so first you start off with lawnmowers, and you work your way up to Rolls Royces, but how else have you changed?

MR. SCOTT: You're not the same man you were three years ago. Nobody is the same person he was even six months ago. The essence of life is change. That may sound pretentious, but it's true. I said once that I didn't want to be the same old Matt Dillon drawing the same old gun in episode 91 as I was in episode one.

MR. MARSHALL: But if you're confronted with the same problems how will you change as a character? Maybe you'll draw a little faster or a little slower, but you still draw and you still shoot.

MR. SCOTT: It has nothing to do with the character as written. The essence of the change will lie in the man himself. He must change, or else it's not really theatrical. There must be some obvious and recognizable evolution.

MR. MARSHALL: He can only become *more* or *less* what he was in the first place. . . . He'll learn more about how he feels when he's subjected to different stimuli. He'll learn how he reacts to them. But nothing more.

MR. SCOTT: When I first went into this thing I spoke of a novelistic concept of character development within the framework of a series. You can pick up any novel—good or bad—and you find a leading character at the outset. Then things happen to him. People happen to him—things and events which change and alter his life. He becomes someone else. This change in him causes other chain-reactions, and by page 500 he emits different wave-lengths than he did on page twelve. Now this concept has been applied very little in series thinking. The sense of growth and continuity has never been developed in broadcast series at all—except, interestingly enough, in the old radio soap operas. This was what kept people interested. Of course, Ma Perkins was always Ma Perkins but there were little changes constantly. In *One Man's Family* the changes were fantastic. If you can do this with a peron's whole personality, rather than in the external aspects of his life, you will have achieved something memorable—something worthwhile.

INTERVIEWER: In an earlier discussion for the *Quarterly*, Paul Monash raised this same point. He had proposed, you may recall, a "vast novel on film" based on *The Young Lions,* and wanted to keep the main characters alive in the post-war era in order to explore their new problems. Monash said his plan would not work because of the "thinking in analogues" he found among those who produce series. By that he meant they could not avoid comparing it to conventional series like *Combat.* Now, if a writer-producer has difficulty in moving this idea forward, what chance has a performer?

MR. SCOTT: He can't do it alone. But if he's very fortunate, he may work with a conceptual mind comparable to the novelist's. There are TV series produced by such minds. One of them is *The Defenders.* Reginald Rose has a strong generalized, basic concept of the situation, and he has been able to keep everything in line in order to assure a flow that moves along a continuity line which is growing. This is interesting—and it's good. Perhaps, as E. G. suggests, the Prestons themselves have *not* grown, but there has been a conceptual guide in that series pointing the way toward growth, and all of us have seen series where this never happens—where everything goes to pieces.

MR. MARSHALL: George's reasoning is beginning to take hold with me now. I think this may be happening in our series. When I first began working with Bob Reed, for example, I was apprehensive because he was young—and an unknown quantity to me. He was a little awkward at the outset and I worried about him. As a father— and as an actor. In one sense, the fictional, he was a young law-school graduate coming into practice with me, and so this made me nervous. And in the real sense, he was a raw young actor who might trip over furniture. And then I became more comfortable with him in *both* senses—as an actor, and as a character. There was a true development in a father-son relationship. I still am not certain that this kind of character development is as deep as the kind you're proposing. I don't think that can really happen. You've got to go from the birth to the grave to tell the story as deeply as you see it, right? You're not going to do that in thirteen weeks—or a year.

MR. SCOTT: You might do it in three years, though. Or five. Matt Dillon certainly hasn't done it, and he's been on the air for six!

INTERVIEWER: Why do you feel that character can grow in your kind of series in a way it has been unable to grow in westerns?

MR. MARSHALL: Now that I've come halfway toward accepting George's position, I would say it is because we are involved with the people who come through our series—with the characters who bring their own stories and situations with them. We must get involved with clients, and we must relate to them. Matt Dillon is the only kind of dramatic character on TV whose simple function is to see that simple justice is done, and if he doesn't have to get off his horse so much the better. It's quick and it's clean and there are no loose ends.

INTERVIEWER: Does this move the argument, then, away from the theatrical and toward the dramatic? Is the western hero simply operating in that simple classic form which forces its own one-way resolution as an inevitable either-or? Are you involved in the kind of immediacies of life where resolutions are being rewritten daily in the newspapers?

MR. MARSHALL: I think that may be the key distinction so far as the development and freedom of range in character is concerned. Matt Dillon says, "He broke the law, and therefore he's got to be brought to justice"; but he can't stop to say, "The law has been broken, but who brought about this situation? What are the conditions that prompted it? Where did it begin and where will it end?" These are the kind of loose endings we face.

INTERVIEWER: Would you say, then, that you are social instruments as much as you are performers?

MR. MARSHALL: You come to sense that. We were banned in Boston for the show we did on abortion, and a month or so after that program *Time* Magazine proposed the same solution—largely that we begin to make a full-scale inquiry into this problem. This is how entertainment serves a function. I don't know how many people subscribe to *Time*, but I know that millions who do not saw our show. It gives you a sense of accomplishment. Your interest increases and so does your involvement. Being in a series like *The Defenders* or *East Side/West Side* is simply not like going to the theatre every night at eight, saying hello, putting your make-up on, and performing until the curtain goes down and it's over. In TV it doesn't end. You are a part of something. There is a continuum which does not exist in the theatre.

I go out and give speeches to Law associations and similar groups. All of the history of the actor as a mountebank, a social outcast and an undesirable—all of the past when an actor was outside the pale—is gone. I'm a member of the community now.

MR. SCOTT: Precisely. You cannot deal with everyday existence and be removed from it. In social work you are directly involved with American life, and the actor becomes involved in the same way. It is a battle that never ends, like Oceania fighting Eurasia in *1984*. Sure, social workers have individual successes at times, but you can't end a play about a social work project like you can end a western, and you can't react *as a character* in any cut-and-dried way. How much do you want to indicate—through your characterization—the overall success or failure of social work as a whole, of society as a whole, of progress at any level of human existence? How much do you want to say? How good is life? How far have we come? Where are we going? If the character of Neil Brock solves this problem one week and another problem the following week, and nine times out of ten comes out smelling like a rose—then the obvious implication is that *society* has come off smelling like a rose. The converse is true.

MR. MARSHALL: You come to a railroad crossing and the sign says "Stop—Look—Listen". I think that's what we're trying to do on these shows. We arrest the attention. We point to the problem. We say, "This is something that we ought to consider—find some solution to. We are not finding it now. This woman is going to lose her child, this man is going to prison. We must consider their problems." That's all we can say. Let's think about it.

INTERVIEWER: How does this approach square, then, with the question of dramatic structure? Is the classic sense of climax and resolution in drama simply passing away? How does this answer Robert Shayon's criticism of the character of Neil Brock—for example—which does not pass through some irreversible crisis? Is dramaturgy itself becoming something else?

MR. MARSHALL: No. We are dealing with a particular kind of

magnetic field here—a field which has continuity. That is the essence of this kind of series drama—time and continuity. As a result, as long as the options are renewed, you carry a different orientation to it. It is a series in which there are openings and closings, but not necessarily complete endings. There can't be, really. If you resolve the main character's problem once and for all some week, the series is over. But this doesn't mean there are no crises and resolutions each week.

MR. SCOTT: If the classic idea of resolution is the goal, then at the end of some forecasted period there should be some true resolution of the central character. There can be change in this sense. Some-day Brock will face this—death, total resignation, incapacity of some kind, a totally new change in direction. But not every week. How in hell can you draw a resolution for the narcotics problem in an hour? It's just not possible. Brock and the Prestons can't resolve it this way. That's why the novelistic concept can mix with dramaturgical and both can still have validity. And that's why a character—at least the major character in a series—does not pass through an "irreversible crisis" every week. We are really talking about the longest drama in history.

MR. MARSHALL: Like the great novels that detail whole decades— whole lifetimes. But for the major character to just drop out of things—well, that's not the point. It's not the point of a news-paper.

MR. SCOTT: But the validity of dramatic characterization in the closed sense of a week-to-week crisis depends on the transient characters in our stories. We begin with them—with their problem specified —and we do resolve that. You recall the wonderful performance given by Don Gordon in a *Defenders* episode last year. He ended up going to the chair—as a result of his own tragic flaw. It was classic in that sense. You can't send one of the Prestons off like that. It would make a hell of a fine episode, but then you bump into the great generalized concept of character evolution you're trying to establish, and you've lost a particular audience.

INTERVIEWER: The mention of audience brings us to that specialized audience within an audience with which you must deal directly—

the representatives of the professions you are portraying. How have they responded?

MR. MARSHALL: I'll yield to George on that one. The attorneys are working within a more rigid professional framework, and I've had very smooth relations with Bar Associations.

MR. SCOTT: Well, the National Association of Social Workers monitors our programs, and they were asked to provide responses— and they provided responses. Many of them were appalled at some of our techniques and *modus operandi*, and many others were appalled at me as a prototype of a social worker. Hell, we tried patiently to explain to them that we were not making training films for social workers. I think the fact that I wear my tie loosened has shaken the very foundations of social work. I don't think they're wrong—but I don't think my attitude is unreasonable either. We're trying to draw attention to social work and its problems. But the letters— some of them—have been rough. "I am a case worker and I can't see that my prototype is anything to rave about." And: "In addition to the program's total and gross misrepresentation of social work practice, I am also deeply concerned about the impact upon the public of the empty and ineffectual portrayal of the social worker. . . ." I've gotten others—letters that say "I'm a social worker", or "I'm a Dean of a School of Social Work", or "I train social workers", and all of these say "Cool it". They say, "You are no doubt getting fantastic opposition to what you are doing—but they'll get over it. You're doing much more good than harm." I get this kind of letter repeatedly and it makes you feel right about it.

MR. MARSHALL: That's what we feel, I think, all the time. That we're close to this thing called life that's happening around us.

9 The Actor's New Opportunities*

TOM COURTENAY

DILYS HAMLETT: a discussion with

ROGER MANVELL and DAVID ROBINSON

ROBINSON: Do you think there should be any special training in the drama schools for film and television?

COURTENAY: I don't think any special technical training is needed for acting in television. When I played in *Private Potter*, I got all I needed from the producer while rehearsing. It's bad for the actor to be thinking of himself in technical terms in advance of working in a play. That's the director's job, not his.

HAMLETT: You get what information you need while you are rehearsing, and I think it would be bad for the actor to be thinking in terms of cameras and shots—that is the director's job not his. It is only too easy to overtrain an actor and make him lose his spontaneity.

MANVELL: Do you think television is a difficult medium—technically difficult—through which to establish yourself?

HAMLETT: No. It represents a challenge after the theatre. The way of working is so entirely different. You just feel you *should* be able to do it, and then you find after all that you can, once you've tried it!

ROBINSON: And films?

HAMLETT: I've not yet worked in films, but to me they represent the chance to give a more *complete* performance than in any other medium, with the guidance of a good director.

---

* *S.F.T.A. Journal, Autumn, 1961.*

From the actress's point of view, I think the situation now is beginning to improve in Britain. Women are being cast, at any rate in the theatre, much more as men are cast—for the particular kind of character that's needed for the play. We're no longer just a set of statistics crowned with a fashionable mask of make-up! I get very angry when the film critics write that we have no actresses here of the same calibre as the Continental countries. Up to now this has seemed to be true only because the producers and directors—particularly in films—just haven't widened their range of choice. They haven't looked for the actresses that are there.

MANVELL: Has this change of attitude, this widening-out in casting actresses, come through the far wider range of character-parts in television drama—and when I say character-parts I mean, of course, character-parts for young as well as for the older women?

HAMLETT: Yes, I think so. A lot of young actresses have made a name through television.

COURTENAY: Tyrone Guthrie said something about this when he was writing about Charles Laughton. On the stage you have to work from day to day, doing the best you possibly can with yourself, the character and the audience. So it's up and down. But with films you can discard what you feel is wrong—a kind of instinctive discarding of any failure: providing the budget of the film will let you, of course!

HAMLETT: I do understand, of course, that casting in films is much more to type, and that the conditions are different from the theatre.

MANVELL: Well, isn't that a limitation in films from an actor's point of view? It narrows him down and, more often than not, includes him out!

HAMLETT: Yes, that may be so. But when it *does* include him in, it gives him a wonderful chance, because the camera magnifies, emphasizes what is right in him *as a person*. You can bring to bear every relevant detail of your personality, mix yourself into the part. They say you can't be as *big* on television as you can on the stage. Everything must be pulled back, understated. But, quite simply, I don't agree. If the feeling is big you should play it big, whatever the scale of the shot. So long as the performance is true the screen can take it. You must go all out if the part, the character, demands it.

COURTENAY: Well, I think the physical presence of the camera near you gives an instinctive sense of scale. You can see or sense the camera, and play on the correct scale for it. In the theatre, the scale of performance is always something of a worry. To whom are you playing—the front row, the middle of the house, the gallery? I play in *Billy Liar* to the middle of the stalls and hope the performance reaches the furthest seats.* But in television and films I feel you can act more in your mind. That's what I like doing. It feels so much nearer the reality of the character.

HAMLETT: I agree with Tom; in television you don't have to worry about projecting a performance the way you have to in a theatre.

ROBINSON: But what about the problem in film of fragmenting the performance day after day?

HAMLETT: I think some actors and actresses are far more affected by this than others. I imagine from what I've read that Irving could never have acted for films. Apparently he did a great deal of preparation before each performance. Whereas Ellen Terry just rushed on to the stage.

MANVELL: So neither of you regard television as the poor relation of the stage and films—I mean from the creative or artistic angle!

COURTENAY: Well, only in one way. Your performance disappears immediately it's over.

HAMLETT: But what an audience you've got whilst you're on!

MANVELL: What about the point of which so much is made by the older generation of actors—about missing the presence and the influence of an audience?

COURTENAY: I like working *without* an audience. I like concentrating on the performance itself, in the way you can when you work for television or films. You aren't concerned with holding, entertaining, worrying about the audience and their differences night by night, or between matinees and the evenings. An audience can actually be a nuisance to the actor.

---

* Tom Courtenay took over the part of *Billy Liar* from Albert Finney in the stage production.

HAMLETT: It's absolutely wrong to say a film or television studio has no atmosphere for an actor. The whole set-up for production, and especially the camera and its crew, creates a tremendous sense of working, of concentration, of feeling for the actor.

ROBINSON: I suppose it's easier to attain what Stanislavsky called "public solitude"—creative concentration without the distractions of controlling the audience as well.

HAMLETT: Yes, it's odd, but it never enters my head during the performance that I'm playing to this enormous audience. I think the actor has to learn three different approaches to his work, so that he can adapt his method of work as he moves from the stage to television and from television to film, and each medium has a different kind of reward for him. The first is performance in the presence of an audience; this is a wonderful thing, uniquely exciting. The second is the reward that comes from reaching out to a vast audience through the television camera and one's instinctive response to the technical needs and the particular excitement of the television studio. And then there's the film, with its wonderful chance of completing the performance stage by stage, detail by detail.

ROBINSON: And the satisfaction's different in each case; I see that. But isn't the end product at which you're aiming—the interpretation of the role—the same whichever medium you're performing in?

COURTENAY: Not really, because you have to do it so differently, and that changes the kind of work you do. On the stage you've got to *demonstrate* more. You *enlarge*, and therefore you lose. With the camera you can pick on small revealing *details*. You can *look* what you want to reveal, or say it normally. You can concentrate, and make the concentration show. That's what I like about television.

HAMLETT: But there are many different *kinds* of drama. Some lend themselves to this intimate kind of performance, some don't. And many different kinds of theatres. You can perform intimately in some, whereas you feel physically quite lost and out of touch with the audience in others.

MANVELL: Why do you think the older generation of actors hates or fears television so much? I know there are many exceptions to this, of course. But so many have expressed either fear or dislike of it.

HAMLETT: Television cameras can be very cruel, unflattering and very revealing and I feel that anyone with a big following, with a big stage reputation and an established stage personality, or even a film star has something to fear in committing himself to this hectic and immediate medium. I feel younger people have grown into it and accept it happily.

10 Comedy on Television: A Dialogue*

SHELDON LEONARD

CARL REINER

INTERVIEWER: We can begin with a traditional question. What kind of comedy is best suited to television?

MR. LEONARD: Comedy must reflect the times, and the answer to that question must take into consideration the fact that the public appetite for comedy changes as the economic and political climate of a country changes. While there is always some demand for certain kinds of comedy, there is also a broad, fluctuating public taste which will account for extraordinary success in a given kind of comedy at a given time. This condition accounts for the remarkable success of a kind of comedy removed from reality like *The Beverly Hillbillies*.

MR. REINER: Taste in comedy swings in great cycles. A kind of comedy that hasn't been seen for a long while will suddenly stimulate tremendous interest. The motion pictures had a cycle of unrealistic comedy during the *Topper* era, and it hasn't been around for a few years. *The Beverly Hillbillies* is creating a new cycle—or repeating an old one.

MR. LEONARD: The social climate points comedy in that direction. We have been trying to make shows in our studios that present comedy situations which are not too far removed from the experiences of the people who are watching them. But there seems to be

* *Television Quarterly, Summer 1963.*

a taste for something a little broader—or even completely removed from reality.

If you consider the matter, the makers of *Hillbillies* are not any more restricted than were the people who made the Keystone Cops and the other old Mack Sennett comedies. They don't have to pay any attention to reality at all, and this makes for a great kind of comedy. This is a hell of a kind of comedy. The talent for making it is a rare one, and I respect it. It doesn't happen to be the kind we are proficient at making, but it shows there are some straws in the wind. Everyone thought *Hillbillies* would click, but it has had such great success that it points to a shift in the public taste again. For some reason, the broad social climate is making people look to entertainment in non-realistic areas. This kind of trend in audience taste is found throughout the history of comedy, and the great comedians were always sensitive to it. Chaplin followed his instincts, but he also trimmed his sails to the prevailing winds. As the times seemed to dictate it, he added more social content to his films.

MR. REINER: And by doing so, he hit. He hit in *Modern Times* and *The Great Dictator*. He couldn't do *City Lights* in the later period. In *City Lights* he was talking about extreme poverty, and by the time he did *The Great Dictator* the public's interest had shifted.

MR. LEONARD: So when you say what is the best kind of television comedy you raise the same questions. What is the nation's interest? What do people want, and need, from their comedy? That's what the best kind of comedy will be, on TV or anywhere else.

INTERVIEWER: Can we consider now the nature of situation comedy? What are the ingredients for success in this approach?

MR. LEONARD: You can define them, but only after the fact. Before you start you have a certain philosophy about a show—an idea of what it might accomplish and how you want to go about accomplishing it. But then you become pragmatic and observe what really occurs, and try to make maximum use of what is happening. As we planned *The Dick Van Dyke Show* we knew that the Morey Amsterdam-Rose Marie combination would let us develop another kind of comedy within the total situation. This would be different from what we expected of Dick and Mary Tyler Moore, and we planned for this. But the subsequent use of the characters, particularly Van Dyke himself, evolved only as we learned what he could do and how he functions best. Then we made the best use of that.

MR. REINER: Situation comedy depends largely upon the general approach you find on a given production lot. One approach has been, I think consciously, to people the stage with comedians—not comedy actors. Long ago when working with Sid Caesar, I learned that it was just too difficult to work a comedy actor or celebrity into a sketch. It just never came off, and so we said let's do comedy with comedians, and if it turns out they can also act, that's a bonus. Andy Griffith was a stand-up comedian before he became an actor. Every show on our lot has tried to follow this principle.

From my viewpoint—and I think as a comedy performer would —I like to load every moment with a possibility for laughs. If you must have a straight scene it should lead directly to something that is going to be very funny. Now, if a comedian is on the stage he will explode to make the audience laugh. A comedy actor will just deliver what the line says.

MR. LEONARD: And we can help the comedian. Once we are certain we have a performer who can get the most out of the comic action, we must provide a good story. If the story situation is good, and the audience is interested in a particular situation, then we have provided some insurance. If the action does not turn out to be funny, we haven't got egg all over our chin.

MR. REINER: If you have found a playing attitude for the actors— if they have a well-defined and clearly identified attitude as a result of their understanding the situation in which they are involved— then the comedy comes up much better. The story line, as applied in terms of situation, must give them a key to their performance—a strong and clearly defined emotional relationship to the events.

MR. LEONARD: An example of this condition was clear in the skiing show, where the doctors told Dick he had a "sprained body". There is nothing terribly funny about that if you look at it detachedly— if you put it in a vacuum. But the story surrounding it made it clear that these multiple contusions would be a terrible source of embarrassment to him—far greater than the physical discomfort—because his wife predicted that if he went skiing he would hurt himself. And so he feels that the fact of hurting himself is almost a reflection on his masculinity, on his role as the head of the house. The comedy grows out of the confrontation between them.

MR. REINER: In any kind of drama a plot is simply the interplay of situation and character. If someone asked me what was the best comedy line I have ever written, I would have to say it was probably a line like "I see", or "Ah-hah!" Because, if the situation is right, that line can get the biggest possible laugh. When I read a script that someone has submitted, I see a number of jokes and I say: "There are a lot of good gags here, but the best joke on the page comes at this point, where a straight scene or straight talk leads into a simple line like *Oh, really*. *That* line will make an explosion because it comes out of a situation in which the attitudes are very strong at that moment."

MR. LEONARD: And this is a result of the integrity and consistency with which you have built a character. If people don't understand the character, the jokes won't work. The most magnificent example of this is the small classic where a gunman pokes a gun in Jack Benny's rib and says, "Your money or your life!"—and then there is nothing but a long pause. And that pause is one of the most effective jokes in Jack Benny's long career. If you looked at it on paper, it would be nothing. If someone who didn't know Benny read it, he would say, "What's so funny about *that*?"

INTERVIEWER: Many critics have suggested that there is room for another kind of comedy—the classic comedy of words or manners, or the comedy of satire like *Born Yesterday*—on television. Yet these, apparently, have not been successful. This has cast a stigma on situation comedy. Some feel it is less than television could achieve.

MR. LEONARD: Well, regrettably, the term "situation comedy" has come to be used in a blanket sense in that it applies to everything except "stand-up" routines. Everything becomes situation comedy, and the use of the term is not justified in the Van Dyke show, which is a comedy of character. The laughs don't originate with the situations in which they find themselves, but in the kind of people they *are*.

MR. REINER: And many of the shows loosely termed as situation comedy do not really seek laughter. They may have a laugh track, but there is no reason for laughs to be there. *The Donna Reed Show* is more often serious than comic. But this is not directly related, I think, to your question. You mentioned a kind of comedy like *Born Yesterday*. This focuses on the essential differences between TV and the stage. Broadway has no close-up, and a good Broadway play has different rhythms; it can't really work on television as comedy.

MR. LEONARD: We've been through this problem again and again. The medium is not designed, fundamentally, to command the depth of people's attention. One who goes to a Broadway show surrenders a part of his individuality and becomes a component in this thing called an "audience". He becomes part of another entity, and, until the show is over and he has to re-orient himself to the reality around him again, he remains part of something else that is not real. The audience does not relinquish this sense of individuality in the home. A phone will ring, a child cries, and they are constantly next to the reality of their own lives as they watch the set. They cannot immerse themselves totally in what they see.

So we seek a partial surrender of individuality, first by developing a relationship between the audience and the continuing cast of characters in a series. The audience feels they know them. And from this basic reason for the existence of situation series, if you prefer the term, we can begin to make further progress toward getting a deeper level of participation in a show. And we do this by seeking things that are fairly close to their reality. Not great and significant abstractions about life and the "comic muse"—but by finding the humor that is, in this sense, human and typical. You have a better chance of getting attention in television if you are dealing with things like plumbing bills that are too high, or kids who don't do their homework. It may not satisfy those who want everything to uplift mankind, but it is human, and it does have a realness. All great comedy comes from that.

INTERVIEWER: Could you say this of *Hillbillies*?

MR. REINER: Why not? Now the audience is looking at the other end of it. We watch these people in that show dealing with the commonplace things of our experience—but in a different way. They are like children. They do stupid things with telephones and swimming pools and cars. Watching them is, for most people who enjoy them, like watching a baby first finding its own navel. This is human too—to watch the stupidity of others. To feel a little bit superior.

MR. LEONARD: We have great respect for Paul Henning and what he has conceived. That's why we can dissect it.

MR. REINER: I'm sure he, above all, must keep asking himself why. Why is *Hillbillies* the biggest thing on television? Why has it swept the country and attracted such massive audiences? He wasn't trying to fool anyone with it. It was an honestly conceived piece because he is an honest guy, and this is his expression. And it's a very good one.

MR. LEONARD: It's too easy for some people to say this was conceived in cynicism—with all that talk about "mass appeal" and the "lowest common denominator"—but it does not answer some basic truths about life *and* comedy. When they framed out *Hillbillies* they knew it would have some wide appeal, but none of them dreamed that it would be such an absolute, runaway hit. You have to examine it and see what kind of monster we're trying to feed. *Hillbillies* is not just a catering to some mass of anonymous slobs that a few people would like to shut out of life. It cuts across all of life—here and all over the world. Great numbers of civilized people enjoy it. There is, without getting too academic about it, a certain amount of social protest in the show—of telling most people what they really like to hear— which is that plain folk are better than rich folk. In this case it's a slight twist. It says plain *rich* folk are better than *ugly* rich folk. But the ultimate human quality is still there. Someone is still getting needled from the point of view of the poor folks, of whom God made so many because he loved them.

INTERVIEWER: Is this the only level at which this kind of satire can be effected on TV?

MR. LEONARD: Openly identified in that way, satire is caviar to the general. Some years back they made a marvelous picture which satirized all of the suave adventurers who were indestructible and invulnerable. I think it was called *Bulldog Drummond Strikes Back*. And despite the conscious kidding, the audience didn't realize that it *was* satire, and ate it up. Satire is an intellectual activity in which it is required that the subject matter be related to the subject being satirized, and very often this is simply beyond the large part of any audience.

MR. REINER: This is the great lesson we learned in my years with Sid Caesar. We often got wonderful reviews for the satire in our shows, and yet we had to couch satire in three or four gags that anyone could understand and appreciate. And if we didn't have those jokes there it wouldn't work—in New York, where a sophisticated audience watched it, or out in the country. Even in our take-off on the Japanese movie, we had to bury the Samurai warrior in straight jokes or no one would have appreciated it. Beyond that, I think that satire itself is a form I've grown less fond of. As you grow older, you get less enchanted with satire. As a kid, you find that the first thing you do in comedy is satire. You take a voice, a sound, a commercial, anything that exists, and you make fun of it. You're not creating anything *new*. You're making fun of— you're commenting on—something that was created before. You pick out a star, or a bad play. But a bad play by a bad author is still more *creative* than the fun a comedian makes of it. Because it exists. The bad play came to life whole—as the labor of someone's real original creation. And as you grow older you come to terms with this. You know the difference. You appreciate the people who create, without making fun of it. This doesn't mean you can create great comedy without making fun of something. You just get a different respect for the act of creation.

MR. LEONARD: When you do high-level satire, where the satire itself is properly disguised, and not too blunt, you lose much of your audience. The other kind of satire, which is closer to just sarcastic comment—the kind like saying "Who do you think you are—Ben Casey?"—is a cheap laugh. It's too easy. And there is very little in-between, I'm afraid. You either go for the cheap, easy laughs, which are close to burlesque, or you go to the sharp and subtle level of great satire, which loses your audience.

INTERVIEWER: Under these circumstances, then, to what degree can, or should, comedy on television attempt to answer the criticisms of those who are concerned about the general state of our social and cultural advancement? The traditional arguments from this point of view center on the general use of TV for escape and the "frivolous", and would claim that this is a mis-use of the medium. How do you coneive your function in relation to these arguments?

MR. LEONARD: I think there should be no mistake about the sense of responsibility we carry. It is, without waving flags, a real aware- ness of the enormous privilege involved in having a half-hour of time before millions of viewers. It produces a sharp sense of respon- sibility to the medium and to the people who are watching it. And this had led us to believe that we can, within a framework of good showmanship, advance valid social comments, valid ethical concepts, valid generalizations about the human condition which have meaning for the audience. The idea of adding a "moral" may seem a little heavy for some critics, and I'll admit that, in the early days of the Danny Thomas show for example, we laid it on with a trowel. Danny would just step out alone on the stage and say. "I don't want my boy ever to feel. . . . "—and so on. We're less corny now, but we still try to get across certain points.

We try to tell a very large audience that it is better to be straight- forward than to be devious. We still try to say that a sense of idealism makes a richer life than cynicism. We still base shows on those time-worn aphorisms and clichés that never seem to lose meaning for people who are trying to make the world a little better than it was. We are happier if this is being done—if it is being said, even in comedy terms. Perhaps those are the only terms that *will* make it stick—and make it lasting.

MR. REINER: This is the best place *for* it to happen. It may not be sophisticated enough for some, and I don't think that matters. If you begin with an attitude that there are moral positions to be taken about life at every step along the way, you can bring it out in comedy at any level. Chaplin did it. A fall-down comedian like Sid Caesar could do it. He would get laughs with mugging or those angular moves of his, but behind it was some comment about life. You can say that the little family squabbles of *The Dick Van Dyke Show* are "frivolous", but most of them carry a strong psychological truth about the relationships of men to women in marriage. The audience sees both sides of the eternal struggle, and they become a little better as human beings because they have seen how the emotional tugs and pulls of the man-against-women struggle resolve themselves into not only real solutions, but the kind of satisfying human solutions which must happen if we are going to live together as people.

That's one of the blessings of being a writer. You can fight with your wife, and then even it up at the typewriter. You can make the truth come out on paper even though, at the moment, your own particular emotions and neuroticism do not allow you the luxury of coming to a real synthesis of the problem. But on paper you are doing it, resolving human conflict, in the cold, clear daylight. And millions of people are seeing this—and understanding it. They're understanding it because it is surrounded with laughter. So, on the one hand, maybe we are "frivolous" to some people with very limited ranges of understanding about how humans live. And on the other hand, maybe we do, because of the nature of the medium—which is reflected in everything we said about satire— maybe we do make some of it obvious. But that ought not eliminate the *fact* of what we are doing.

INTERVIEWER: Moving, then, from the social values of comedy to some specific techniques of bringing a show to life, can we assume that you approach every show with a basic situation carefully worked out in advance?

MR. REINER: Every show has to have a "reason to be". There are many reasons for a show "to be", and they don't come out of anything more than the desire to do good comedy—at a basic level. We just finished a show we have been trying to work out for two years. We knew that Dick Van Dyke could do an hilarious bit on Stan Laurel, but we could not find any reason for it to happen. Finally, we used the simplest reason for bringing it about— a variety show within the format. It never occurred to us because we have been doing situation comedy, and needed a story. Then a very small story was worked out around the cast taking over a hotel for an evening as a favor to a friend. The reasons for it was to allow a situation in which a variety show could take place, and in which we could let all of our performers, who are musical performers too, show this side of their talent in a way that we knew they could.

INTERVIEWER: In writing jokes, do you let them evolve out of the basic situation or do you invent jokes which are then applied to a situation?

MR. REINER: It must develop, basically, out of a situation. Danny Thomas is a great man to study if you want to see how this works. He once said, "If you talk long enough, straight enough, and if you have a funny bent, you will talk funny sooner or later". It must evolve out of people and the way they are. I can't be serious for too long. Someone can be saying something serious and I'll start to make funny noises. When Danny hears someone talking seriously and profoundly, after a while he just can't stand it. A real comedian will be given a straight line, and he just ends up switching it to a funny line. It's built into comedians.

MR. LEONARD: There are two basic approaches to developing a story that work for us. The first, of course, is to find a story that deserves to be told, and that couldn't be told in an anthology show as a straight story. Then we find comedy terms in which to tell it. The other approach is to work backward from a sequence, like the Stan Laurel thing, which is just too good to let go. You find the story that can hold the sketch. It's not as effective, but it sometimes works. Van Dyke does a great drunk act. We had to find a way to let him do it within a credible story.

MR. REINER: And that show, incidentally, offers a commentary on the way in which we have to learn to deal with censorship in its various guises in TV. There are pressure groups, codes, a variety of ways in which you are told you can't do something. Like every other shortcoming in the medium, conditions like these make you more inventive. You have to advance what you want to say—and you find that, by living with these conditions, you often come up with something better than if you had just said it in a direct way.

Dick could play a drunk—and he could do an immediate switch from drunk to sober and back again. It was supreme comedy, and we had to find a way to let him use this tool, because for some people there is nothing funny about seeing a drunk on television, and these people have a way of scaring others into seeing things their way—no matter the cost in terms of a brilliant comic inventiveness. So we worked at it, because it bothered us, and we developed the idea of putting him in a post-hypnotic state—where every time he heard a bell he *thought* he was drunk, and when the bell rang again he *thought* he was sober. The sin was taken out of it. It was much funnier—and we got twenty drunk scenes instead of one without offending anyone's sense of propriety.

Censorship can work to your advantage. It's there, and you have to acknowledge it. But maybe it's good that it is there. It makes you find new ways to let expression come through. In the long run, comedy needs to keep inventing, to keep saying things that don't offend, but aren't stripped of everything that's human—and funny.

11   Social Problems in TV Drama: Sex and Violence*

ROSALIE CRUTCHLEY

KEN TAYLOR

ROSALIE CRUTCHLEY:

I WOULD like to say at the outset that I don't believe in shielding children from the truthful presentation of either violence or sex. But I am not a supporter of a continuous display of violence to no purpose on the screen. I am, in fact, appalled when violence seems to be taken lightly. I think parents ought to explain to children who, at an early age, watch Westerns and crime stories on television that the kind of "off-hand" killing that goes on in such productions is utterly unreal; death is simply taken for granted, whereas in real life there is always some reason—social, political, psychological— why people are killed, and the reason is an important part of the truth about violence. Violence to me is never normal; it is always a sign of some individual or social disturbance that needs resolution. And the truthful presentation of any act of violence should show what the nature of that disturbance really is, not why it is wrong.

I believe most women, whatever they may say, are inwardly opposed to violence, though I know they often, through mixed motives, possibly fear, encourage their menfolk to be violent. Women are protective of life, and are not likely to respond to that fashionable, destructive Bond figure. The Bond cult seems to me a
particularly to younger people—because it actively en-
them to assume that violence, coupled with a synthetic

urnal, Summer 1964.

form of "high life", is attractive and makes for sexual success. Perhaps it does, but I consider this a disastrous way to influence young people, and there is no doubt the influence can be very strong indeed.

So I accept that we must see violence on the screen, but in its true light, showing the evil and the waste that it represents. Writers and producers should surely try to move away from these incessant forms of crime as entertainment and only reveal the true effect on people and society. That it why, if we have these plays about crime and social and psychological disorders (as I admit we need to) I prefer it in the form of, for example, *The Defenders* or *Z-Cars*, and not the violence-for-violence-sake types of dangerous, bogus entertainment.

My attitude is the same about the presentation of sex relationships. It seems to me wrong not to show these truthfully to children who have reached the age when they are capable of understanding enough of the situation involved (very young children would be bored, anyway, and therefore unimpressed). Sex is part of all life, whereas violence, one hopes, need not be, and writers, producers and actors should in my view see to it that it is the truth they are portraying. So there should be no need of censorship. But if these relations have to be drained of the truth in order to present some unreal or pretty picture about something everyone will, in some way, experience, often at an extremely youthful age, then we do great harm; our job as adults is to arm children, not shield them, to protect them by giving, not withholding, knowledge of what may happen, good or bad, in their own relationships with each other. Shielding children is wrong, and the parents who do this are partly responsible for weakening their powers of resistance.

For instance, I consider it is extremely dangerous the way sex relations are treated in some women's magazines, or the equivalent on films or television, where every relationship seems in some degree falsified. Now this is the kind of thing from which I would try to protect children, and if necessary censor that kind of presentation, rather than the genuine realistic portrayals that so often seem to shock parents who are unable to face, or object to facing, things as they are, however difficult. Censor unrealistic romance, by all means, because such nonsense is particularly dangerous nowadays for very young girls and boys, who should be prepared as early as possible to face life realistically.

I simply do not understand, fundamentally that is, why there is this opposition, primarily by women, to the more exact and truthful presentation of sex relations on the screen. After all, in this age of comparative freedom their daughters are very likely—at a surprisingly early age—going to experience sex to some degree. So I would hide nothing. On the other hand, I agree with them when they object to the portrayal of the sleazy way of life in order to make quick money, exploiting, as some forms of the press do, human degradation for the sake of sensational entertainment. Commercialized sleaziness can be just as artificial a concoction as commercialized romance. For instance, my youngest daughter, aged twelve, saw one of the recent Purple Heart programmes; she was horrified at the desperation of these adolescents and said they seemed "so unhappy"—there certainly seemed no question of her being drawn to that way of life. In other words, the programme was an honest one. Though she realized people did these things, and as a result showed sympathy for them, she regarded them as sick and in need of healing.

I think the effect of television on children remains comparatively small in those homes where any form of active upbringing is taking place. The home atmosphere usually wins. But if children are allowed to look at television endlessly without having any compensating values given them, then I would accept that the ceaseless presentation of thoughtless crime, violence and sleaziness on the screen must in the end affect their outlook. And I would hope that all of us who work in television must realize the huge influence it has and feel our responsibility very strongly.

KEN TAYLOR:

IT was about four years ago, when the ITA had just intervened to ban a play of mine, that I first noticed the press using the phrase "sex and violence". At the time I was irritated by the conjunction. Unfair to sex. . . . The general feeling then, which I shared, seemed to be that sex was a good thing and violence wasn't—except perhaps bull-fighting, which was art anyway. Now—a good deal of agonized thinking and re-appraisal later—I am happy to accept the catch-phrase both for journalistic convenience and for the way in which it defines the subject area of censorship in relation to instinct, the artist and society.

Sex and violence, Eros and Thanatos—the two poles of the creative and destructive impulses which are the elements of the life force. The basic data of the life situation is presented in these two themes—that life must reproduce itself and that it must destroy other life to live. The most primitive and natural preoccupations of the artist are with copulation and with killing. The most basic preoccupation of human society is with the regulation of these two functions. In any organized community the fundamental rules prescribe what we may or may not eat and go to bed with. The forbidden instinct creates the dream and the dream is realized by the artist. In this sense you could define art as censorship defied.

Any attempt finally to resolve this conflict between the artist and society is therefore bound to fail. It is inherent in their character. In our own time the problem has become especially acute through the simultaneous expansion of the popular arts and the collapse within society itself of a regulating ethic. It is one of the interesting features of the complex relation between the artist and society that the most fruitful periods of artistic expression are those in which society is securely based in its attitude towards the eternal verities through some form of generally accepted religious ritual. The tension between man and what he fears is then reduced to a level at which the artist is most free to use instinctual material for creative purpose within an agreed convention. In our own civilization these pre-conditions have almost ceased to exist.

This is a difficult time then for artists—and perhaps especially for those working in the popular media of films and television. We exist in a society without faith, freed from the ethical restraints which define conventions and burdened by the lack of a convention which would relate us to the facts of our existence. When nothing is unspeakable, the unthinkable cannot be defined. The great truths in consequence are either debased or denied. Sex is for giggles. Death is for giggles too. The artist's subject-matter being meaningless, he retreats into the absurd. The tragedy of *Dr. Strangelove* was that it offended almost no one. The contemporary sin against the Holy Ghost is to be deeply moved.

Descending from these lofty generalizations into the smoke and blood of battle, here are my own prejudices and working preoccupations. Both by inclination and persuasion I am a Puritan, which means that I find myself in almost total conflict with the contemporary scene. Because I am concerned in my work with fundamental and sometimes ugly truths, I have been accused of striving for sensational effect. Because my attitude towards my material is deeply serious, I am also accused of being obvious, sententious and a bore. These charges are all valid—and I have not yet found a way to avoid them. Certainly there is no greater heresy today than to affirm the importance of human intelligence, dignity and sensitivity against the joint forces of commercial exploitation, mass vulgarization and soggy intellectual hedonism masquerading as the New Enlightenment. The good ladies of Birmingham* would have my support in their campaign if they were truly devoted to the defence of human values against the erosion and encroachments of modern barbarism. Civilization is a frail thing—and the pressures of the twentieth century have subjected it to forces which it may not survive. Sigmund Freud was a great scientist and thinker, but few philosophies can have been more debased than his in the coinage of popular misconception. Freud struggled with the problems created for the individual by the conflict between instinctual drives and the necessary, restrictive forces of social organization. His name is used now as the excuse for rejecting the validity of any form of social or personal restraint. So far as films and television have assisted in this process, I believe that their influence has been detrimental. Man is an animal— this we must accept. But he is an animal that has created a moral order.

The true artist is concerned with total reality. The ladies of Birmingham would restrict us to what is "nice". To accept their limitations would destroy the very function of the artist. Bad in itself—but not so serious as what might follow. For, by masking the extreme nature of our peril, we should increase the probability of our own self-destruction. To men who hold the Bomb, "Know Thyself" has become the categorical imperative above all others. In this sense the artist's obligation to defy censorship has never been so compelling—the danger that we may anaesthetize our sense of protest, never so great.

Let me be quite precise. I would not ban the strip clubs, the nude films or the horror movies—let alone dear *Fanny Hill*. The great

---

* This refers to The Women of Britain Clean-up TV Campaign which was launched in May 1964 in Birmingham, England.

merit of a free society is that it can know itself for what it is. I should be more inclined to ban the TV sociologist who implies that love can be equated with lack of sexual restraint, or the TV politician who maintains that self-aggrandisement can be the highest virtue. But even these must be allowed their say. I should ban no one then—but I should seek to amplify if possible the still, small voice of human conscience.

For I believe we have an obligation (Oh, how sententious! Oh, what a bore!) to recreate a sense of moral purpose in our society. We have a duty to emphasize that men and women possess brains as well as sexual organs, that love is more important than fornication, and that gentleness and wisdom have more human value than a pair of tits. If these things are no longer true for us and have no meaning, I hold that the sooner we are obliterated by our own stupidity the better it will be.

We cannot Ban the Bomb—and we can only learn to love it if we first loathe ourselves. Those who reject the facts and those who try to make us worship brute reality—of whatever kind and from whatever motive—place us alike in peril.

II

ART AND TECHNIQUE
OF TELEVISION ACTUALITY

The Camera and The Event

A. WILLIAM BLUEM

IT is a truism that television coverage of the events and circumstances which constitute "news" has introduced an entirely new dimension to journalism. The printed press has always implied its devotion to those vaunted masthead terms of trust—"fairness", "objectivity" and "impartiality"—but newspapers and magazines generally have been political instruments from the start. As "journals of opinion" their business has been to support as much as report. The class-room ideal of journalism as an impartial recorder of change may never have held true significance until the cameras arrived, and despite the efforts of many who would make American television the servant of one or another of the power classes within our society the cameras manage to prevail.

We may acknowledge that the man who aims the camera or edits that flow of aural and visual signals upon the small screen can exert considerable control over the impressions which millions receive. It is also true that the mere selection of an event for televising can somewhat alter the nature of that event. Heisenberg's Uncertainty Principle, which lies behind quantum physics, establishes that in making observations on a system it is necessary to exchange energy and momentum with it—a process which of necessity spoils the original properties of the system. To some this describes with precision the relationship of TV cameras to events they record. Even the London *Times* has opined that "although they may not necessarily spoil the meeting . . . they (TV cameras) certainly modify it for better or worse".

It is, of course, far too late to begin the retraining of those tradition-bound newspapermen who continue to espouse the illogical theory that a printed record of a happening is mysteriously less capable of distorting, or even corrupting, the nature of that event than is a filmed or electronic version of it. What film and television report differently they need not report less honestly. Indeed, there has now accumulated sufficient evidence to suggest that such reports are more true and impartial than their printed counterparts. While a man who speaks in public or in a private interview surely knows he is at the mercy of the note-taking reporter, never has a politician dared suggest, upon seeing himself in a televised interview, that he was being "misquoted".

The presence of the camera irritates vested socio-political interests even more than it does journalistic interests, in so far as the two can be separated. This is because the validity of the camera recording lies in its neutrality. Democrats who celebrated the graceful style and photogenic qualities of Kennedy view with alarm the rise of former film star Ronald Reagan, whom they regard as "manufactured" as opposed to "genuine", while Republicans who cursed the Kennedy "image" are overjoyed with the "star" qualities of their candidate. Naturally, according to who is winning, television is alternately damned as a corrupting force in politics or praised for its capacities to reveal "the truth about a man".

Interesting variations of this phenomenon occur in the South, where those who would prefer to see desegregation advance at a speed more convenient to them are inclined to regard civil rights demonstrations and televised coverage of them as complementary aspects of the same evil. For the racist in the deep south the networks have no business "making more" of the event than *they* think it deserves, and there is a strong sentiment that "things would work out alright if the TV people would let us alone".

Such attitudes are shared in far less conservative quarters. Over-zealous liberals also have dreams of controlling the meaning of the image. Perhaps the classic example of how resentment against television's neutrality can corrupt even supposedly "objective" social scientists is recorded in a study by two University of Chicago sociologists, Kurt and Gladys Lang, who attempted to prove that the televised record of a parade in honour of General Douglas MacArthur's return to Chicago in 1952 was "biased" in MacArthur's favor. To no one's amazement they proved what they set out to prove. Parades *do* have a habit of glorifying those they are intended to honor. It is a commentary upon the "scientific detachment" of the Langs that they would equate those automatic decisions which any director who is responsible for televising a parade will make with some kind of "right-wing plot" to make a hero of MacArthur. Had they attacked those who conceived the *idea* of the parade their bias would have been as obvious, but their complete lack of understanding about television's relationship to events would not so blatantly have been revealed.

The Langs, it turned out, discovered that there were many empty spaces along the line of march which the cameras did not televise. Further, as these scientific investigators mixed in the crowds they discovered people who were *not* cheering. These, our self-appointed television directors insist, should have been electronically noted. This failure to recognize that the reason for the existence of the event is also the primary reason for televised coverage of it poses an alternative to what the Langs implied was a "pseudo-event"—the "non-event". At best, their argument suggests that the Langs are fighting in a back-to-back stand with their less liberal counterparts in the south. Both kinds of reaction suggest only what valid investigations into communications behaviour have long since concluded— that people tend to perceive only what they want to perceive.

It is probably a good thing that American television news and actuality coverage has finally entered its "cool" phase. There is no evidence to suggest that the attempt to employ the medium in an angry editorial manner at a national level is producing desired results, no matter how many print-bound theories of journalism's "function" are expounded. It is well to honor Murrow for what he tried to do, but perhaps that "Golden Age" is also past. Our understanding of how people use the medium grows surer, and as we consider journalism's function of "giving light that the people might find their way" we may also ask whether television reportage cannot give *more* light by applying *less* heat. If this medium, with all of its dynamic characteristics, continues in the time-honored print tradition of exhorting, pushing, arguing and contending, it may lose its greatest powers for inducing positive social understanding.

Some of these judgments are supported, enlarged upon, or openly contradicted in those essays which deal with news, actuality and documentary in the following section. One can be certain, after reading them, that journalists on both sides of the Atlantic carry fierce pride in their profession. They are, in an electronic age, acutely aware of their responsibilities as well as their commitments.

12 TV Journalism: A Dialogue*

REUVEN FRANK

DON HEWITT

INTERVIEWER: We might begin with a quotation which appeared in the May issue of the *Quarterly*; one originally borrowed from the British TV journal, *Contrast*. In it, Maurice Wiggin, a British newspaperman, made some sharp observations about TV news. Among other things, he suggested that the medium had never reached its ideal; that real news was incapable of being pictorialized; and that the medium largely disappointed those who saw a bright journalistic future for it. This is the classic argument from the "newspaper point of view", we assume, but it might be a good point at which to begin.

MR. HEWITT: Yes. It reflects that school which still thinks television has completely abandoned the word. I don't know why someone can't get as much from listening to Huntley, Brinkley, Sevareid or Howard K. Smith as he can from reading. Perhaps the specific comment is a direct result of the British habit of underplaying the newscaster—of making him anonymous. His personality is kept apart from what he is doing, but we've let our American newscasters become personalities in their own right—probably bigger personalities than Lippmann, Alsop or Scotty Reston. That's because people can identify them. They know them and are fond of them.

INTERVIEWER: But doesn't this lend credence to the arguments of those who insist that television is a "personality" rather than a "news" medium.

---

* *Television Quarterly, Fall 1962.*

MR. FRANK: No. To begin with, most of the argument is old-hat. Oh, some who raise it may be sincere, but most are just being defensive about their vested interests. The newspaper-versus-television argument has always postulated the *ideal* newspaper against television-as-it-exists. That's a weak-enough argument in America, but it's ridiculous in Britain. When is the last time anyone saw an *idea* in the *Daily Sketch*? Or even in the *Mail*, which is a pretty good newspaper? Some of their editorials are written at a level which would embarrass the American grammar school boy. Which are they talking about—the *London Times* or the *Guardian*—or the mass circulation papers?

The same argument is raised here. Someone will wave the *New York Times* over his head in symbolic justification of 7,000 American newspapers that use barely twenty paragraphs from the AP foreign budget every night and do nothing of their own.

It's a false argument. Unless it says, "Is television living up to *its* ideal as well as newspapers are living up to *their* ideal?" it can't be a real argument at all.

MR. HEWITT: And even if we assume that perhaps we should be compared only with the *Times*, there are other factors to be considered. The *Times'* directors and stockholders are concerned with only one problem—putting out a quality newspaper. The board and stockholders of a network must consider news as one small part of their total concern. If all the money, time, energy, and resources of NBC or CBS were poured into news operations only, then the comparisons of ideals would be valid. We are not the be-all and end-all of network television.

MR. FRANK: I'm not sure that point is as relevant as it was a few years ago. In fact, you could logically make just the opposite case—that we in television are practicing journalism in its purest available form. I say "available", not ideal. I see that *Time* is contemplating entering the art gallery business, the ticket agency business, the Cook's tour business. I see the thrashing about of the *Saturday Evening Post* in an attempt to stay alive. We all saw the scuttling of *Collier's*—some say for cynical reasons, and others that it was the victim of a Madison Avenue whispering campaign far worse than the worst of the so-called rating games in television. And the newspapers themselves spend more and more time, space, and effort on circulation-building stunts which are much farther removed from the duties of journalism than anything the people we work for would ever think of asking *us* to do. The stunts may originate in the business or circulation offices, but it is usually a damned good reporter who draws the assignment of interviewing the winners, and it is often a skilled and experienced old rewrite man who writes the original copy.

For one reason or another, everyone in a television news shop, down to the copy boy, knows more about each step in our process of "publication"—to use their term—than most print journalists. Whenever there is a compromise we are all aware of it. Newspaper people live generally in blissful ignorance of far more basic damage being done to their product. When they criticize us—and I don't refer only to the critics—they match us against the rosy image they formed as cub reporters or students.

Moving to the larger picture, television news programs rarely do anything to increase their own circulation. When they try, they do it badly. Experience proves that the only way they can increase their own circulation is by putting out better programs. The competition among them is direct—but it is for news. I'm not sure this virtuous result stems from virtuous causes. For one thing, we haven't the time for gimmicks and contests. That leaves us the written word— publicity in print—which runs up against the vested interest of the people who might print it. I am sure the influence of this vested interest is not conscious, but you have to be a fool to assume it's not there.

So, coming back to Don's point about news not being the sole or even the prime function of television networks, I think at least we have come to the time when it is an inescapable function. I think that henceforth the networks will be unable to get out of news, or even reduce it substantially. It is quite possible for a corporation which publishes a newspaper to stop publishing that newspaper and continue for a long, active, and profitable life as an economic unit. Not so in television.

INTERVIEWER: Let's move to the day-to-day aspects of this argument. Do you get direct criticism from newspaper colleagues? Do their points seem reasonable?

MR. HEWITT: We get it all levels. Last week a newspaper TV critic criticized us for using an end-piece on "Miss America". But the day after it printed the criticism, the same paper ran a three-column picture of the "Miss America" candidates on page two!

It's flattering, in a way, when they expect more of us than they do of themselves. The critics will not excuse us for the daily sins of their publishers.

INTERVIEWER: Now we've shifted the "they" from general criticism of TV as a news medium to TV critics on newspaper staffs who judge news programs.

MR. FRANK: Yes. I suppose this is the most annoying aspect of it. We put on a program which has a news-value in its own right. The critics will say it was a terrible bore, but the news editors at the same papers will put the story on the front page. It happens day after day.

MR. HEWITT: That's true. There was a recent case in which a re-viewer said that a *Meet the Press* episode did nothing but "generate a lot of heat and no light". His paper ran the story of that interview as a lead story on page one on the same day. If the TV critics aren't qualified to determine the news policies of their own papers, how can they set standards for news coverage?

MR. FRANK: And they get their functions confused. Too many of them fall into the great trap of confusing television's coverage of a "live" news event with the nature of the event itself. I think it's fine for someone like Arthur Daley to say "It was a lousy ball game", but not for the same judgment to creep into a critical column.

The essence of TV coverage of a "live" event is that we do not have control, and should not have control. I am always embarrassed at national conventions when someone from the national committee comes along and offers control of the event to us. They want our opinions. Hell, it's *their* convention. We are there to report it.

MR. HEWITT: That's a point. We ran a "school" for politicians once—the worst possible thing we could have done. That's just not our business. We are in the business of providing a big conduit from a convention hall to the TV set in somebody's living room, and we enable someone to see what is going on as best we can.

When we cover an event like a convention, or a space-shot, what we're really trying to do is what the Scripps-Howard masthead claims it does—"give light and the people will find their way". I think we have done that far better than they have.

We probably are not always the best *reporting* medium in the world, but we are the best *acquainting* medium. Because of television, and radio to a lesser degree, the name James Hoffa is no longer just letters in cold type. Hoffa is a living, animate man because of television. The fellow listening to his car radio hears the name "Willy Brandt" and, because of television, he visualizes somebody. He's more involved with, and interested in, the story because he is acquainted with either the person or places represented in that story.

MR. FRANK: And it pushes even deeper than that. One of the major reasons that news is on television at all is because people watch it. Even if you were to make the argument that regularly-scheduled daily news programs perform their function badly—not as well as newspapers, not as well as historians, sociologists or the people reading off rock tablets—even if this argument were made overwhelming, television would still have to provide news to justify its existence. You put on such programs because you have command of the audience. It's a fundamental responsibility—and a real function, whether it's a single news program or the whole network's output of news and public affairs. It's a duty you can't avoid.

We do have the words, and that's the first basic duty—the getting out of a fast-breaking news bulletin. We have the ways of getting them on just as fast as radio.

MR. HEWITT: They say radio is faster than television. That isn't so. More times than not, a fast-breaking bulletin moves faster on all three TV networks than it does on radio. That's mainly because the television newsrooms are more on the ball than radio newsrooms.

MR. FRANK: A second part of our duty is the regularly-scheduled daily news program—Cronkite, Huntley-Brinkley, the ABC shows. You can put news on in this framework and it is accepted. The personalities are accepted in the home. I don't care if they are "stars". Some of them are and some of them aren't. If they have any skill, they will perform in such a way that the information gets over and is reasonably succinct. I don't think it will often equal the total information of a two- or three-column story in a newspaper, but it exceeds—and I'll stake my reputation on this—it *exceeds* by and large the scope of news, both foreign and national, in most news-papers in the United States today. We have the reaction to demon-strate this truth. And this is amazing in itself. I recall when NBC started its news-on-the-hour experiment about ten years ago. Stations loved it. People loved it. Out of the cornbelt came the cry for more foreign news. The press does not handle it. They have abdicated their responsibility in this area, and so we moved in.

And in the process we've learned our trade and our craft. In the early days—at both networks and perhaps more so at mine—if it wasn't picture it wasn't news. There is still a lot of that. Network TV is a dozen years old. Gutenberg was long ago. That's a fact, not an apology!

MR. HEWITT: And when we came of age, network executives stopped second-guessing us. There was a lot of "You've got to have more pictures", or "Swayze's on too long", or "Edwards is on too long". It took us a while to prove ourselves. Now they don't second-guess anymore.

MR. FRANK: To be fair with them, it did take time for us to learn our business. But we discovered the things that words must do and the things only pictures *can* do.

An example of this distinction came out of the Alger Hiss trial. It went on day after day—a continuing story would be told over the same old pictures of Hiss, or his attorney, or the prosecutor, or the jury, going up and down the steps at Foley Square. We saw those pillars at Foley Square day after day—and that's pretty dull and there was no reason for it. We all did it. We sent down a cameraman or two and we always got those pillars.

Then one day there was a sequence no newspaper could have matched. Alger Hiss left the courtroom, walked to the IRT, went down and got on a train, and went home. And one of our men had the ingenuity, which you either have or don't have, to follow him. He went down and took pictures—of Hiss sitting, quietly reading a book. People were swaying. This was a dimension. Everybody knew about Hiss by then. The information was moving. But this was an experience that couldn't have been gotten otherwise. No newspaper writer could have captured it as well in those forty or fifty seconds.

I daresay Alger Hiss on any other day would have been dull.

But at this time he was the single figure in a national drama—and we followed him alone as he walked out, down the steps, and as he dropped his dime in the turnstile. There are some who would say this isn't journalism. I think it is. I believe it is.

MR. HEWITT: That's one great contribution. And it's part of a greater contribution I think television journalism has made. Because of television there are no more "hicks" in America. The guy on Main Street in Ashtabula or Okmulgee knows as much about John Glenn, the Berlin Wall, Fidel Castro, as the guy on Broadway or Pennsylvania Avenue. This wasn't always so.

INTERVIEWER: Was this only television? Didn't radio begin it?

MR. HEWITT: It began it, but it didn't carry it to the extent television has. And it's important to understand that what the American has learned doesn't come from, or begin and end with, *CBS Reports*, NBC *White Paper*, or ABC *Close-up*! He knows it from the daily shows. He may not know why he knows it, but it is because he gets it night after night.

MR. FRANK: The best example is the Hungarian rebellion. We *lived* the Hungarian Rebellion, and we got Americans involved in it. Americans are interested anyway. There has been a fantastic growth of sophistication in this country. We're all about the same age here— and when we were in high school would you have imagined the American taxpayer arguing not about the idea of foreign aid, but simply the amount of it? How much is what we argue about. There are no frontiers left for Americans except those we just can't get into. Americans don't know anything about Red China because we can't get there.

And I think this is the result of the fifteen-minute TV news show every night. We expanded the horizons and created the interest for *White Paper* and *CBS Reports*. We don't claim it as anything personal. It just happens that way. There are very few managing editors of newspapers who don't watch at least one TV news show. One major mid-western paper always had the front page make-up of the *Times* bulldog edition cabled back, and now they have added our program make-up. I really wish we had more outside-TV competition. It would be good for us. The competition now is awful.

INTERVIEWER: Let's turn to the matter of the news-selection processes you carry out. As you know, it is a common argument that television *makes* something news even if it isn't news, simply by virtue of having treated it. Does the argument have a basis in fact?

MR. HEWITT: That's the way the *Times* operated for years. They *said* it was the lead story, and that's what made it the lead story.

MR. FRANK: There are no objective criteria. I always thought "objective" was a useless word in that sense of its usage. It belongs in laboratories and logic courses. There are no objective criteria by which to judge what "news" is. There is only an accumulated body of tradition and the personal intelligence of a man who, in full possession of that tradition, makes it operative. It's news because we covered it. We covered it because we thought it would be news. If it turns out to be what we expected, it's news. It isn't what we expect— it's not news.

MR. HEWITT: I think we are the most responsible journalists working in all media today. Television journalists in general have a better eye for prejudice, a better feeling for balance, and less personal predisposition to push causes than all the others. Now when I say "balance", for example, I don't intend that it be carried to extremes— the kind of "stopwatch" balance which says "How much time have we given Eddie McCormack and how much time have we given Teddy Kennedy?" You just know, over a period of time, what the proper balance is. And an example of what I mean by not "pushing a cause" might be found in a feature story we did the other day. It was discovered that one of the pieces of furniture in the White House was not the authentic antique it was supposed to be, and to cover the story we used a clip from the original White House tour with Mrs. Kennedy. Well, we got some criticism for it. Mail and phone calls telling us we were "anti-Kennedy", and so forth.

I would have used the same piece, and the same treatment, whether it was Mrs. Kennedy, or Barry Goldwater's mother, or Martin Luther King's grandmother. It was a good story and it made no difference.

I've said to my staff that it is important that they do not presuppose anything. You can't approach the school issue by supposing the segregationists are "bad guys" and the integrationists "good guys" or vice-versa. You can't approach any story in this way.

If you consider the daily shows and add to them such programs as *CBS Reports, White Paper* or *Close-Up!,* you can say this is a better page in American journalism than has ever been written before. The public is more knowledgeable, and there's a greater sense of responsibility on the part of the people who put these programs together. They soul-search, they write and rewrite, they edit and re-edit, and they put more of themselves into television journalism than has ever before been put into journalism of any kind in history.

MR. FRANK: I defy anyone to watch up to a year of television output by the American networks and give me an accurate judgment of the political opinion of the people who own the network. There are few newspapers in America in which you can't determine that by reading a single issue.

INTERVIEWER: Perhaps it's time that we considered the growth of other kinds of news and news-documentary programs. Can we begin to classify some of these according to type, and also consider how they relate—in approach and technique—to "hard-news" programs? How, for example, does a *Brinkley Journal* differ from a Frank McGee program? What effects will such shows as *Eyewitness* have on plans for a half-hour daily "hard-news" show?

MR. FRANK: These forms are still shaking down. *Eyewitness* goes a step beyond the daily news reports, and gives greater consideration to a single story. The *Brinkley Journal* is unique in that it is conceived and built around his personality.

MR. HEWITT: Just as CBS built *See It Now* around Ed Murrow. You don't say, "Let's do a journal—someone go find me a Brinkley". You start with him. Murrow began like Brinkley. He used three or four stories. Then it was cut to two, and down to one; and then from the half-hour to the hour.

When you take programs like *Eyewitness, White Paper,* or *CBS Reports,* you find them treating subjects treated on daily newscasts, but they expand upon them.

Yet even the "hard-news" programs on TV—and I'm not sure what that means—are different from radio "hard-news" treatments. Radio is primarily concerned with the news of the last twenty-four hours, but TV daily news shows will get into at least some of that "news of the times we live in" which isn't essentially "hard-news" and yet never give it as much treatment as the longer news-documentary shows. We seem to get into an area that radio would leave to its public affairs shows. We can get out the bare fact that 86 people were killed in Algiers, but with film we can do two or three minutes of background as well—offering something more than just pictures of 86 human beings getting killed.

MR. FRANK: And there's another reason for the deeper "hard-news" treatment, too. Radio programs tend to be the continuing product of a newsroom, but a TV news program is the specific and individual product of a small group whose only major responsibility *is* that program. And so the interchange of ideas in a group is more important. You can work on all levels. You can be two weeks ahead, or six months ahead, or five minutes ago.

INTERVIEWER: But isn't it true that, as you move to the "greater consideration" in the weekly reports or news-documentaries, certain factors change? Doesn't "dramatization of fact" put these in a class quite apart from the "hard-news" way of treating a subject?

I recall, for example, the reaction to Ed Murrow's original McCarthy show on *See It Now*, and the approach used in *Harvest of Shame*, where a number of strong visual techniques were used to force home a point.

MR. HEWITT: Of course, the longer "in-depth" news-documentaries do follow a theme or take a point of view. They have a beginning, a middle, and an end. They come to a conclusion, but they do not necessarily make a recommendation. They don't state a network position, although sometimes the very fact that the show is done says, in effect, that a network thinks people should be thinking about the problem.

But beyond that, I think it has to be understood that personality has got to come through. You can't end up with a bland product. A strong personality sees it in a certain way, and it is not editorializing any more than in a daily news show. The Brinkley or the Murrow or the Sevareid has got to come through.

MR. FRANK: Pictures are like words—they are not facts—they are symbols. Whatever is selected will create a point of view. There was a wonderful story in the *Times* recently about a voter-registration meeting—in Georgia, I think. And the reporter used a sentence describing a deputy sheriff who was holding a five-cell flashlight in his left hand and smacking it heavily into his right palm. This symbol just popped out at you from the word-picture and you just felt the tension—"Everybody's happy here—what are *you* doing here?"—that was generated.

Selection always creates a point of view. The question is not one of *objectivity*—but *responsibility*. Objectivity is a screen we hide behind. It's just a word. These programs cannot be done by computer. They have to be done by people. People must react. People who have no interests aren't worth anything at all to you. You are looking only for people who are sufficiently disciplined to approach a subject responsibly. "Fairness" is not an objective criterion. It is subjective. "Fairness" is not "equal by the stopwatch".

So you are pushing too far by asking us to generalize the differences—generalize the functions—of news and news-documentary. These programs are the functions of the people who do them.

This brings up the matter, then, of decision-making. Every program has a large staff—platoons of people are needed to get anything on the air. But decision is restricted to only a few—a few people within the unit who are sympathetic with each other. Out of these people will come the myriad decisions. What film do you shoot? How do you edit it? How is it written? How is it spoken? And these become a unified whole. Successful programs are consistent in this way, and *CBS Reports* is about as good an example as you can get.

Consider Murrow's treatment of the migrant workers in *Harvest*. If you were writing a book about migrant workers you'd make a big point about cattle being watered and exercised every four hours, while human beings travel for a full day without rest. It wouldn't be a fiction book, would it? Nor would it mean anything to take a picture of a bus going ten hours without a stop unless your program was ten hours long! That way you could get across the idea of boredom—like some of the new art-films.

But this was an important point to be made. So they compressed. The method they chose was to contrast that with cattle trains. Other equally skilled but different individuals might have used another way to illustrate it. My inclination would be to get two or three cameras at the point where they got off the bus and get lots of faces as they got off. It's my experience that this is the *best* way to tell a story. But they made their editorial point—an important point in the exposition—that way, and it worked.

But setting down "differences" between one series and the other is just a trick. It keeps newspaper editors happy, it keeps salespeople happy; it gives them something to talk about. Producers are nobody to the general public. So you devise formulas to explain these differences, and if you are lucky and intelligent, the formula somehow reflects the fact.

MR. HEWITT: And the man, or the few men, who are at the top in this effort must have a soundness and a dignity in approach that commands respect. It is not enough just to be controversial and attract attention. Oh, you could say that there's a network hypocrisy in what happens to some men who begin to get controversial, but you have to look at it in a larger context. Friendly's "point-of-view" can be controversial and hard-hitting, and yet give the network prestige *and* revenue. Another fellow, and there are examples, can stir up excitement and controversy and do it so well that he makes the cover of *Time*—but a month later he's *gone*. The networks will put up with trouble, and they assume that their best men must be given their head even if it means trouble. There's a basic honesty there. A recognition of the terrible need for this kind of thing. But if the man cannot somehow command respect inside and outside the network, then the hell he raises is just not worth it.

INTERVIEWER: Let's move to the specific problems of technique then, and consider some of the developments of very recent years. A "school" has evolved, as you must be only too aware, which is seeking to get rid of the "voice-of-doom" technique and to substitute a newer, more intense and subjective camera and editing style. Is it having a strong influence? Does this evolving technique have a real place in the kind of programs we have been discussing?

MR. HEWITT: There are a number of things you can do with techniques of this kind, but not everything can be handled that way. You have to pick and choose the subjects to be handled with the subjective camera technique.

MR. FRANK: The school has opened up some things for those who were willing to watch certain techniques. They taught us nothing editorially. The basic trouble with a subjective technique is a lack of respect for the skills involved. You can use a subjective camera and still be in focus.

MR. HEWITT: I've seen it evolve, in some cases, into almost a Disney technique—something to be watched with a class of photographers. In a recent show I found that I lost the thread of what was being said and ended up fascinated with the zooms and the cuts and the out-of-focus. When a cameraman or director upstages his subject matter it's a bad show. In special events it is essential that as few of television's shenanigans be put between the viewer and the subject as possible.

MR. FRANK: This principle extends over the whole field of public affairs. Technique is of no interest to the public.

MR. HEWITT: Unless it really complements the subject. At a convention you might use a trick "super" to single out someone, and it has a natural attention-flow connection. You complement, but you don't *impose*.

INTERVIEWER: Let's turn to the future—and to the entire question of an evening network half-hour news program. We know it has its proponents as well as its detractors. What are some of the positive and negative factors involved in such a move?

MR. HEWITT: The half-hour is coming, and probably should, but it's hard to say that we haven't stumbled on to a good thing with the present fifteen-minute show. It has been successful—it is informative, so naturally you're reluctant to tamper with it. Perhaps the longer programs—*Eyewitness* and "Instant Specials"—can bridge the gap. I'm not sure of this.

MR. FRANK: I think the reason for the proliferation of forms, particularly in the half-hour weekly things, is that there are functions that a continuing news-vehicle should undertake, but can't. I think the fifteen-minute dinner hour news program is a hangover from the most successful days of radio news and has no relevance to television at all. I'm tired of fighting cartoons. People are willing to give more attention to news. The half-hour news program can be properly done and be successful. But it must be the largest journalistic undertaking in history.

MR. HEWITT: It would certainly mean an upheaval in accepted practice if each network were to do a full half-hour in the morning and the evening. With all of its full resources assigned to it—everything channeled into it, including all the reporters—it could be extremely successful. But our immediate problem, I think, would be the reporters—especially at CBS, where our technique is to use film mainly for illustration of a correspondent's story. Our men are split up on a dozen assignments now, and it's hard to get the reporter on the spot when you need him.

INTERVIEWER: But after such administrative shakedowns, would the result be worth it? Will the half-hour work? Will it offer a better, deeper dimension in news?

MR. FRANK: Yes. We could go back to fundamentals in the *transmission of experience*. Information of itself is everywhere, and in the fifteen-minute news programs you have such compression that you cannot carry out television's real job of transmitting experience. A half-hour show would not just be putting in twice as many bulletins, or putting two Huntleys and two Brinkleys back-to-back. It is substantially more than that, and would cost more than just double the present cost.

It would operate at all levels, just as the good newspapers used to. You have to have special correspondents—you have to have the general flow of information—you have the regular problems to answer; but I keep coming back to the real possibilities of transmitting experience—of giving that new dimension of information that is not contained in words alone and is applicable in every situation where human beings are in contact. In conflict, if you prefer.

What could the extra time mean? It could mean a seven- to ten-minute "takeout" every night. What is it like to starve to death in Algeria because they can't make up their minds about the kind of government they want? Now we could find the symbolic thing that opens this up, that illuminates it. Television does that. It illuminates the news. It *pictures* much better than it *explains*. You can pick on little things, and by examining them you cast light over a larger area.

This is the function of pictures. It is as true on the tube as it is in the theatre. It is as true in fact as it is in fiction.

This is what the half-hour news show will let us realize and explore. You wouldn't do it all the time. Most nights you would use prepared materials—some prepared for a long time. Everybody else does it. How much of a paper, except for the front page, is written within the last twelve hours? Yet all of it is relevant to the news of the world that day. That is journalism—the recording of change.

13 News Presentation in Britain*

GEOFFREY COX
Editor, ITN†

TELEVISION as a medium for news has great strengths, and some limitations. Our aim in ITN is to make the most of those strengths, and to offset the limitations, so as to give viewers a daily service of news which can be readily understood, and which will hold their interest.

The most obvious way in which television is a strong news medium is its ability to depict on the screen an event exactly as it happens, or as it happened. "See it Happen on ITN", was the slogan with which we went on the air in 1955 and the perfect example of this is, of course, where one can bring an Outside Broadcast direct into a news programme. This was done on the Winter Hill air crash, and on a number of occasions from London Airport. The arrival back of Mr. Macmillan from Moscow was covered direct in ITN bulletins, as were traffic scenes on the Kingston By-Pass on Bank Holidays and from London Bridge during the London bus strike. As a technique it is particularly effective. The natural impact which any OB possesses seems to be curiously reinforced by its appearance in a programme which normally deals with what has happened, not what is happening. It is almost as if the viewer feels unconsciously that he is getting double value, and relishes it.

Few events, however, fall within times and range which make

* S.F.T.A. Journal, Spring 1960.
† ITN is a non-profit-making company set up by the British commercial television companies to supply their news service.

their direct portrayal in a news programme possible, and so film and video-tape recordings look like remaining for very many years to come the main instruments for this direct portrayal of the news. Where the cameraman has been able to catch an event just as the page, if not of history at least of the day's news, was turning, it is possible to present the news on television with an impact and an economy unrivalled in any other medium. The classic cases of this in recent years were the scenes of the Hungarian uprising, and again the landing of the American troops in the Lebanon. The exultation of the shabbily dressed, bandoleered crowds when the Soviet star was toppled from the Communist headquarters in Budapest, or the spectacle of the American landing craft moving inshore, the ramps coming down, and the marines charging ashore past the incredulous lines of bathers and ice-cream vendors, gave the exact flavour of these events in a way which took columns of space in a newspaper. They provided not only their own story, but to a large degree their own interpretation. Only a minimum of commentary was needed. Where natural sound of the event is available the impact is even more effective.

We have always placed great store in ITN on hard news film of this type, and are prepared to run it at considerable length, so that it not merely illustrates the news, but tells it. In 1956, when we got our first film back from our cameraman with the invasion forces at Port Said, we used eight minutes of it in a 13-minute bulletin, and every frame of it was worth while. There is no doubt that in television, as in the popular press, when you have the pictures that tell the story you must give them the space to do their job, even if other news has to be boiled down to headlines.

The other strength of television, which we have sought to exploit in ITN programmes, is its capacity to portray not only events, but the people in the news. The television interview presents to the public the people in the news, big or small, with a candour, directness, and, I believe, honesty which is unparalleled by any other kind of journalism. Until television came along the public had to rely, in making its assessments of its leaders and would-be leaders, either on still photographs, or on the estimates of the cartoonists or of the writers of profiles. Still photography can be highly selective—as anyone who met Hitler in person, after seeing him portrayed in the idealized German photographs, will remember. All cartooning and written studies are essentially subjective. Though there is also a selective element in the choice of film, the chances of the true personality of a man or woman coming across on television are much greater than in any other medium. I believe that because of this the British public have a much truer version today of their leaders than at any other time in history.

In establishing the proper techniques for interviewing people on television, we have found it essential that a television reporter should ask direct, pointed questions, and that he should, if this is necessary to get at the facts of a story, be prepared to press his questioning hard. The reasons for this are largely technical. You cannot summarize film, you can only cut it. The television reporter must therefore couch his questions in a form which will produce short, succinct answers containing the meat of the story. He has to get the interviewee to do, as it were, his own subbing. And one of the ways to do this is to keep the questioning succinct, even curt. For a woolly question will almost certainly evoke a woolly answer.

It is also the television reporter's responsibility to press for a reply when one is not forthcoming. This aspect of television interviewing has come under fire lately. But done correctly it in no way justifies the charge that it is "trial by television". The television reporter—and the television news service—have a positive responsibility to see that issues are thoroughly probed. Otherwise a news service would not be presenting the facts as it has found them to be, but simply giving people in the news a platform to present the facts as they chose to present them. News interviews would become just a series of *ex-parte* statements, no doubt with some clumsy attempt at accuracy being made by trying to balance one *ex-parte* statement against another in the same or subsequent bulletins. I do not see any way in which a news service on television can do an honest job of reporting unless it is entitled to challenge, and challenge hard, statements made to its cameras.

There is, however, one important limit which must be put to the interviewer's rights. He must pose his questions with a genuine desire to arrive at information, and not to score a debating point or, for programme purposes, to try to stir up a row or a sensation. In particular, he must not abuse his ease before the cameras in order to discomfort someone else. Provided this line is drawn—and certainly

ITN reporters have very clear instructions where to draw it—then the dangers of the television interviewer exploiting his powers can be readily avoided. Within these limits, however, the freedom of the interviewer to cut his way through verbiage and evasiveness must be allowed.

So much for the main strength of television as a news medium. Its main limitations are that it is in no way a journal of record, to which people can turn back should they wish to study a picture or a story in detail. For this reason court cases are difficult to report on television, and so are Parliamentary debates. Yet a great deal can be done by the skilful use of diagrams, film and maps to put across complex facts and documents. The main items of the Budget can be clearly and effectively presented if diagrams, and in particular animated diagrams, are used, and provided they are held on the screen long enough for the viewer to take them in.

Perhaps the biggest problem for a television news editor is the "situationer", the task of bringing his viewers up to date on an ambling, shapeless, but important story like last year's Foreign Ministers' conference at Geneva, or the present disarmament conference. This is a story which the cameras cannot tell, and for which television is forced back on to what is virtually a radio report with the reporter in vision. A certain amount can be done by the use of the sound camera to give atmosphere and authenticity, so that the reporter delivers his report against the background of the place where the conference is being held, or by bringing up film underlays to illustrate his points. But even if this is done very skilfully—and Brian Connell, Reginald Bosanquet and John Ardagh have all shown for us that it can be so done—the viewer's attention is liable to wander unless the report is kept short and pointed. Probably the most effective way with this type of story is to do these reports only at intervals, and then to give them a good spread of space, with the full complement of diagrams and maps. But certainly the daily political or diplomatic situationer which the newspapers can carry has little place in a television bulletin. At best it amounts to no more than an extended headline.

Television has incidentally proved itself a surprisingly good medium for reporting crime. A filmed story of a major robbery or a murder brings through not only the drama, when such exists, but also the squalor and sordidness which mark so much crime, and make it so much less glamorous than it is often depicted to be. Which is all to the good.

From our earliest days we have deliberately set aside part of the inevitably limited space which news can command on the air for human interest stories. It is sometimes argued that these have no place in a hard news bulletin, but should be relegated to a specific news magazine programme. This is a view which I do not share. Such stories are an invaluable element in a regular news bulletin. Not only do they provide some relief to the harder news, but they also ensure that viewers who might be deterred by a diet of hard news will stay tuned in—and so are likely to take in at least some of the hard news as well as the lighter items. A light-hearted "tail piece" to a bulletin also helps to keep viewers with you to the end.

I have left to the last one of the most important elements in a television news bulletin—the newscaster. The personality of the man who reads the main items of news, who links the whole programme together, is of the utmost importance. His is the greatest single impact. He personifies the service, and gives it to a great degree its style and character. From the outset ITN has set out not only to have as the central figures in its news programmes men of personality, but also to have them take a big part in getting as well as presenting the news. They work as interviewers in the studio, reporters in the field, and as the writers, or re-writers, of their own bulletins. We believe that in this way the authority of what they are saying is substantially reinforced. If the man who gives out the news is seen also as one of the men who gets the news, his contact with the viewers is steadily strengthened. This in its turn, it is true, poses certain problems. If you are going to send newscasters out on stories, particularly abroad, you limit the number of days each week or each month in which they can appear in the studio. In the early days of ITN, when we did practically no overseas reporting with sound cameras, we found two regular newscasters, with one holiday relief, both efficient and effective. Now we find a minimum of four to be essential.

Across the years, without deliberately setting out to do so, we have arrived at a format for ITN programmes which I would define as roughly that of a popular newspaper of the air, with a blend of hard news and pictorial and human interest items. We have intended steadily to drop the set, newsreel style items—the beauty parades and the street carnivals. Instead we look to action stories and in particular to sport for our main pictorial elements. Where we have the great annual spectacular events, such as Trooping the Colour, we try to add a further dimension by interviewing spectators, or Guardsmen, before and after the parade. Above all we are trying every day to find new ways of using the camera as the reporter's notebook, to allow people to see and hear news as it takes place, or as it is described and discussed by those who took part in the making of it. Jeb Stuart, the great American cavalry commander, once described his aim in war as being "to get there fustest with the mostest men". Not a bad slogan for a television news organization is to "get there fustest with the mostest cameras—and the bestest reporters".

14 TV in the American Political Campaign*

TOM WICKER

KENNETH P. O'DONNELL

ROWLAND EVANS

TOM WICKER

IT seems to me that this monstrous thing that has been unleashed in the last couple of decades has several characteristics that are having profound importance in politics.

The first characteristic is the tremendous impact and drama that comes through from a well-conceived and well-conducted political broadcast. The prime example, of course, is the famous series of Presidential debates in 1960.

The next is the national character of this impact. It is obvious that the most, and the best, political broadcasting is done on the national networks, and my impression is that most viewers pay more attention to network political broadcasts than they do to local political broadcasts.

The third characteristic which is obvious to all is the enormous cost of political broadcasting. The Gore Committee reported that about $4.7 million was spent by both parties on radio and tele-

* Television Quarterly, Winter 1966.
If ever one questioned the dominant campaign role of television, the following statements from people who have lived in the midst of the fray should settle doubts once and for all. Two of the observers are journalists, TOM WICKER of the New York Times and ROWLAND EVANS of the New York Herald Tribune; one, KENNETH P. O'DONNELL, has been special assistant to Presidents Kennedy and Johnson. All agree the medium offers unparalleled opportunities for spreading the word quickly and with effectiveness; all agree, too, that it has its limits.

vision broadcasting in 1956, and even with more free time available—and more sophisticated use of that time—it has been reported that over $3 million was spent on the national contests alone in 1960.

Finally, I think we have to consider demands made upon the cast of characters by television. These range from the very smallest detail to matters of immense importance. On the one hand, at routine news conferences reporters are often asked to stand up to ask their questions. Now that may seem a small matter, but what it represents, as everyone knows, is an accommodation to the television camera. It doesn't make any great difference, but it is an accommodation, and from that low level the accommodations creep upward in scale and importance.

We might consider the fact that many candidates for office now appear before the public in cosmetics. Again, make-up may not seem important, but it does begin to lend a tinge of falsity to the process. In this connection we might recall some observations made by Richard Nixon in his book, *Six Crises*. In a discussion of his preparations for the second debate in 1960, he wrote that he had not been at best advantage in the first debate, and he said he knew there were three things which he had to convey in the second. One was knowledge of his subject, the second was confidence in himself, and the third was that he "had to be sincere". I would submit to you that when a man goes before the cameras with the determination to be sincere, the last thing he's going to be is sincere!

Now, considering these things that are inherent in the nature of political broadcasting, I think our politics have been altered or shaped or influenced in a number of ways.

Obviously, television in the campaign raises out of all proportion the dangers that are inherent in political fund-raising. More money is simply demanded, and when more money is demanded it has to be raised. And since it has to be raised, the dangers in the process obviously are going to be even greater than they have been.

Secondly, television puts greater emphasis on, and it rewards in higher proportion, something that is not intrinsically related to political questions and political issues, and that is the production and merchandising of talent.

Anyone who saw the 1964 half-hour broadcast of Senator Goldwater chatting with former President Eisenhower on his farm at Gettysburg, and compared that—an expensive, time-consuming and carefully planned sort of thing—to the very brief spot the Democrats ran showing the hands of an unseen man tearing up a social security card, will understand that the one spot had immensely more impact than the half-hour program. Yet, in either case, there wasn't much political knowledge conveyed. The merchandising and the production were what counted.

I have read that Mr. Ronald Reagan of California, who is apparently content to continue his acting career, is being "re-modeled" by an advertising and public relations agency there. He will come out of a long seclusion as a sort of two-tone sports job. He's tailored, he's painted, and he's produced for the camera. I'm not opposed to Ronald Reagan at all. I know very little about him, But I find this process, whether it's for a Democrat or a Republican, basically offensive.

I think it should next be pointed out that because of all this there has been an almost immeasurable increase in the public's interest in, and knowledgeability about, candidates and races. This is due not only to the broadcasts of candidates themselves, but to the extremely widespread and costly efforts of television in news and public affairs programming. During a Presidential campaign, for instance, if the air is not saturated, it is certainly dripping with politics—with issues, speeches and faces. All of this has lifted the level of American interest in politics. And this has been particularly so in every case where a television debate—something on the order of the 1960 Presidential debates—was conducted in a campaign. Before and after such debates the level of public interest rose.

Obviously a debate in itself makes for high drama. It's a public clash between men, and it personalizes and concentrates the intrinsic clash which is the race for office. And incidentally, it has created a whole new type of issue in American politics. If one man ducks out in a debate the other man goes through the whole campaign charging him with not being "willing to debate the issues".

The next point to be observed is that television can actually shape the content, the outcome, and the nature of a campaign. Let me cite a couple of examples.

The New Hampshire primary of 1964 was the first of that year. It was, for all intents and purposes, the opening of the Presidential campaign. Because it was, the television cameras in particular (and newspapers to some extent, but without the same impact) saturated the New Hampshire primary. My impression is that Senator Goldwater was not prepared for this. I don't mean "prepared" in the way of having facts—he wasn't prepared for what it would do to him, for how he would have to respond, and the pressures that would be on him. As a result, Goldwater never escaped, in my opinion, from the first impression he made upon the general American public in the New Hampshire primary. That is when the social security issue was pinned on him. That is when the nuclear bomb issue was pinned on him. That is when the warmonger issue was pinned on him. He never got out from under this. The first exposure in New Hampshire shaped the whole campaign, and I predict that this is going to happen time and time again in the future.

By way of further example, Mr. Nixon once said in a private conversation that he believed that if Goldwater ever had a chance to win the general election after having gotten the nomination, he lost it on the night of his acceptance speech. There was tremendous interest—millions of people watching—at that moment when he had the greatest opportunity to bind up the wounds of the party. Either by design or by oversight, he reopened them with his remarks about extremism, and by reading out of the party those who he said did not agree with him. Here was a specific instance of how the whole shape of events can be influenced by one dramatic and climactic episode on TV.

Having been in Washington throughout the period, I believe that the single most successful moment of President Johnson's tenure in office came within the first five days, when he addressed the Congress on Wednesday after having become President on Friday. I don't think that he could ever have recovered from a bad performance at that time. At that point he made the necessary presentation of himself to the public with the necessary words.

The next thing I would call to attention is that television tends to soften what we laughingly refer to as "the issues" in a campaign. TV puts tremendous emphasis on blurring over the hard questions of choice between two courses. Few people, after all, sitting in their living rooms with the children around them—and with the opportunity to switch the channel and get *Man from U.N.C.L.E.*—are going to listen to serious discussion for a half-hour on the international monetary problem, on civil rights, or other complex issues.

Beyond that, television reaches all shades of opinion simultaneously. You can't address yourself just to liberals or conservatives or to Democrats. You're addressing yourself to anybody that turns on the set. Therefore, while you may make a very hard and pointed speech on one issue which may attract a lot of Democrats, there may be many more Republicans watching, or vice versa. So you have to soften your tone somewhat. Television, I think, demands less in the way of reasoned analysis and discussion of issues. TV demands punchlines, slogans and impressions that the candidate can put across.

In this connection, if you read the 1960 debates—read them in text today—it is difficult to say that either candidate really won on the basis of the issues. I have heard it said by people who heard those debates, particularly the first debate, on radio rather than saw them on television, that they thought it came out about even.

Finally, I would make two more points that are perhaps the most important. Television came along at about that time in our history when there began to be a massive shift in our population from the farms and out of the cities and into the suburbs. And I think that the conjunction of that shift and television has helped to weaken if not erase party loyalties. For this reason I do not subscribe to the thesis that Democrats move to the suburbs and become Republicans. Rather, people who move to the suburbs take their political tendencies with them.

Once in the suburbs, however, it's much more difficult to stimulate that tendency toward party loyalty of one kind. Voters have escaped the ward captain, the city club, and the social pressures that Republicans might find in small towns and on farms. Suburbanites— lacking this polarity of city on the one hand and farm on the other— become much more open to party switches, to taking independent stands, and to voting for "the man".

Since TV does reach members of both parties simultaneously, and since it does tend to blur issues and put emphasis on men and on generalities, these patterns have moved together. In the past 15 years emphasis has been taken off the polarity of our party system. People are not so sharply Democrat or sharply Republican as they once were.

Since national coverage is the best and the widest with TV, even those living out in the small towns and far from Washington have developed more interest in, and know more about, national politics and national candidates than they do about local politics and local candidates. They have developed, in my view, a more personal sense of participation in national politics, in Presidential campaigns, and in the activities of the President than they have in their local candidate for Congress or for the state legislature.

I raise the question whether this may not be a key factor in what seems to be the increasing American acceptance of a large and powerful centralized government in Washington. Television brings government into the home. The people participating in government are personally, immediately and constantly in the living room. This is not true of the members of legislatures and city councils.

Finally, I want to make the point that the voracious demands of television must not be allowed to reach the fundamental institutions of our politics. I find it regrettable, for instance, that the national nominating convention is being written off by many people as an anachronism, as a bore, as too long and unnecessary. I don't agree with that at all. In my own view, the national nominating convention is something like the grass in the prairies. It grew out of the United States, and what it's all about. It is a part of the way our parties have developed and our federal system and the great ethnic divisions of the country, as well as the great geographic divisions. I think that the national convention is something that is as natural in our system as the Presidency itself.

Now it may be very true that all those favorite sons are a great bore to the home viewer, but all those favorite sons play an important part in the deliberations and results of a convention. It may have been true that in 1964 Senator Goldwater and his supporters put off the platform debate on Civil Rights until late in the evening, in the hope that the Eastern viewers would have gone to bed and wouldn't see it. That may be true, but isn't that a legitimate political move on the part of people who have the power to control something? The point is that while the convention may be a bore, and while it may go on too long, it's an intrinsic and useful part of the system. And if anybody's going to adapt, let TV adapt to the convention and not the convention to TV.

I would say also that however TV may change political tactics and strategy—no matter how it may influence the ways that people campaign—it isn't fundamentally going to change American politics.

Nothing is going to change American politics until America itself changes because our political system seems to grow so naturally out of the kind of country this is.

What we're really talking about here is the way the face of politics is shaped and the way the skin of it may be stretched. But not the way the heart of it functions.

KENNETH P. O'DONNELL

ATTEMPTING to adjust a candidate and a campaign to a new medium is a very difficult problem—one I don't think we have solved. In the 1964 campaign we did not get what we thought were maximum results. We did not arrive at the most economical and effective blending of a candidate and a medium.

Campaigning has been drastically altered by television. We have progressed from "speeches" at a rally through radio and now into a brand new medium which has upset, to a degree, the monopoly once shared by radio and newspapers. Now we must deal with the sight-and-sound interjection of a political figure into a medium which is available to all of the public. It is a change of major proportions, and we are still adapting to it.

Let me extend some specific examples of how TV has worked changes in the art of campaigning. In 1952 Adlai Stevenson was an unknown and rather obscure Governor of Illinois. Largely as the result of the influence of President Truman and the party operation, he was suddenly thrust into a national limelight as the Democratic nominee for the Presidency. Reluctantly, he accepted the nomination. I think that politicians and academicians alike, however, would accept him as one of the great public speakers of our time. And TV reflected him as a great orator, a sincere man, and an intellectual. He was a new type of politician, suddenly entering the lists. And just as suddenly he became a great national figure and ultimately a world figure. His dramatic appearance upon the political stage was through television, and without TV he would never have become so prominent.

In the same year—the same day, really—a distinguished Governor, perhaps the best in the history of Massachusetts, was a keynote speaker on television. And he destroyed himself, politically, because

he did not understand the medium. He was not aware of the difference in acoustics. He was not aware of the type of picture he
projected, the "image" (whether we like it or not) that he projected.
Three months later he was defeated by 14,000 votes by then-
Congressman Christian A. Herter.

Governor Stevenson, of course, had not been trained for TV,
but he came through with the obvious sincerity that was his. We now
have fears about "the image" and Hollywood movie-stars seeking
office. But I think they're unfounded. The single exposure may
have its effect, but as the years went by Stevenson continued to
maintain the same high standards. Whether we voted for him or
not, his intellectual integrity continued to be carried by television.
Even those who would not vote for him would listen to Stevenson.
They wanted to hear his ideas, his thoughts, and know what he
could contribute to the dialogue of our intellectual community.

Party politics aside, Adlai Stevenson became a great American
statesman. TV was a factor in his acceptance, and John Kennedy
was to come along and harvest what Stevenson planted. Kennedy's
rise was absolutely a triumph for television. In 1956 Kennedy, a
reasonably obscure Senator, went to Chicago, where like dozens
of other candidates (and primarily for home consumption) he was
a talked-of candidate for the Vice-Presidency. But first he went on
television to introduce the narrator to the convention. Then he
nominated Adlai Stevenson—and suddenly he became a national
figure. He could not, however, have maintained the stature of a
national figure unless he continued to appear—day after day—for
the next three years. On *Meet the Press*, on *Face the Nation*, on
panel shows and interviews, he maintained his position within the
framework of potential he had established at the convention. He
continued to discuss issues on TV with an intellectual depth that
people required, desired and demanded.

It is true that television thrusts people into prominence, but in
order to remain there they must have the qualities of greatness.
TV cannot manufacture them. It can only transmit what is there.
It's too easy, I think, for politicians to blame TV or the press if
things seem unfair. Generally speaking, it's still up to the candidate
to attempt to "fit in" by himself. He must project the issues in a
campaign in a way that people will find compelling. If he cannot,
they will not watch him on television.

We would also do well, I think, to stress the fact that any Presidential candidate has a TV opportunity which is generally not given to gubernatorial candidates, Senators, or Congressmen. Lesser candidates are exposed to some degree in what are really paid advertisements by city councilors, aldermen, and people in their particular communities. But the President is allowed a single, specific opportunity for massive exposure at one moment at a convention. It is then that he produces ideas and issues that interest the people, and it is up to him to impress upon the people the simple truth that he is the gentleman in whom they must place their confidence. Television gives him a vehicle, but it does not give him the weapon to elect himself.

The primary campaigns present a host of varying challenges in the area of proper TV usage. We learned a great deal in Kennedy's campaign. We went to the states of Wisconsin, West Virginia, Nebraska, Oregon, and Maryland; and in each instance we had to take different positions. In all of these campaigns we used advertising agencies only to purchase time. The issues, and what went into the candidate's presentations, were determined by Mr. Kennedy. A few of us who were with him would advise him, but he knew what the issues were in the state. He knew which would be most effective and he addressed himself to them.

The two most effective television political programs I've ever witnessed were planned in a period of five minutes. In West Virginia, the President, with Franklin D. Roosevelt, Jr., appeared in a fifteen-minute program which dealt with religion. This was the major issue, as we all recall, in West Virginia. It was never rehearsed, and without question, in the judgment of most people who saw it, that program was one of the most effective television presentations they had ever seen. We repeated it in Oregon, following the same format, with Congresswoman Edith Green. Both of these efforts, in our opinion, were the most effective we did. Once we began to campaign for the Presidency, it is my judgment that our television efforts—after being put in professional hands—rapidly deteriorated. The professionals don't really understand the issues, and they begin to ask the politician to tell them what issues they should be producing shows *for*. This reverses the nature of the strategy.

One of the major problems we face is adapting television to the campaign itself. On the campaign trail we would try to block out a TV plan while we were moving six and seven days in every week. TV put great demands on schedule planning, and on relationships between our needs and the needs of local forces. In a normal cummunity the political leader does not want to rush into television. He wants the candidate to meet the local ward leaders, the mayor, the sheriff and others. To him, TV is an obstruction, and it's very difficult to blend all these forces into an effective unit.

I had hoped that at some point we would be able to think things through and perhaps come to some agreement about what makes an effective television campaign. But things change so rapidly that we are into another campaign before we have been able to arrive at any conclusions. We do know, however, what major problems we face, and one of them is the great advantage which our media extend to an incumbent President. Obviously, the incumbent has the kind of access to the public media which is not available to the other candidate.

The first important revelation of this advantage came with the Suez Crisis in 1956. Governor Stevenson was running an effective campaign at the time, but those of us working for him did not feel he would be elected. We did think he was at least in a position to help our local campaign tickets despite an Eisenhower victory. We were working hard to assure that the tickets would not go down with him. In the middle of the campaign, however, the British, the French and the Israelis attacked the Suez Canal. General Eisenhower appeared on television as the Commander-in-Chief of the armies. In reality—and in the eyes of the electorate as well—he was the man whose responsibility it was to handle our military problems. As such, he dominated the news for two days. This was in late October. The election was nearly over, and there was no possible answer that the Governor could make. In 1964 the situation was reversed. The Russians changed leadership in October, and President Johnson went on television to explain what the change signified—what the possible future views of the Russian leadership might be. A week later the Chinese exploded an atomic weapon, and the President again went to the people, via TV, to explain its meaning.

Now the fellow who is not in office is bound to feel at a disadvantage in such cases. No one was really interested in Senator Goldwater's views on the change in Russian leadership, any more than they would have been in Stevenson's thoughts about Suez. This is a unique problem, and as one with an interest in the historical evolution of TV and politics, I know of no answer to it.

The other problem stems from TV's capacity to control, in a way, a candidate's statements. This may occur more in the minor offices. Here TV reporters use a somewhat different approach from the newspapers. The reporter can ask a question—with a microphone in his hand, and with a television camera on the candidate's face—on a very controversial issue. A candidate, for valid reasons, might not want to answer it at the time, but on TV he is always in danger of appearing evasive. If he attempts to "duck" the issue, they keep pushing that microphone into his face. This is very difficult for candidates, and tends to put the television newscaster in a rather different position than a newspaper man. This problem, too, must be faced.

Despite these difficulties, I am not at all pessimistic about the role of TV in the political campaign. We are not on the brink of a political world in which the cheap or phony will somehow triumph by television. Any candidate, no matter how glamorous, will have to stand the test of time. He'll have to discuss the issues, and discuss them in impromptu fashion over long periods of time on television and in the newspapers. He will face the probing of very learned and distinguished gentlemen who have spent their lifetime in the business of journalism and politics. One must really stand the test of time in offices of responsibility, so I don't think the future runs to movie stars or good-looking candidates or "images". John Kennedy was attractive, of course, but he had the intellect, the governmental know-how, the wit, and the intelligence to stand before a press conference every two or three weeks and discuss any issue that came before the United States Government. I think this was the lasting imprint that he really left on the American people, who believed that he understood the workings of our Government and that our nation was safe and secure in his hands because he worked at it.

ROWLAND EVANS:

THE exploitation of television by politics is one of the modern wonders. Consider, for example, the television-age Presidential campaign. These are the days when not one but two entirely separate, disconnected campaigns are waged by each candidate. This was true to some degree in 1960, to a greater degree in 1964, and will dominate future campaigns. Campaigns are waged concurrently by different teams of the candidates, advisors and experts, who sometimes go for days and weeks without even seeing or communicating with each other.

Campaign number one is the traditional political exercise: the candidate stumps the country, holds press conferences, moves from city to city, is seen in the flesh, talks to voters and makes speeches. Campaign number two is a sort of *sub rosa* television campaigning. It's canned—taped in late August and early September in five-minute bits, and then allowed to seep out over the airwaves near the end of September, all of October and early November. It moves into the living rooms of the country.

These two campaigns are so disconnected that the reporter who covers the traditional conventional campaign never sees the un-conventional TV campaign. Last fall, while touring with President Johnson, reporters never saw the short five-minute spots that were canned much earlier and concurrently, perhaps, with a TV speech that he was making out on the Trail. We never saw those, and yet some of the experts who worked with the President are convinced that the living-room campaign was fully as important in getting votes as the conventional campaign.

Despite the importance of the living-room campaign, TV will never substitute for the historic, traditional campaign. It does not affect, in my opinion, the dynamics that make it essential for a Presidential candidate to go out and be seen in person.

Further, I think that the argument that campaigns should be reduced in length because we now have television is erroneous. I don't think you can have too much exposure in a Presidential campaign. Let me cite one example. Leaving aside the TV debates in the 1960 campaign, if that election had been held in mid-October, Mr. Nixon almost certainly would have won. And I think the explanation is that it took two months in 1960 for what I believe to be the essential sterility of the Nixon campaign to come through. Voters don't catch the full impact of a personality because they see the man on television all the time, or because they listen to his speeches. It takes two months, sometimes three months, for the full impact of a Presidential campaign to strike home. The fact that we use TV so much in politics today should not, and will not, shorten Presidential campaigns in the future.

Now let us consider some implications of the marriage between politics and technology. I was very surprised in 1958 when I first observed the use that a candidate can make of this medium. I accompanied Mr. Nixon early in the '58 Congressional campaign, and his custom upon arriving in a city was to go at once to a television studio where he engaged in a crossfire of questions with four or five reporters. What surprised me was the kind of questions that would be asked. Many were the ugliest, meanest, nastiest questions you could imagine. They impugned Mr. Nixon's honesty. They slighted his personality. They questioned his motives. After the second of these engagements, I asked him why he subjected himself to that kind of punishment and abuse. He told me that he planned it that way—that he always called the television studio and made sure that the reporters who were to appear with him were the toughest reporters in town. He told me that exposure to hostile questions automatically created sympathy in the audience. And I found, as I investigated this, that Mr. Nixon was absolutely correct!

We might also consider other aspects of the raw power which TV can bring to politics. First, it exposes voters—who normally would never be exposed—to the candidate of the other party. A reliable study showed that during the Stevenson-Eisenhower campaign of '52, 44 per cent of the Stevenson voters watched between 20 per cent and 50 per cent of the televised speeches of General Eisenhower and Mr. Nixon. How many others, who may have favored Stevenson at the onset of the campaign, changed to Eisenhower because they saw him in their living rooms? Yet these same voters might never have taken the trouble to attend a speech delivered at a local rally by a Presidential candidate.

Had it not been for the televised Army-McCarthy hearings in 1954, the Senate might never have censured Joseph McCarthy. And you may recall what happened to Estes Kefauver as a result of the televised crime hearings. He became, almost overnight, a major national political figure.

Shortly after he moved into the White House, I asked President Kennedy about television and politics. He answered—and I quote—"Television gives people a chance to look at their candidate close up and close to the bone. For the first time since the Greek city-states practiced their form of democracy, it brings us within reach of that ideal where every voter has a chance to measure the candidate himself." If, as Kennedy said, television really does give every voter a chance to measure his candidate, does it also give every candidate an equal chance to be measured? I consider this the most difficult question in politics today. The answer is, of course, no— there is not an equal chance for each candidate to be measured—and the reason is money.

Money has always been a vital ingredient of politics, and television is obviously increasing the financial demands on each candidate. This, I suggest, is the one conspicuous area in which politics has not caught up with technology. I don't think the gap is as important as some commentators would have it, however, particularly in view of the fact that Congress, by repealing Section 315 in specific cases, has made it possible for the major candidates to appear on free time either in debate or in other forms of contention. The questions, despite this, are far from answered.

Finally, I would offer some brief comment on this matter of whether television is truly a builder of demi-gods. I know TV has been criticized for its use by politicians. It is said it offers the perfect medium for those who have the knack of talking glibly. I discount this as a factor in political life today. It took no television to make Huey Long what he was, and the most cursory view of history will turn up any number of examples which attest that a politician-demagogue does not need TV to build himself up. Quite the contrary, in exposing the candidate "close to the bone", TV may make the rise of demagogues less likely in the future.

15 Reporting British Elections*

PAUL FOX

JOHN GRIST

PAUL FOX, Head of Public Affairs Programmes, BBC Television, discusses the presentation of the October 1964 General Election.

The reporting of the General Election results on television is, without doubt, the biggest and the most complex operation undertaken by the BBC. That was established back in 1959 when Grace Wyndham Goldie and Michael Peacock master-minded the operation. At that time I was one of its 20 million viewers.

Five years in television can mean half a lifetime. But even with the Rome Olympic Games, half a dozen satellite programmes and innumerable "instant specials" behind me, I was still staggered by the immensity of the General Election Results programme, 1964.

Fortunately the young maestro of the last Election was able to shed his BBC-2 duties long enough to be the overlord again this time.

With the possibilities of a spring election always likely, detailed planning for what was almost a 24-hour programme began in earnest in the autumn of 1963, though there had been many discussions before that to settle major points of coverage. The team on the screen was never in doubt: Richard Dimbleby, of course, at the centre of it all for his fourth General Election†, flanked by Robert

* S.F.T.A. Journal, Spring 1965.
† Richard Dimbleby until his death in 1965 was the doyen of BBC commentators and compères for programmes on current affairs.

McKenzie and David Butler. To them we were able to add two post-
'59 arrivals: Robin Day and Ian Trethowan. With Cliff Michelmore,
these six highly experienced television professionals made our studio
base safe and secure.

The behind-the-screens team was more difficult to get together
in one place at the same time. The luxury of a permanent Election
Unit—such as exists in the American Television Networks—is not
possible with our flexible electoral pattern.

When the Government of the day happen to pick the eve of
Olympic week for its date at the poll, then television producers face
two headaches. And when those Olympic Games, with their unique
satellite facilities, practically clash with the incredibly involved
technical requirements for a General Election, then engineers face
outsize neuralgia.

The major editorial problem we faced was, to put it simply,
how to sort the wheat from the chaff. When the results flow in at the
rate of 150 an hour—as they did at the peak of Election night—how
do you spot the key results that could bring about a change of Government from the dull and predictable results? And having spotted the
ones that matter, how do you find the time to keep them on the
screen long enough for any worth-while comment?

Our answer was a "rush result" service. Obviously the quickest
way of getting the result that matters on the screen is to point an
outside broadcast camera at the Returning Officer. Clearly that can't
be done everywhere. And even if it were, we'd get hours behind, as
well as slightly tired of the time-honoured phrase . . . "and I therefore
declare the above-mentioned . . . duly elected. . . . "

Even so, 61 outside broadcast cameras were swung into action
in 39 locations. Among the key constituencies covered live were
Billericay (which, with Cheltenham, Exeter and Salford, traditionally
leads the declarations race) Smethwick, Devon North, Huyton,
Bolton, Stockport, Cardiff and Kinross.

But the bulk of the results flowed into the news room that was
set up on the studio floor either over the telephone from reporters
engaged by the BBC or from the Press Association. In important
marginal constituencies special telephones had been installed so that
the results could be broadcast as quickly as possible.

This telephone reporting service was shared with the radio
services and formed the basis for our "rush results". Once the result

was telephoned in, the news could be on the screen within 12 seconds of the call.

Though that time was not always met, these intensive preparations—smoothed out during a number of dummy runs—paid off handsomely. Due to the closeness of the race, as well as the fast flow of results caused by the growing number of overnight declarations (432 were declared overnight this time compared with 387 in 1959) the normal results—the ones held by one party or the other with five-figure majorities—went to the back of the queue.

Even though one realizes that the electors of East Grinstead and Easington and Belfast South were eagerly waiting for their own results, comment and analysis on the results that mattered, and the trend they conveyed, was far more important.

A computer, from Elliott Automation, had been installed in the studio to provide detailed statistical analysis as well as a projected forecast of the final outcome. While no one—not even the computer—foresaw clearly how close and tense the final hours of the Election would be, the detailed breakdown of results made available by the careful advance programming of the computer was invaluable.

To the results, the comment and the analysis, were added a large number of interviews to make the story of that night and the following day complete. Among the speakers who had been invited in advance were Mr. Harold Wilson, Sir Alec Douglas Home, Mr. Jo Grimond, Mr. George Brown, Mr. Quintin Hogg and many others. Winning and losing candidates from many parts of the country, as well as innumerable electors, rounded off the election picture. Though street interviews have become commonplace on television, on Election Night and Election Morning, the voice of the people matters a great deal: whether it's from the fruit market in Glasgow, the side streets of Smethwick or striding across Waterloo Bridge.

For the first time, the Election Results programme was more than just a domestic operation for the British electorate. The BBC offered all its facilities to foreign television organizations and on Election Night the Television Centre was host to 17 countries.

The three American networks—NBC, CBS and ABC—had been installed in a special studio overlooking the major election area. By the skilful use of satellites, some of the highlights of the BBC's programmes were transmitted live on American screens, interpreted by commentators Chet Huntley and Charles Collingwood, who had come to London for the Election.

In addition to the Americans, 16 European countries took excerpts from the BBC programme for live transmission on the Continent. And this wasn't just Western Europe. Czechoslovakia, Rumania and East Germany were among those who saw our Election in common with 20 million British viewers. There were some European enthusiasts—particularly in Sweden—who stayed up beyond 2 a.m. to watch the flow of results.

Out of the many memorable moments of an exciting 24 hours, I still recall the shocked face of Patrick Gordon-Walker at Smethwick; the timed-to-the-minute departure of Harold Wilson from Liverpool just as we came on the air at 8 a.m. on Friday and the brisk interview George Brown gave to Robin Day when Labour's victory was assured. The tensest moment? Two out of a hundred strong claimants vie for first place: the Kruschev news two and a half hours before we ever went on the air and the audibility of the radio telephone link with the train that was bringing to London Harold Wilson—still not 100 per cent sure that he was Prime Minister.

JOHN GRIST, Chief Assistant (Current Affairs) BBC Television.

THERE are hazards in the way of those who make political programmes that are specific to their particular trade. In this context political programmes refer to programmes, or items in magazines, on either network that deal with the issues and personalities of Party Politics. This is a narrow definition which is acceptable only in this short article.

The most obvious hazard concerns speakers who, in their other role, are legislators and Party spokesmen and will decide, or wish to decide, the future of the organization of which the staff are junior members. Producers and others can find themselves living in a world on tiptoe, as though one false move with the Rt. Hon. "X" or Sir "Y" will plunge their world, and that of their hierarchy, into catastrophe and darkness. This is bogus thinking, but still held in some quarters. It is still necessary, however, to repeat at intervals, for the people on both sides of the camera, that there is no hard evidence either here or in America that a seat, an election, an empire or even a reputation have been lost or won in one television appearance. There is equally no evidence that a production or interviewing error has ever got anybody the sack—although I am not sure that this ought to be true. For a long time too much thought was given to the dangers of politics on television and not enough thought or ingenuity used in its presentation. The punch-up or the dramatic confrontation tended to replace programme thinking. The other way out was the prestige game; the shows where the catering department was supreme and the photographer gets half the rehearsal time and nothing interesting happened except the gossip downstairs afterwards.

There used to be a belief, and perhaps there still is somewhere, that it was a good thing to have MPs in programmes. The theory, a product of the uncertain atmosphere that usually surrounds the future of television, rested on the fact that by an appearance in television the MP would be well disposed towards the organization. Apart from being an insult to all MPs the idea created such problems that could only be solved if the House of Commons formed itself into a choir which broadcast regularly. But whether the idea is dead or not it points to a particular hazard that programmes are not there to have people in but to communicate with an audience.

However pure the motives of a programme and however careful and accurate the treatment, both producer and contributor will occasionally be shocked by accusations made against their integrity and intelligence in the name of those two Bs—bias and balance. To some extent the broadcasting authorities in the past have been less than honest in that they tried to imagine some form of ideal political eunuch above it all, free, independent and pure. Vulgar earth men would make rude noises about this and be suspicious of the whole idea—and in human terms, of course, it was impossible. There are no doubt millions of people who are totally impartial in all political issues today, but they are likely to be of little use in television and especially in current affairs where, above all, curiosity, interest and understanding are needed. All the men I know who are involved in this work have predilections towards certain people and policies and Parties, but I do not think this stops them from making fair and objective programmes, and being perfectly acceptable to all Parties. If most of the people in one programme, both staff and contributors, have a similar set of Party prejudices, and this shows in their work, then the Parties have a legitimate cause for complaint.

There is, or should be, a basic difference between the politician and the broadcaster. In the last analysis one is on the outside looking in at the people working at their business of politics. The public have a right to expect that their reporters and commentators are not taking a hand at the game when nobody is looking. It may be that we in this business in both networks, and the Parties, should think a little more about the ground rules here.

The strength of television in this country is just that it has a reputation for objectivity in current affairs. It has reached a new and larger audience who can trust its output because it is not being loaded according to any one social or political theory. It is for this reason that attempts to "editorialize" must be prevented in the regular daily and weekly programmes of current affairs, however many channels there are. To present a point of view in a regular programme whithout attempting to be objective would achieve little that was new and would work against the best interests of television. Television has an enviable reputation for the presentation of news and current affairs not shared by Fleet Street, and this is something that must not be thrown away. It may well be that there are not sufficient outlets now for those whose ideas are not conventional and that minorities of one sort or another do not have sufficient time on the air, but if this is true this is a reason for new types of programmes, not for a change in basic policy.

Politics and the work of politicians sometimes looks as though it is a private game without much relevance to the life of ordinary people. It is hard to think of a change of government in terms of a game, but the criticism does have some validity. In the past ten years television may have helped that image of detachment and led to some of the disenchantment with political life. Politics on television at one time seemed to be people endlessly arguing with each other from set beliefs in an abstract world. It was good humoured, entertaining, but not somehow very relevant.

The earlier problems of reporting politics as it is—warts and all— have been overcome; the recent election showed considerable progress. In the future it will need more ingenuity, research, more resources, but the basis of it will be the professional fascinated by his work, interested, stimulated by the clash of ideas and personalities and generally relishing his somewhat hazardous occupation.

16   The Political Interview*

ROBERT McKENZIE

ROGER MANVELL

MANVELL: There has been a great deal of discussion about political interviewing on television which, many people claim, imposes a kind of inquisition on politicians. Do you think this is a fair comment?

McKENZIE: No. I would take exception at once to the implications behind both "imposes" and "inquisition". First of all, a politician is quite free to accept or reject an invitation to be interviewed. There's obviously no compulsion whatsoever of the kind the word "inquisition" suggests. Besides, there are all kinds of built-in safeguards to ensure the interviewer will atempt to be as fair as possible to politicians drawn from any of the parties. If an interviewer allowed his own personal viewpoint to direct the line of questioning, he would rapidly become unusable on any of the present channels. Most of us, I think, quite honestly attempt to reflect the questions than an informed viewer would have liked to put himself had he been in the position to do so. Therefore, the questions posed might be said to originate from several successive different points of view which are both to the left and the right of the politicians concerned.

However, you can't, of course, guarantee what the net impact of any interview is going to be; that's one of the pitfalls in this kind of work. The politician, after all, may have a weak case, or his case may be full of loopholes, and so he may in consequence appear to have been worsted by the interviewer. You can't always guarantee

---
* *STFA Journal, Spring 1965.*

the interview will end in an apparent draw. The interviewer's job, as I see it, is to examine the politician's case as closely and fairly as he can, and it is quite possible, as a result of this, that he may appear in the guise of a victim.

MANVELL: But what about the manner in which the questions are put?

McKENZIE: An interview, if it's to hold the public, must at least be spirited. Sometimes the interviewer may give the appearance of trying to outwit the interviewee. Perhaps the pace may appear too fast for him, for instance. But part of our job is to make the interview sparkle, and there are often occasions when the interviewer is in fact far more experienced in television technique, and so at his ease, than the politician he is questioning. But I would maintain that if a politician has really got up a good case, he can't fail to make a respectable showing. If he hasn't—well it's a precarious situation for him if he accepts to be interviewed in the circumstances.

MANVELL: And he has the right, of course, to refuse to answer certain questions, if he wants.

McKENZIE: Certainly. Or he can duck them, or flannel, or, like Hugh Gaitskell used to do, become a past-master in the technique of re-phrasing a question to the advantage of his case. You know, politicians often give answers which are completely illogical in relation to the questions put to them; then you get the kind of interview that's like a stretch of dialogue from *The Caretaker*. Viewers may well not notice the illogicality of these interchanges.

MANVELL: Do you think all responsible politicians should master television as a prime means of communication.

McKENZIE: Yes, I'm sure they should. Television as a means of communication between the politician and the electorate is more important than the press and far more important than the public meeting. On each television appearance he makes, a politician will be addressing more people than a Member of Parliament in the nineteenth century addressed in a lifetime. It's sometimes said that these television appearances tend to place too much weight on, or give too much influence to, politicians who have a special flair for broadcasting. Well, if I had to assess a man's honesty or political capacity, I'd far rather judge him from the way he showed up under interview than from his performance on a public platform. The interview represents a far more exacting kind of test, and one that comes nearer to the way in which we judge people in the circumstances of normal living. A man firing off from a platform is not being tested nearly so critically.

MANVELL: Well, this implies that television has introduced not only a new factor into our democratic system of government, but one which may well have a profound effect on humanizing and maturing the relationship between the politician and the people.

McKENZIE: Yes. Television, in my view, has strengthened, not weakened, the nature of democracy in its human relations. By bringing politics into the living-room, by enabling ideas to be communicated in an intimate, domestic setting, television is an important reinforcement of democracy.

MANVELL: To what extent do you think individuals and organizations with special interests to plead should claim a citizen's right to be heard on the air?

McKENZIE: I'm in favour of maximum opportunities being given on television to organized interests which have what we might term relevant causes to discuss or promote—for example, the steel interests, or groups concerned with the abolition or retention of capital punishment, or CND. But they should be cross-examined. One of the reasons why I want to see more channels is because this will give us greater opportunities for discussions such as these. It's because we've had too few channels that it has often proved difficult to give the kind of interests I've mentioned proper opportunities to put forward their views.

MANVELL: Or because those responsible for television have had cold feet over it?

McKENZIE: Or because there exist closed-shop agreements between the principal political parties, which have, for example, until just recently kept the Scottish and Welsh nationalists from presenting their cases in the party political broadcasts. Also, we seem too afraid still of the extended interview. There ought to be far more one-hour interviews, such as are frequent on North American radio and television. In the last Canadian elections, for example, the party leaders in turn took part in one-hour interviews from eleven o'clock to midnight on Canadian television. I once did a one-hour interview with Tom Mboya for Canadian radio and I think one got a far better understanding of African nationalism than is possible in a short interview. In this country we seem afraid of interviews that last longer than ten or fifteen minutes. This is not long enough.

MANVELL: Do you think the electorate here is entitled to more than they get at present in the way of actual criticism of policies and politicians by political commentators on television?

MCKENZIE: I think there should be as wide a variety of direct comment of this kind as possible. Only recently, for example, have the broadcasting authorities permitted journalists to give their own views about the performance as well as the policies of individual politicians in programmes such as *Gallery*. It came, as it were, along with the political satire and diatribes in TWTWTW.* But there is still nervousness about allowing this sort of thing during an election period. I believe in the maximum amount of political comment and analysis.

MANVELL: To what extent should political comment be allowed to appear in other programmes than those which are specifically dealing with these issues?

MCKENZIE: Well, again, as widely as possible, with due regard to the nature of the programme. It's obviously quite right in the general magazine-type programmes such as *Tonight*.

MANVELL: Yes; but what about the satiric entertainment programmes?

MCKENZIE: Excellent, I think, so long as there is a proliferation of such programmes, and a *variety* of satiric viewpoints reflected in them—not just one. It would be intolerable, for example, if there were only one or two newspapers or weekly journals of political comment with a marked political bias.

---

* TWTWTW. The familiar abbreviation of *That Was The Week That Was*, the first of the BBC's regular satirical programmes on social and political topics. Compèred by David Frost.

MANVELL: Which brings us to the key point—the distinction between the press and television broadcasting as media for political comment. Should the television channels be allowed editorial freedom?

MCKENZIE: I don't myself believe that television is an appropriate medium through which to pursue a single political line, angling the presentation of the news, for example, from some pre-determined point of view.

MANVELL: Why?

MCKENZIE: Mainly because there are too few channels for this kind of limitation to operate to the public advantage. If there were very many channels operating under a variety of controls, then it could become acceptable if certain channels adopted a known editorial line.

MANVELL: Even granted this, should the news, on television, as distinct from editorial comment upon it, remain un-biased?

MCKENZIE: Yes, I think it should. The presentation of news should always remain independent of party political editorialising.

MANVELL: Though perhaps presented with associated, editorialised comment?

MCKENZIE: That's all right. You must, as I see it, make a clear and continuous distinction in the mind of the viewer between the newscaster who tells you what has happened and the commentator who represents a particular viewpoint upon it. This being so, then I'm in favour, as I've said, of having as many different viewpoints expressed on the air as possible. I think the regulations that govern television and politics should be constantly reviewed: for example, the inhibiting rule that during an election campaign, no candidate can appear on television unless all the other candidates in the constituency he's contesting also agree to appear as well. Surely, so long as each of them is offered the same opportunity, this should be a sufficient safeguard.

MANVELL: Lastly, what about televising Parliament itself?

MCKENZIE: The televising of Parliamentary debate, in my opinion, will come, and it should come, initially in the form of an edited telerecording put out at night. And I would like to see a few of the major debates of the year televised live and in full. After all, Hansard is published as a verbatim record; why shouldn't we see the record as well? But, naturally, this must be dependent on having more channels available. As for the suggestion that televising Parliament would have some kind of adverse effect on the nature of the debates, I just don't believe it. When some of us were promoting the idea that Party Conferences should be covered by television, we were told that the effect would be dangerous—everyone would be talking to the camera. But this hasn't happened. People wrapped up in their speeches don't bother to talk to the cameras, and far from these telecasts having an adverse effect on the public, I think they have greatly increased the interest shown in political affairs and debate.

17 The Craft of Interviewing*

HUGH DOWNS

MIKE WALLACE

We might begin by ascertaining whether you hold some special philosophy toward interviewing. Is it a unique art or craft? Why, for example, do interview and talk programs have greater apparent success with British TV audiences than with American?

MR. WALLACE: I think we must separate the interview from the regular talk program at the outset. Interviewers are not "talkers". The function of the interviewer is to talk no more than necessary. His job is to encourage the man sitting across the table from him to talk.

As for the success of talk programs in London, I suppose the British are more addicted to the talk show, both in radio and television. Men like Malcolm Muggeridge and Robert Morley have great followings because—somehow—the British seem to be brought up to be better talkers than Americans.

MR. DOWNS: I am aware of the great number of talk programs in England, and some of them are very good. But often a talk program can become random and aimless if it does not have the focus that a good interview must have. One of the remarkable qualities of Mike's interview technique, for example, is its deliberate direction.

It is my belief that there is no such thing as an embarrassing

---

* *Television Quarterly, Summer 1965.*

question in a good interview. There is always the matter of taste, of course, in a question. It might be loaded in such a way that the listener becomes confused—or it may take advantage of an ineptitude on the part of the guest. But Mike's show seeks participation, and asking those frank questions which are in the mind of the viewer really constitutes the whole art of interviewing. I have always felt that my ultimate function is simply to represent the natural and healthy curiosity of the viewer or listener.

MR. WALLACE: You must also remember that when Hugh does one of his *Today* interviews, he is not just a reporter who is digging for facts. He is not only reporting, he is actually editing and publishing at the same time. This is a difficult and complex job. The discussion we are holding now, for example, is different from an ordinary live television interview because both Hugh and I will have a later opportunity to see a transcript, and we can make sure that we have said what we intended to say. We will have the right to say "Let's get this out", or "This is what I meant here". You will condense and rearrange it, and we can see it before it is frozen in print. But the TV interviewer has only a few fleeting minutes to accomplish the same goal, and under pressure. Nobody else in any other medium must work under those conditions which make broadcast interviewing unique.

MR. DOWNS: Yet an audience member is not exactly like a reader. The reader will sense that the print piece has been polished—that it has been culled from a lot of material and that skilful editorial ability has been applied to it. The audience for a TV interview, however, recognizes the nature of the work and how it is delivered to them. They can be more compassionate when they know that a person is on the spot, and they will settle for what comes out within such conditions. Mike pioneered this approach in his old *Nightbeat* show and the audience responded to it. That lack of perfection which is an inescapable element in my own daily interviews is somehow understood, and in large measure forgiven, by the audience because they are aware of our problems.

MR. WALLACE: We ought to recognize, too, that the function of the interviewer will alter in different types of programs and with different kinds of guests. Many interviews—perhaps the bulk of them—are purely informational. But there are also interviews which are devoted to pure entertainment. If I am interviewing Woody Allen I am not really after information. I am virtually a straight man, just setting up jokes for him.

But the informational interview can have controversial overtones. I may have a guest who has aroused a great deal of curiosity because he is disputatious, and I want to push him, prod him, and encourage him into making more direct statements of his views. I try to confront him with an attitude he has held in the past. Perhaps he has changed his position. I may operate on the hunch that he hasn't made his change of mind public, and I will try to confront him with this private change.

MR. DOWNS: Certainly the objective is truth, but elements which will mitigate the incisiveness of the interviewer as he digs for it must be considered. Certain aspects of taste will influence him, as will simple compassion, and this poses a dilemma. If, out of compassion, a questioner lets up on a guest the interview can become vapid and hypocritical. There are some viewers who may say, "That's good. The guy is a human being after all"; but many others will say, "I don't give a damn about his feelings. I want to know the truth." This group wants the interviewer to keep after him. You have that obligation to the viewer you represent, but on the other hand you feel odd about really putting on the heat in order to get at the truth.

For five years I worked with Jack Paar, who, contrary to what some people have been led to believe, was not a villain. He was not malicious, but because of his personality he could be more incisive than many people who have made life-long careers of getting infor mation out of people. He just asked a question in a certain way and *bam*! I don't think he was hurting people. I think that one of the conditions which led to his remarkable, and not undeserved, success is a certain morbid curiosity in many viewers. They didn't tune in to listen to his skill or maturity, but because he had that raw, direct quality which brought out the truth in such a way that TV seemed an even more powerful medium than it is. He had the knack of asking the basic question right off. When he interviewed Harlow Shapley the first thing he asked was, "Is there a God?" A question like that would unnerve even a distinguished scientist like Shapley.

MR. WALLACE: It may seem strange, but when you consider it there is a certain time of day when questions like that become more appropriate. The kind of question Paar used to ask on the old *Tonight* show could not be asked by Hugh on his morning show. It seems to me that after eleven o'clock the threshold for acceptance of pointed questions is somewhat lower.

MR. DOWNS: That's a coincidence. I never discussed this matter with Mike, but over the years of broadcasting I got the same feeling. I once wanted to do a magazine piece called "The Prude Curve". The observation is true, but it isn't because the audience make-up changes. There are subjects you can touch upon as the hour grows later that cannot be broached at other times. At quarter to one in the morning you can bring up topics and use words—and we did— not because there were different people, but because the "curve of acceptance" seems to drop. This creates additional problems when you are pre-taping because editorial handling and time-placement can bring about entirely unanticipated reactions. A taped discussion of incest or birth control intended for late evening might be played on a morning show and bring on strong criticism.

We are touching upon the entire question of appropriateness and taste in interviewing now, and I wonder if you would comment upon the increasing tendency to bring "kooks" on the air—people who see flying saucers or who have far-out notions on any subject. Is this dangerous in the kind of interview where confrontation is an objective? Perhaps what we are really seeking are your own standards for selection of interviewees.

MR. WALLACE: It will inevitably depend upon the interviewer's taste and judgment. I don't welcome the self-conscious "kook". It might be useful to salt the schedule with one or two in a season, but it can be a delicate matter.

MR. DOWNS: Doesn't the American stage pose an analogous question? There are human beings, it is true, who are handicapped or crippled, either physically or emotionally, but if you people the entire stage with them it reflects not so much the world as it is as upon the nature of the playwright's outlook. Has he really made

valid comment on our lives? The same question faces the interviewer—more acutely because he is not dealing with fiction. It is
not real or editorially honest if you select too high a proportion
of such way-out types. This is as untrue as eliminating or ignoring
them.

MR. WALLACE: You can destroy your own credibility when you bring
too many of that kind to your show. I would readily admit that
my old *Nightbeat* program occasionally came near to vaudeville
when I resorted to the piercing, rather than the penetrating, question.
The audience sensed what we were doing and so these lapses did
not serve us well in the long run.

But let me differentiate between the two kinds of questions.
The piercing question was instituted purely for shock value—like
a telegraphed punch. The penetrating question was used to honestly
seek information and a point of view. The latter kind of question
seeks to generate sparks between one idea and another idea. It is
not employed—as the piercing question is—merely to hurt or to
raise a little hell. The end result of that approach may be entertaining, but it wears itself out very fast.

If your goal is an adult and mature, if abrasive, way of getting
vital information, then almost any question is a sensible one. The
least palatable approach is not simply in interviewing "kooks", but
in creating a "kook" environment around normal people. Some
performers now on TV do much of that.

MR. DOWNS: I think the guests will survive even that, but the show
may die. Some guests on the Paar show complained that he "made
them look bad", but I disagree. Nobody can make an interviewee
look bad, although he can make himself appear ridiculous. A guest
may be neglected or abused—or even misused in some ways—but
if he looks bad he has done it to himself.

MR. WALLACE: I feel we do not attach enough importance to the
manner of presentation. The visual effects which can add dramatic
value to an interview should not be neglected. Ted Yates designed
the visual presentation for *Nightbeat*. It was his idea to shoot it over
the shoulder, thus making the interviewer more anonymous. He felt
that the audience must see the interviewee's face in a tight closeup
in order to reveal the thought process in action. When a penetrating

question was asked you could see it hit. You'd see the reaction begin in the eyes, and this made for a kind of drama superior to many others on TV. And the lighting was blocked out so as to contribute to the starkness of the setting. Incidentally, there is a crucial distinction between radio and TV interviewing. Radio time is cheap and more of it is available, whereas in TV the half-hour and hour required for proper depth in an interview is simply *not* to be had. And I think it's impossible to develop a good and sensitive interview in less than half an hour.

MR. DOWNS: Thomas Mann wrote that one of his characters "got used to not getting used to a certain situation", and that's the way I feel about time in television. There is too little of it to begin with; there are too many interruptions. I have had to learn to work with it. You find out how much time is available and you try to use it in the best way possible, but interviewing interesting people under such restrictions is like walking a shore filled with interesting shells and stones. You know that if you linger too long at any spot you will fall behind.

*Is there a real dramatic structure in a good interview? With
a beginning, middle and end, and point of climax?*

MR. WALLACE: Absolutely. You can only hope that you'll have the wit, flair and ability to respond to the flow, in order to make the interview more and more interesting as it builds. In order to do this you have to know your person pretty well. You must know what he has said in the past, and what his point of view on various subjects is and has been. The interviewer must research what others have said on the subject or about the person being interviewed. But there should definitely be a story "line" in the interviewer's mind as the interview begins.

MR. DOWNS: That's a sound framework, but I would differ to this extent: I have found it possible to lose freshness and perspective if I am too well versed in a subject and the viewer is not as completely informed. In theory, it seems to me that some ignorance can be virtuous. If you have an interesting person, it may be helpful to follow a line of simple adverbial questions: "Who are you?" "Why are you here?" It is a theory, but it will work in practice with stimulating guests. I like to be well prepared, but if I know the subject too well I begin to follow inside routes and the viewer is left behind. I would at least enter a brief against over-preparation.

MR. WALLACE: Well, you could have fooled me, because I thought you were a superb interviewer who knew what he was doing and was capable of performing in such a way as to make me believe that it was spontaneous.

MR. DOWNS: I think I rely on ignorance more than that. I majored in it at college.

> *Do you try to ask the question that hits at closely guarded secrets? Do you often ask questions that will annoy the interviewee?*

MR. WALLACE: I have, especially in the past. A device I will occasionally use is to ask a question and, if I get only half an answer, let "dead air" take over. The interviewee may find that the protracted silence is too much for him, and—so—frequently the pudding comes tumbling out.

> *In that regard, do you often find yourself dealing with the compulsive talker? How do you treat this kind of situation?*

MR. DOWNS: I don't find many of that kind, but I was a bystander on the Paar show on that horrible night when Mickey Rooney spent 25 minutes digging himself into a hole 50 feet deep. My toes curled in my shoes and at one point I wanted to try to rescue him in some way, because Paar just sat there and let him go on. It was a masterful use of technique. Later, when Rooney wanted to sue Paar, someone asked, "How do you sue a man for sitting by and watching you dig yourself into a hole?" This is actually what he did. Rooney couldn't stand silence, and Paar simply sat there and looked at him. It's a hell of a technique. It can also be a very cruel technique.

There are all types of interviewers and interviewing techniques, but maybe the technique of listening is most neglected. There is a type, especially among the amateurs, who has simply never learned to listen. I call him the "Yeah, well . . . " interviewer. He will begin by asking a person how long he has been in the city, and while the guest is answering he is already thinking of what his next question will be. If the interviewee says, "I've been in New York for 155 years" this chap will blandly say, "Yeah, well where do you go next . . . ?" If you don't listen to the answers it can't be much of an interview.

MR. WALLACE: By the very act of listening you can get a fine interview. A man coming to a TV studio for an interview is, after all, in a formidable situation. There are lights, cameras, mikes, distraction. Your function is to try to wipe all that away and establish a chemistry between you and him. You do that by listening. You do it by responding and directing the flow of conversation, and if you do it well there is a moment of truth—a moment in that time period when your eye suddenly fixes on his and you are talking to each other. He has forgotten all the distractions and this is when the best interviewing happens.

MR. DOWNS: During the early days of TV—no more than a dozen years ago—the interviews were carefully blocked and written out. A director would tell a guest, "Mr. Blank, when Mr. Wallace asks you this question, address your remarks to camera three." It wasn't long before the guest was ready for a strait jacket. He had no idea what was happening and couldn't begin to keep track of things. It is up to the medium to bring its techniques to the person who is not familiar with them. It is up to the interviewer, the director, the cameramen and everybody else to make the guest feel at home. The most vital skill is to listen carefully, and probably the next most important is never to ask a guest to look into a camera. Television is at its best when it is eavesdropping.

MR. WALLACE: Playing the cameras is a mistake. Many politicians do it. Jack Javits constantly does it, and it's very distracting. You ask him a question and he immediately turns directly to the camera and away from the interviewer. The audience—I think—prefers to have a sense of eavesdropping on a conversation between a guest and an interviewer.

MR. DOWNS: The reasons for that preference are not hard to find, either. Audiences have become immune to being talked and shouted at. They have seen too many loud and abrasive commercials, too many political speeches. A curtain drops in front of their eyes.

Mike, have you ever tried to tell a politician that he might be better received if he didn't talk at them?

MR. WALLACE: Time and again, but it is difficult to break the ingrained habits of politicians who insist upon speaking to their constituents. I think the most effective political spots I have ever seen were those run by Bobby Kennedy in his senatorial campaign. People came up to him on the street to ask questions, and he answered them directly. The camera was there just as a bystander, taking candid shots. He never looked at the camera, and so it was believable. There was candor and conviction in it.

This was the kind of sequence they used in a CBS Reports *on the Kennedy-Keating race. Are there any special techniques that can be used to get by the routine statement—the foggy political speech?*

MR. WALLACE: Most politicians I know are quite in command of an interview. They know the devices that will be used as well as the interviewer knows them. If you want a straight answer you simply have to be dogged. You must go after it and keep after it, as Lawrence Spivak and his colleagues on *Meet The Press* do so well.

I will never forget an interview with Wayne Morse. He led me by the nose despite all the doggedness I could summon. He was going to use the show as a platform, and I could not shake him loose.

MR. DOWNS: The political interview is not a specialty of mine. I occasionally get one, and once when I did, Senator Clark managed to make me look inept and ineffectual. I recall that we were discussing an amount of money in the billions, and I suggested that three million or so was a drop in the bucket. He replied, "Well, maybe three million isn't much to a radio announcer, but to me it is an important amount of money". It was a wonderful put-down. I had just stuck my neck out so far and he whacked at it.

MR. WALLACE: I thought Martin Agronsky used to do a superb job of political interviewing on the *Today* show before he came to CBS. He conducted a very low key—if insistent—interview, and he got his answers. He got them remarkably fast, too, because he wasn't given much more than twelve minutes.

In closing, what interviews did you find particularly memora-able? Who is the most stimulating kind of guest?

MR. WALLACE: The best kind—not just for interviewing but for any stimulating television—is the person who builds upon his own ideas. Articulate writers and lawyers are excellent. Actors, by and large, are dull because they talk only about their current work. But an artist, a writer, a poet—anyone who deals with ideas—is fine. Frank Lloyd Wright stands out in my memory. He knew why he was there. He wanted to talk about his ideas and stir up a little controversy. He was almost self-conscious about it. He wanted to have some fun and excitement.

MR. DOWNS: The real delight is someone who wants to tear up the floor, not be agreeable. Frank Lloyd Wright is the perfect example— a real joy and challenge. He would lead off an answer with an airy "My dear boy—" and you knew you were working with a genuine master of stimulating conversation. That makes interviewing the most potentially exciting form of television.

MR. WALLACE: It certainly does. Wasn't it Ed Murrow who once said that people armed with their own convictions can compose compelling literature while they are speaking? That's TV at its best—in a talk, a documentary, an interview—anything. Conviction.

18 Television in a Democracy*

ROBIN DAY

THE Pilkington Committee,† whose membership was distinguished by its lack of journalistic, editorial or political experience, was obsessed by what it conceived to be *good* broadcasting. It ignored the problem of how to achieve *free* broadcasting, or at least *freer* broadcasting.

In the last ten years television has taken a few nervous steps in the right direction. Topical reporting has been immensely invigorated. But we have nowhere near reached a television system which reflects the rich variety of British opinion, or which presents political issues with the vigour worthy of a mature democracy.

What disturbs me is that so many people appear to think of television's future as first and foremost a question of *control*—how to stop this, restrict that, prevent the other. I believe that it is wrong to start by seeing the issue as one of control. I see it primarily as one of *freedom:* how can television be built into the broadest possible platform of democratic opinion? Arguments about the rival merits of BBC and ITV, about public-service television versus commercial—these are of secondary importance. Both systems can produce topical

* *SFTA Journal, Spring 1965.*
† *See* footnote page 30.
Robin Day's experience during ten years as a television commentator has brought him into intimate contact with the problems of politics on TV. He believes the key issue is how to build television into the broadest possible platform of democratic opinion. In this article Mr. Day presents a revised version of a chapter in his book *Television—a Personal Report.*

programmes of high quality. (The BBC, justly proud of its own current affairs programmes, is not ashamed to be the purchaser of commercially sponsored programmes from America in this field.) Both systems can stimulate—or suffocate—free expression of opinion. If both are always required to be "impartial" and forbidden to take sides, then their output is bound to be restricted. This restriction must remain so long as TV remains in a very few powerful hands (public or commercial). *But if the editorial control of programmes is spread among as many different hands as possible, we could enable television to fulfil a truly democratic function; the diverse and independent expression of free opinion.*

The purpose of control in television should be to *create* opportunities for freedom of opinion, not to restrict them. There must always be limitations on free expression, but by the laws of the land— libel laws, obscenity laws, and so on—not by a few television executives who sit down and decide in their wisdom what issues the public shall see discussed and what individuals shall discuss them.

The object, then, of a democratic television system should be not simply the impartiality of a few, but the independence of many. One would have thought this was a fairly unexceptionable proposition. After all, this is what we want to see in newspapers. Why not in broadcasting.

One must gratefully record that some progress has been made. The last decade has seen many healthy developments in the handling of current events on TV. These, however, are only relative achievements. Though television journalism is now more robust and virile than it used to be, it still has to work within the emasculating confines of "impartial" broadcasting controlled by a very few people. There is a long way to go. There is concern about the monopolistic tendencies of Fleet Street, and the closing down of newspapers, but the Press today is a far more diverse and vigorous institution than broadcasting. If take-overs and closures are endangering the free expression of newspaper opinion, then it is all the more important that television should be built into an alternative platform of expression.

One important way of achieving this would be the televising of Parliament, about which I have written in detail elsewhere.* The relevant point here is that by televising Parliament the cameras

---

* *The Case for Televising Parliament*, published by the Hansard Society, 1963.

would transmit to a new public a forum of democratic opinion which would be independent of the Press, and independent of the television authorities. What is more, it would be a forum independent of party orthodoxy. These last two claims may call for justification. By saying "independent of the TV authorities" I mean that a televised Parliamentary debate would be an entirely different matter from, say, a *Panorama* discussion which is initiated, devised and "cast" by a producer. A televised debate in Parliament would not be a producer's creation but would be the coverage of a public event. The selection of extracts would be a matter of professional news judgment. In that sense the televising of Parliament would establish a forum "independent of the TV authorities" because the TV authorities would be reporting, not creating, the occasion.

Perhaps more difficult to justify is the claim that Parliamentary television would afford a forum "independent of party orthodoxy". What about the whips and party discipline? The fact is that although party whips are cracked in ruthless fashion—particularly when the Government has a narrow majority—members on all sides still express themselves fearlessly on the floor. They may vote loyally in the lobbies, but nonetheless speak their mind in debate. This is what the cameras would show, and the televising of Parliament would bring before the public many MPs whose lack of orthodoxy makes them rarely acceptable to TV producers who have to arrange a "representative" discussion.

The televising of Parliament would, however, be only one way of making television a more adequate platform for democratic opinion. No one supposes that Parliament is the only source of opinion and criticism. One must therefore look for a system which would enable television to reflect much more effectively than at present the vigour and diversity of contemporary opinion.

How could such a system be achieved? First, three broad principles should apply:

1. The responsibility for topical programmes should rest in as many hands as possible.
2. Those in charge of topical programmes should be able to express their opinions, subject to the ordinary law of the land.
3. The opportunity to run a programme should be on the basis of merit, not money.

How would these principles work in practice? In order that there should be the maximum diversity of control, programme-makers would be allocated certain times of the week for their transmissions. They would have no responsibility for any other programme, but they would have complete responsibility for their own. They would produce, edit, and present it. They would indemnify the "publishing" network against libel. They would be chosen (by whom will be suggested below) so as to offer the widest possible representation of independent opinion. There would not just be *Panorama* and *This Week* and one or two other "impartial" programmes presenting a so-called balanced view. There would be a range of independently edited programmes which would match, and maybe exceed, the variety of opinion we can find in the Press. Just as we now have, for instance, a *Spectator*, a *New Statesman*, a *Tribune* and an *Economist* reflecting various shades of the political spectrum, we could have a matching variety of independent (not impartial) TV programmes.

At present the only programmes organized on this principle (i.e. programmes for which BBC and ITV are not responsible) are the party political broadcasts which are "devised by and presented on behalf of" the party concerned. *The political parties are the only people who have separate television time to state their views on current issues as they wish and how they wish.* Why should this be tolerated in a mature democracy? Democracy apart, these broadcasts are done by the very people who would be expected to produce dull television—professional politicians. One or two of them may also be professionals in television, but political orthodoxy can rarely be a setting for liveliness, frankness, or originality. Under the system I am advocating, professional television journalists—editors, producers, reporters—would have access to television to present programmes free of any political orthodoxy, and to express opinions.

Lest I be misunderstood, it is right to say that "impartial" broadcasting in Britain has done its best, and a very good best. But the limits of journalistic freedom which can be achieved within the strict bounds of "impartiality" have been reached. *The time has come to introduce a new concept into British TV and radio—the independent expression of opinion.* Broadcasting in Britain has hitherto been content to attain independence from political control, but has not yet sought *positive* independence, the right to express opinions. It is the difference between freedom *from* and freedom *to*. The one is an immunity, the other is a right.

The duty observed in British television today is the duty of trying to seem to be fair to most of the people most of the time. This is a reasonable aim in a system where broadcasting is in the hands of a very few big groups. The future development of television should not be so restricted. We should move towards programmes which are diversely controlled, and which are as free to express opinions as books or newspapers.

Years ago, political controversy was rare in broadcasting. Now it is common. "Balanced" debates are part of our regular television fare. TV arguments, once so revolutionary, are now familiar in many homes. This is all to the good. We are accustomed to clash and controversy on the screen. Now we must take a step further towards grown-up broadcasting. We should aim higher. Television needs some independent, committed voices doing on the screen what editorials and articles do in the Press.

How would a system such as I have suggested be financed and organized? There are at least two possibilities, which apply to both television and radio, and which could be used to open up local as well as national broadcasting. It could be operated by the BBC (or a new public corporation) if the charter was amended to provide for the transmission of a few editorially independent programmes produced by outside persons.

Alternatively, or in addition, it could be operated under a commercial system, with revenue from advertising. There would be a Broadcasting Commission which would establish its own transmitters and studios. It would receive all the advertising revenue. Out of this it would commission a wide variety of individuals or groups to present programmes using its technical facilities. The Commission would allot time on a basis of professional merit, plus diversity of opinion. It would say: "Submit us an over-all budget and plan for your weekly or fortnightly programme." If it approved, the Commission would engage the programme for a given period and offer its facilities. It would have no editorial control of, or responsibility for, the contents of the programme. Obviously the professional quality of the production would determine whether the contract to produce it was renewed.

Some of those who might be qualified to produce programmes

might not be millionaires. A considerable number of small, independent, free-lance groups of producers and journalists could be commissioned to provide regular programmes, in much the same way as books or articles expressing independent opinions are commissioned by publishers. Advances of money could be made out of advertising revenue to assist in starting operations. The basic facilities—transmitters, studios, office space—would be provided by the Commission out of public funds which would be repaid as advertising revenue came in. Current affairs would, of course, be only one element in the programmes. A similar system of commissioning independent programmes could apply in other fields, locally and nationally.

The technical limitations on channels and frequencies make it inevitable that access to TV and radio time should be under some sort of authority, but the Commission suggested in my scheme would be different in character from the BBC or the ITA. *It would originate, but not control. It would select, but not supervise. It would be a publisher, not a producer.* It would not be responsible for programme content, once the choice of programme-maker had been made. This choice would be made openly, and independently of political pressure.

I have given the outline of a possible system. It would not be without imperfections. Nor is the BBC or the ITA. I put it forward for critical discussion as the basis for a new sector in broadcasting to supplement—not to replace—what exists at present.

Television has barely begun to serve democracy. Even if the fullest and most adventurous use of TV is made at future general elections, this will not be nearly enough. Democracy does not function for only three weeks every few years. There are two hundred or more weeks in between elections. If television is to serve democracy to its utmost capacity, it must be continually presenting political opinion on a much broader and freer basis than at present. One step towards this end would be the broadcasting of independent editorial opinion as suggested in this chapter. I have also advocated the regular televising of Parliament. The development of local broadcasting would provide a further platform for public discussion and a new link between politicians and their constituents.

Our Parliamentary leaders do not yet appear to have grasped the fact that television and radio offer them today a closer link with the people than has been granted to any statesman since the time when Pericles addressed his whole community in the city of Athens.

During the thirty years since television first flickered into British homes the attitude of politicians towards it has changed from ignorant disdain to fear-ridden desire. The instinctive reaction of politicians to the problems of television is to think in terms of restrictions, controls, limitations, when what is needed is freedom, diversity and independence. Hitherto the timorous answer to the challenge of television's power has been to *contain* it, by keeping it in a very few "impartial" hands. During the next quarter of a century let us *distribute* the power of television, so that in 1984 television will not be an Orwellian instrument of mass hypnosis, but will have long been built into a broad and open platform of democratic opinion.

19 Documentaries and Dollars "This Fair Conjunction"*

LOU HAZAM

THE millennium of TV film documentaries has not yet arrived.
Perhaps it never will. But the giant strides that television has recently made in this field promise, in the years immediately ahead,
a steady growth in number of documentary programs which will
not only increase public understanding, but make a significant
contribution to the art of film-making as well.

Much has been made of Mr. Newton Minow's contribution to a
renewed emphasis upon documentary. We, too, agree that it has
been great. But long before he appeared on the scene the networks
were aware of the need to present more, and better, documentaries.
At my own network (and I do not discount the remarkable achievements at other networks) *The Way of the Cross* was completed before
the famous Minow speech, and *Vincent Van Gogh: A Self-Portrait*
was begun and well underway before he launched his assault. Yet
one must still agree that he is probably the documentarian's best
friend—simply by dint of waiting off-stage.

But while Mr. Minow may be a force in assuring the continued
presentation of documentaries, he can do little about their quality.
The two factors, it seems to us, that are most responsible for the
steadily maturing art of TV documentary are sufficient money to
make them, and sponsors willing to buy them.

It is ridiculous to assume that on one day almost no one knew

* *Television Quarterly, Winter 1963.*

how to fashion a worthwhile documentary, and on the next almost everyone did. All of us had marched quite a way along the road to learning about documentaries before the medium encouraged us to do what we knew we could do. But without a doubt, money alone spelled a good deal of the difference between *knowing how* and *being able* to do the job.

Who would have believed, only a few years ago, that we would ever be given $100,000 to produce a television documentary? Yet in this season alone four of our NBC projects are budgeted at over this figure. You can do many things with a hundred thousand that you cannot do with twenty, and we are getting this money today because network officials have finally come to recognize that, with few exceptions, any true quality in production requires it.

And not only the networks have come upon this realization. Not so long ago, even prayer couldn't unearth a sponsor for a TV documentary. It was believed that the audience for such programs was infinitesimal—so small as not to be worthy of serious attention. Today, on every network, few major documentaries take to the air without sponsorship. Sponsors have discovered that the audience is far more significant than they had imagined, not only in numbers but in composition. This has been a tremendous boon to documentarians. For while it is true more often than not that the networks fail to recover their full production costs from these sales, they nevertheless recoup some part of production costs and generally get their full price for the time sale—just as they do with *Wagon Train*.

What specific improvements in the documentary art has all of this permitted? First, with so much at stake, we are given real encouragement by our employers. In the "old days" we were merely suffered, but now we are given more time to prepare a program. Money can pay for the needed time.

We are now able to range the world with our cameras, and are thus no longer forced to depend on what we can find in film libraries. In addition, correspondents—able, albeit expensive creatures—are often sent with us as observers-on-the-spot for news documentaries. This is a marked departure from simply stepping into a studio a few days before show time to "recite" a script against film which correspondents had no part in making.

The new budgets have enabled us to afford the services of

imaginitive cameramen, knowledgeable directors, and excellent writers. Many times, previously, we were sent out to make film documentaries with live-program directors who knew little of film-making techniques, and with news-camermen who had previously shot little more than two-minute news sequences of fires, accidents, or sound-on-film statements from Congressmen emerging from hearings in Washington.

We are now able to hire researchers—recognized experts in their fields—to study a subject before we pursue it, and to inform and advise us. And, happily, we can often survey locations before we actually arrive at them.

We are now permitted to shoot more than just minimum film requirements, and select from this wealth of film the particularly good footage we need to fashion the best show. This permits us to enjoy that wonderful tool—"choice".

We can now send that once lowly, abused and suspected person, the script-writer, out into the field, where he can "see" for himself, "sense" his story, and help create it on the spot. This enables him to endow his scripts with much more believability.

Finally, the increases in budgets have enabled us to shoot in color if we wish.

But perhaps nowhere is the new aspect of the TV film documentary more clearly evident than in the knowledgeable use of film-making techniques. Now sufficiently supported by budget, more than anything else on the technical side they are serving to transform the once-plodding documentary—primitive in treatment and bereft of artistry—into an absorbing slice of life.

Rarely, for example, does today's TV documentary commit the unpardonable sin of talking its audience to death. Whole sequences are visually planned to speak for themselves—telling the story through a moving assortment of related shots, each planned to succeed the other in such a way that words are not needed at all. Gone forever are the scenes of white oxen in India pulling a plow while the narrator (voice over—as if hastening to serve up his conglomeration of facts before the picture gives out) runs the entire gamut of statistics on Indian agriculture, presenting facts which have little or no relationship to what is being witnessed on the screen. Instead, today's film-makers shoot specific material which covers each important point being made by the narrator—i.e., the types of agriculture being practiced, the workers in the field, their home life, the economic result of their efforts, and so on.

Film-making techniques are maturing as rapidly in the editing room as in the field. Whatever estimates we make of the date when a film will be ready for airing will allow generously for editing time. This permits the most careful selection and use of each frame of footage, giving us time to try a variety of options in approach to an individual sequence before deciding upon the best one.

At one time, TV film editors were often regarded as technicians whose job required little artistry. Now the editor—at least among the knowing—is given a voice in the final decision on each sequence, and he often contributes the basic idea that takes the work beyond that mere "stringing together" of film which advances the story. In *The Way of the Cross*, editor Connie Gochis—nominated for an Emmy for his work last season—created the sequence of the convulsed world, that followed upon the crucifixion of Jesus, with film "run-outs" from the end of each reel—footage that the cameraman and director never, in their wildest imaginings, might have considered to be useful.

This brings us to the abstract use of film—something seen quite often in one-reel Art films, but rarely on TV. Not only in *The Way of the Cross*, but in *Vincent Van Gogh: A Self-Portrait* (for his insane spells) and in *Shakespeare: Soul of an Age* (for the witches in *Macbeth*) we ventured into this area, particularly to treat ideas that could not be handled by a normal, straightforward use of camera. Today, our cameramen are instructed and encouraged to give us footage of this type when they feel it is called for and can be useful to us in the editing room. This freedom has resulted in such creative innovations as Scott Berner filming Miami at night with an exciting made-in-the-camera super-imposition for *U.S. #1*, and Guy Blanchard creating the *Macbeth* witches out of water bubbles and light reflections. In short, we are no longer fearful of such film.

Two other points are worth mentioning—both reflecting the dollar's contribution to documentary's new look.

First, music. With increased budgets we now have the wherewithal to pay a composer for a hand-tailored, original musical score. This is of singular importance, since music is that essential ingredient which serves to combine all the diverse units of a program and weld them into a single entity. It establishes mood, creates effects, accents important points, and carries the viewer from one scene to the next in the proper spirit. Formerly, music was regarded simply as "background" and was selected from those records or tapes for which clearance was available.

Today, however, those seeking to make films of stature enjoy much greater latitude in music use. The music is constantly improving in such documentaries, contributing considerably more than just "background". Since the composer is forced to write to exact time—10 seconds here, 12 seconds there, up 3 seconds, segue to a new theme and under narration for one minute and twenty-eight seconds, etc.—his is an especially difficult creative enterprise. But many composers have learned to do it and do it well, despite the handicaps we have imposed upon them. In addition, producers and editors have learned to cut entire film sequences to music— often fitting the picture to the score, rather than the reverse, and thereby sometimes securing an added effectiveness that would never come from simply dropping in music after all else is fixed and immutable.

And the dollars have led to a second important innovation in the TV documentary—its stars, men of performing ability who can command a public in their own right. Given money, we are now able to hire their talents to help us, thereby escaping the need to use announcers, or newsmen narrating film that has nothing to do with news. Thus, Lee J. Cobb gave us a memorable Vincent Van Gogh, and his performance was matched by an equally facile Martin Gabel, who narrated the program. Van Heflin accompanied us along highway *U.S. #1*, and his on-the-scene voiced-sentiments might, on other lips, have created far less impact. James Mason guided us 4,000 miles up the Nile; Sir Ralph Richardson presented our Shakespeare show, with Sir Michael Redgrave voicing the excerpts from the plays. Without Sir Michael, or a performer of equal stature, and forced to rely upon the questionable abilities once assigned to us, our program on Shakespeare literally would have been impossible.

There is nothing new about stars on TV, but there is something decidedly new about stars on documentaries. Normally, of course, the public expects the star always to be seen on camera, but our star usually is not seen—simply heard. Yet we have had no complaints. And aside from the high talent they bring to bear in our behalf, they often draw audiences to our documentaries because of their name-value alone—attracting many people who would not ordinarily watch such fare. They "dress up" the new documentary and give it a totally different flavor from some of the undistinguished presentations of the past.

These, then, are some of the reasons why the TV film documentary is maturing, and some examples of how it has matured.

Do we continue to have problems? Of course. Few enterprises in TV are conducted in an atmosphere of sweet peace. Creative people, as a consequence of the arrangement of their genes, are often emotional people—impatient with rules and rebellious by nature. Administrative people, of necessity, are a generally rules-abiding people—conformists by nature. Maintaining the bridge between both is sometimes a difficult and trying job for the producer—himself invariably a hybrid. The conflict between the desire to produce a work of artistic distinction and the more understandable, and acceptable, need to produce a commercial success endures, but is slowly breaking down in face of repeated evidence that both can be accomplished in one and the same show.

Finally, the production schedule in documentaries—as with similar schedules throughout TV—is rarely considered inviolate. Normal and unforseen business developments will repeatedly confound it, and much energy is spent in fighting to preserve the essential time needed for a proper job.

To these one might add many other trials and tribulations. We are plagued by such questions as "Why does it take so long to write script?" (Often we shoot from a treatment and no script at all, for lack of time.) Or "Why don't you go for a finished film the first time around, instead of proceeding through such slow and laborious stages?" (There's a phrase for you—"the first time around!") Or "Is all that editing-overtime really necessary?" The list is endless.

Despite all this, every network continues to press forward with documentaries—producing and presenting the kind of factual shows which at one time not long ago were only fond dreams. At the same time the old saw about documentaries never being able to draw "the kind of audience" a plot-construction type of show draws is being put to bed. In our own experience, for example, our *Nile* program, we were told in hallowed tones by those who fill their day with such scripture, drew a "30-market multi-network Nielsen Raring" 33 per cent share of the audience, outrating such formula fare as *The Untouchables, Naked City, Combat, Hawaiian Eye, Rawhide* and ABC's movies.

But perhaps the most surprising testament to the documentary's new status was evidenced in the 1961 "Emmy" Awards. Three documentaries—those Cinderellas of the "yore" of television—competed with such programs as *The Judy Garland Show* and *Victoria Regina* for the top prize "Best Show of the Year". They were *Walk in My Shoes* (ABC), *Biography of a Bookie Joint* (CBS), and *Vincent Van Gogh: A Self-Portrait* (NBC)—one from each of the major networks. No, none of them won. But the fact that they were nominated indicates that the documentary, like the automobile, is here to stay—thanks to the combination of the money made available by enlightened networks, intelligent sponsors, an eager new public, and a friendly F. C. Co. "Smile heaven upon this fair conjunction. ..."

20 A Form for Television*

GORDON HYATT

A DRAMA critic once said, "I don't know how to criticize television, for it hasn't any form of its own". This is the hard and simple truth, for no matter how closely one examines the medium, it seems that every type of presentation is basically derived from another medium.

Consider these five categories: (1) theatrical film, (2) the game show, (3) live coverage, (4) studio drama, and (5) news. Each of these forms had an independent origin in a medium outside television, and yet every kind of TV presentation can be classified within these broad "forms".

Into the theatrical film category may be fitted every dramatic or situation program now on celluloid. They are all, in essence, simply "small" movies, made to fit a specific time and format. The only essential distinction between today's *Laramie* and yesterday's *Riders of the Purple Sage* lies in the method by which it is exhibited before an audience.

What of the game shows and live coverage now on television? The game shows, of course, are all holdovers from radio, with a few visual elements added. Most of the current programs are direct descendants of *Doctor I.Q.* and *Can You Top This?* In live coverage, whether it be vaudeville on the *Ed Sullivan Show* or a Thanksgiving Day parade, nothing essentially new is added by television other than an immediacy of presentation. While immediacy may be highly prized

* *Television Quarterly, Winter 1962.*

at World Series time, the techniques of camera placement and proper alternation of visual images were established by newsreel men in the '20s and '30s. The electronic camera replaced the film camera, and nothing else has been added.

Studio drama has all but disappeared from the video scene, despite the fact that some of TV's most memorable moments, and its greatest writers, emerged from early experiment. But the mere fact that men like Gore Vidal, Tad Mosel and Paddy Chayevsky have moved easily from TV to motion pictures or Broadway suggests that they never were creating a "new TV drama", but had merely admirably crafted and adapted stage plays and playlets or motion picture shooting scripts.

In news alone are new techniques of reporting evolving and new technical equipment being perfected. It is here that television seems to be shaking the Alistair Cookes out of its stew and creating a form of its own. The medium's highest refinement of technique to date is the television documentary. *Variety* calls it the "telementary", which is a useful name for our purposes here.

The telementary usually includes certain ingredients. First, there is a commentator, host or correspondent—a man whose personality and delivery sets the overall tone of the presentation. He usually speaks from a studio, and graphic arts and scenic elements derived from the program's material often supplement his appearance. To this is added film—shot in any number of ways, from the revealing "candid" methods to production interviews filmed on locations appropriate to their subjects. The live and film portions may be counterpointed by the use of sound, also recorded on location; or with special sound effects designed to enhance or comment upon the meaning of the images; or with music, originally written or prerecorded material, carefully synchronized to underscore and understate the mood of the entire piece. Superimposed titles, animation, and all other tools of film and television technique can be used to point up the intent of the presentation. But it is the *intent* that holds the key to successful telementary presentation. The intent, the point-of-view, when combined with all of the techniques, makes the new form.

The form is that particular combination of original film documents and original writing, edited and presented with a sharp and critical point-of-view which attempts to discover the truth of a situation. The situation may reflect the public world, hitherto the province of newsmen; or it may concern the private world, hitherto the province of writers, poets, and artists. The telementary is not documentary film in the theatrical sense—it is the unique product of television's techniques and personalities which, in the final analysis, constitute its form.

Producing telementaries has become a serious and dedicated profession. No one could disagree with this observation after seeing an accurate telementary indictment of inhumanity, of prejudice, of short-sightedness in public life or indifference in private individuals. As in any serious work which communicates the ideas, feelings and vision of the creative man, it is the aim of the telementary to reach the audience's intellects, their emotions, their senses of righteousness and humor—the sum total of their sensitivities. It should produce an emotional response from the viewer. What results from this depends on the intent of the presentation. Viewers may be aroused to action. They may develop a new personal insight into a subject or merely be made more aware. An individual's response is usually conditioned by his own inner resources. It is the purpose of both art and communication to reach those resources and stimulate response.

Dramatic television at its best evokes such response. So does a dedicated newspaper editorial, a memorable speech, a significant film or a drama of integrity. These are the forms of mass communication, the ways we approach the truth, and the ways we make our fellow man sensitive and aware. With the telementary, television has entered this search for meaningful expression. It has joined with dedication, with eyes wide open, and with the strength of moral conviction.

The fields of expression for the new form have just begun to be explored. They have ranged far and wide, from the portentous *CBS Reports* presentation, "The Year of the Polaris", to the sharply critical study by NBC's *White Paper* of "The U-2 Affair", or the sensitive, highly personal ABC *Close-Up* examination of the American negro, "Walk in My Shoes".

These programs begin to compare in significance with some of the best of television's studio drama. The latter were subjective presentations of literary integrity approaching essential truths as the producers *saw* them, not as the producers *found* them. These men aimed at understanding and communicating human experience. Critics must decide whether the drama of the negro as viewed in a documentary study has the validity of the insights evoked by a Langston Hughes. Will some forthcoming study of tenement life reach the same quality of insight, humor and truth attained in Paddy Chayefsky's "Marty"? Perhaps not, but the telementaries will at least aim that high. At moments they will suggest a poet's vision; at times they will suggest a dramatist's power.

Perhaps the telementary is one of the most acceptable approaches we have today for getting at the truth. Our highly developed world of communications continually pushes hard facts at us. We are brought into contact with news and newsmakers faster and in greater-documented detail than ever before in history. The President's statements are no longer only reported; we see his news conferences. We are brought into the United Nations, into hearing rooms, into courtroom corridors. As a result, first-hand material and actual presence is becoming commonplace. The telementary is one significant attempt to move beyond the mass of surface representation by adding meaning to cold evidence.

Consider the opposite editorial directions being taken by *The New York Times* and *The New York Herald Tribune* as evidence of this growing need to deal with masses of fact. The *Times* daily grows in bulk and weight, fulfilling its calling as "the paper of record". Meanwhile, the "Trib" moves hesitatingly but significantly in another direction as it seeks a format which will provide an overlay of analysis and understanding upon these facts. Its aim is to distil and pinpoint the meaning of facts and provide a form of daily news interpretation based upon facts.

But the daily paper cannot always bring the sum total of a situation to the reader. News has a continuity. It unfolds slowly, as life itself does. The total meaning of a developing situation, as in life, may completely elude the daily reader. For example, it took weeks before the real and subtle issues at stake in the Newburgh, New York, welfare dilemma were made clear. At first it appeared to be a simple case of too many free loaders. In time it was shown to be rooted in local, state and national problems—a complicated story. To grasp the meaning of the Newburgh welfare situation a reader would need a total presentation. He could have turned to a news magazine like *The Reporter*—or he could have turned to television. We can hope that he compared both. To understand life, man turns to the forms of mass communication and chooses from them in light of his own experience. Mass communication must provide the choices.

Finally, two observations about what the telementary is *not*. First, it is essentially different from the documentary film. Great documentary films like Robert Flaherty's *Nanook of the North*, Pare Lorentz's *The River* or the *March of Time's* "Battle of Britain" are basically studies of place and event recorded at a particular time of history.

Nor is the telementary an expanded theatrical newsreel. Remember the newsreels? Think back and you will recall those glimpses of a king and queen on tour or a dictator reviewing his army. These snippets were mere visual supplements to facts already reported by newspapers and radio. You saw them days after the event, when you got to the theatre. Imagine, for instance, a documentary-newsreel of an incident of the 'thirties—say the Panay Gunboat affair. By the time a significant, cumulative report of its material reached the public it would have resembled *Nanook of the North*. It would have become an historic document.

But television has a place and a time for a single effect, a total effect. It creates, if you like, an "instant audience". It reaches the viewers much in the same way that a periodical reaches the newsstand; not in the way a history book reaches the bookshelves. Its effect can be calculated in direct proportion to the timeliness of its appearance.

Each telementary that you see is a new attempt in the use of this new form. It is a distinct form, separate from news magazines, from documentary films, from the public forum, from the broadcast speech and from daily journalism. When a medium has begun to perfect its form, endless variations will develop for the men who use it and who attempt to create a style within form. We can hope that the style will continue to develop and mature.

20a The Impact of Vision*

ANDREW MILLER JONES

MORE than 14 million sets, over 120 hours of television per week, an audience of 17 million for *Steptoe and Son*—four times the total number of people who saw *My Fair Lady* during its record-breaking run at Drury Lane—a regular audience for *Panorama* and *This Week* far greater than the circulation of the most popular daily newspaper, a viewing figure for *Monitor* and *Tempo* larger than the readership of all the "intellectual" weeklies put together; clearly television is the most pervasive influence in our lives today. Not without reason is television the most sought-after selling medium for mass-produced consumer goods. Undoubtedly it has impact.

Yet how much do we really know about how this impact is achieved, and how much of the impact is due to the ideas content and how much to its presentation? It was once said of television by a distinguished Director General of the BBC that far too much attention was paid to presentation and not enough to programme content —possibly a fair enough comment on some of the programmes at the time, which were often dressed up with visual gimmickry not strictly relevant to their theme; he then went on to say that provided the content was satisfactory the presentation was of no importance. No successful producer would agree with this statement today. All would assert that content is always conditioned to a greater or lesser degree by the manner of the presentation. This they feel instinctively

* *SFTA Journal, Spring 1962.*

or they would not continue to be successful or indeed continue in television. Yet how many of them really know why their programmes have impact or how much greater that impact could be? In the absence of a proper codification of practice based on scientific research, or even the existence of a body of informed independent criticism more perspicacious and philosophical than is to be found in the daily and weekly newspapers, how could they?

Such principles of production as there are seem to be of the *post hoc propter hoc* kind—such and such method was tried in a programme which was successful, or certain previously accepted conventions were flouted, therefore this method is good or those conventions unimportant. The vogue phrase now is "brutal production". The success of TWTWTW,† which in the stress of topical production broke all previously-accepted rules and conventions, is held in some quarters to indicate that they are of no importance. It does not seem to have occurred to these pundits that TWTWTW succeeded for quite other reasons and in spite of its disregard of established techniques. Its *enfant terrible* character, its lack of inhibition, topicality, good writing, cast, variety of image and pace were sufficient to compel attention. But the production was rough, the composition often bad, geography sometimes confusing. In the fantastic rush of production it could scarcely be otherwise. But this is no argument for ignoring these things. If the Prime Minister, Lyndon Johnson, de Gaulle, Kruschev, were televised at a table, discussing whether at dawn the following day they should throw the bomb at one another, such a programme would have tremendous impact regardless of whether it were shot upside down, out of focus, phase-reversed, in a fog, regardless of poor sound and confusion about who was sitting where. All of which is not to say that such a programme would not be *more* shattering if it had been impeccably produced.

Technique, rules, conventions, grammar—call it what you will— is only important when it aids communication. Put another way and at its lowest—good technique, like good grammar, should be unambiguous and unobtrusive. At its highest it should, like good advertising, take into account the physio-psychological characteristics of its audience, an audience of one.

---

† *See* footnote page 161.

In fact the only justification for technique is whether it antici-
pates the psychological need of the individual before he is aware of it
himself. Good technique is not a matter of slavishly applying a set
of rules, though the rule of thumb may help the beginner in television.
It is much more the result of an ability on the part of the producer
first to put himself in the position of a viewer. People are more like
one another than unlike. The producer may be more highly educated,
more specialized in his knowledge, certainly more aware of the
technicalities of television than the majority of his audience, but
these differences are small compared with what he has in common
with them. As a human being the chances are that he reacts in the
same way to external stimuli, only he must be more aware of his
reactions. In this way he can identify himself with his audience.
Second, he must have a visual imagination so that he can see in his
mind's eye what he proposes to put on the screen, and then—
metaphorically exchanging his producing hat for his viewing hat—
he must appraise the effectiveness of his programme in detail as a
viewer, and modify it accordingly. If he is then satisfied with what
he sees, he has only to cope with the technical problems of realizing
his "vision" on the screen. Granted the ability to identify himself
with the viewer, and a visual imagination—the ability to envisage a
succession of pictures on the screen with their accompanying sound—
it follows that his technique will be good; he will have communicated.

Unhappily, it would appear all too frequently that either or
both of these faculties are lacking in producers. In some they may be
latent but undeveloped, in others perhaps non-existent. It may even
be that some people are visually blind, as others are tone deaf,
which is not to say that they are unaffected by visual stimuli any
more than the tone-deaf are unaffected by sound.

How visual should television be? Is there too much sound radio
on television? Is there too much talking head? The days are gone
when an editor of the early *Panorama*, fresh from sound broadcasting, could express surprise that such effort went into showing
things when they could be said. Almost everyone working in television today pays lip service at least to the power of the image, but
how many of us really appreciate the relative importance of what is
said and what is seen? There would seem to be a case here for
independent scientific research, as there might be for aptitude tests
to assess the powers of visualization in would-be producers. Ameri-

can psychologists assert that we remember 20 per cent of what we hear and 30 per cent of what we see, and that combined with sound and vision instruction we remember 50 per cent of what we see and hear.

It is generally admitted that if the attention is assailed through the eye and through the ear simultaneously the eye will win every time. How much more difficult it was recently to concentrate on the highly coloured and evocative words of the Onlooker in *Under Milk Wood* when Donald Houston was shown acting, over-acting perhaps, in big close-up, than when he was more distant and there was relatively less movement on the screen. The image assumes greater importance when we consider that those who leave school at the minimum age—the majority of our mass audience—are estimated to get through life on a vocabulary of 800 words which they habitually use and a further 2,000 with which they are familiar but many of which they do not fully understand. It is also said that until a person has acquired an abstract vocabulary he has to visualize before he comprehends. But though vocabulary is a concomitant of education, it is not necessarily an indication of intelligence.

If these assumptions are reasonable, and experience seems to indicate that they are (though it would be valuable for them to be scientifically tested with television specifically in mind), the image plays a much more important role in communication than seems to be commonly accepted, if only to give significance to unfamiliar words and concepts. This is not to underestimate the importance of words. Pictures by themselves do not tell a story until they have been made meaningful either by words or by context, and preferably by both. The same picture can be given a completely different significance when used in different contexts, as Christopher Mayhew pointed out in *The Listener** some years ago, when he used a picture of a smoky industrial town both as a symbol of Britain's wealth and an illustration of the appalling living conditions to which so many of her people were condemned.

But if words are important to make pictures meaningful, so is the time-relationship between words and pictures. Once its significance is understood a picture makes an immediate impact, but time

---

* *The Listener*. A weekly journal published by the BBC; primarily concerned to reprint the text of talks and discussions given in the Corporation's sound and television services. First appeared 1929.

is necessary for the meaning of words to become apparent. If this is accepted, and given that the eye distracts the ear, it follows that words must precede the picture to which they refer and must be overlaid on pictures from which the interest has been exhausted. Any new and unexpected stimulus in these pictures will distract the attention from the words being spoken. Even the order of words in a sentence becomes of paramount importance. If this seems self-evident, any week's television will provide a dozen examples to the contrary, and not only in informational programmes.

If, as seems to be the case, so many producers (with of course many notable exceptions also) ignore these basic principles, may not the explanation be in English education which is heavily biased towards literary rather than visual appreciation? Shakespeare, Keats, Shelley, Hopkins, Eliot, Auden, are required reading in every school, and enthusiastic teachers are there to encourage an interest in literature and a love of language. But how many schools look upon painting, design, an appreciation of colour and form, as anything more than an optional extra?

In theory of course there is a great awareness of the importance of design in television, and many designers of outstanding ability are employed, as visits to television studios will frequently show; but all too rarely is it apparent when the producer has used their work on the screen. It was interesting to observe in the International Exhibition of Television Design mounted by the BBC a year or two ago that there were many brilliant elevations, striking coloured photographs of sets in the studio and impressive-looking models, but not a single example of how the designs appeared on the screen. Yet what the audience sees is all that matters. Consciously the audience (or most of them) will be unaware of poorly composed and badly conceived pictures unless they are very bad indeed. But they will not be unaffected by them. The high priests of advertising, knowledgeable in the mysteries of hidden persuasion, know the value of layout and composition, and, abetted by top-flight film directors working anonymously, have applied it to television commercials, some which in this respect put many professional television producers to shame. If more producers knew what they wanted to put on the screen and considered why, and had more designers thinking in screen terms to help them, it is more than likely that design costs would be drastically cut in spite of the increased salary list.

Television at this point in its development is an exciting medium to work in. There has recently been an influx of lively young minds, fermenting with ideas and a desire to express them. They accept nothing without question. It is right that they should do so, and it is likely that old methods of presentation which have been complacently accepted because they were technically workable and convenient will be drastically changed and not before time. It is to be hoped that these new producers will challenge everything, but neither accept nor reject anything without rigorously applying the viewer reaction test to what will appear on the screen, and then endeavour to make it more effective, before committing themselves to a technical course of action. Perhaps they will question the convention of the armless news-reading torso, and consider that the viewer might be more involved if there were visual evidence that the news was being read, and that the sidelong glance was directed at something. Perhaps they will realize that the set of a head on the neck and the attitude of the body and the shape of hands can powerfully supplement the enlarged features of the face in depicting personality. Perhaps they will rigorously prune away all unmotivated movements of camera or artists and eliminate distracting irrelevant material.

At the same time it is to be hoped that they will realize the value of relevant movement and visual variety as a factor making for interest.

The remark in a *Punch* cartoon some years ago, of one lady to another in a launderette, that watching the whirling smalls through the window of a washing machine was almost as good as the telly, was more than a comment on the triviality of television programmes. Variety, whether imparted by movement or by change of camera viewpoint, is as important in television as in good writing. No writer would think of repeating the construction of an effectively turned phrase in sentence after sentence. Yet the very big close-up dominates the television screen. Quite apart from whether this is the most revealing method of presenting personality, the vision does little to help maintain the viewer's interest. Once he has become familiar with the shape and set of the features and has explored every hair and wrinkle, there is nothing to help concentrate the attention on what is being said. Nothing to stop him from pouring another cup of tea, looking for cigarettes or moving about the room for one purpose or another while still listening to the spoken words, which he will do with greater or less attention according to his interest in the subject under discussion.

This is not to plead for arbitrary changes in camera work for the sake of variety. The introduction of new visual elements not strictly relevant to the theme can equally distract from communication. It is a plea, however, for the introduction of as much variety and texture into a programme as can arise naturally and unobtrusively out of a given situation. Above all it is a plea for the recognition at all times of the personal and informal nature of the medium, and for the realization that however diverse the reactions of the millions of separate individuals who make up the television audience to the *matter* of a programme, their unconscious reactions to the manner of its presentation are likely to be the same.

It has been suggested that some producers/directors instinctively know the factors making for interest, and that others responsible for what comes out of the television set do not know that there is anything to know.

Perhaps at this stage in the development of television a study of its most effective use should be undertaken, which would validate or disprove present production practices. Psychologists suggest that a variation in a person's normal blink-rate is an indication of attention, and have designed apparatus to record blinking. They have also devised a method to indicate precisely where the eye is directed when confronted with an image an how the eye moves over it. Research of this kind could only be undertaken by a university department with considerable resources behind it. It would be a proper subject for study by a Centre for Experimental Cinematography and Television on the lines of the one in Rome, which has been suggested for this country by Thorold Dickinson and Sir William Coldstream of University College, London.

In this way could be built up a body of expertise which would be professional in the true sense of the word, and the appraisal of programme values by those who make their living in and by television could then be based on something more viable than personal predilection.

21 The Individual Approach: Television Actuality*

RICHARD CAWSTON

AUBREY SINGER

JOHN ELLIOT

SINGER: I remember that I was once encouraged to be original and wildly experimental. That was a long time ago before television became big business, and both getting and keeping large audiences became the primary object of the operation. Getting and keeping audiences is not, unhappily, a situation that encourages originality in one's productions.

CAWSTON: The extreme example of that, of course, is the United States where I've been recently; the proven article is the accepted thing, the successful stereotype. But I tend to look at this problem rather differently. I am primarily a documentary film-maker working for television, and for me every job has to be a prototype. For that kind of work I believe that to a large extent unless you are original you fail. We had to get away from the conventional patterns of cinema documentary, the hackneyed "interest" picture, the documentary sewage which was in danger of invading television. It was

* SFTA Journal, Spring 1962.
Richard Cawston and Aubrey Singer discuss with John Elliot originality in the presentation of actuality on television. Richard Cawston is Head of Documentaries, BBC Television, after making such television films as *The Lawyers*, *This is the BBC*, and *Television and the World*. Aubrey Singer is Head of Outside Broadcasts Feature and Science Programmes, BBC Television, but was at the time of this discussion Assistant Head of BBC Television Outside Broadcasts with special responsibility for feature. John Elliot is now a freelance writer, but was at the time of the discussion a Group Producer in the BBC Television Drama Department.

absolutely necessary to find new ways of doing things because television consumes so much. I find one's work in this medium dates so rapidly in style and approach. You've got to keep fresh in order to keep up with the constantly changing period in which you are working. And you've got to have the complete confidence of your employers, so that they trust you to get on with your work in your own way.

SINGER: In the end, whatever your technique, it's your personal standards that really matter, while at the same time you try to keep up with the ground rules of your day and age. Of course, technique dates rapidly; for example, people can accept much faster cutting on television now than they used to in the past. But as far as personal standards are concerned, you've got to be master of your own ideas, in advance, and then make them work on the screen.

CAWSTON: Well, I'm never master of my ideas in advance, I think this can be too limiting—I have a firm overall plan but many of my detailed ideas come pretty late in the day, mostly in the cutting room. My ideas tend to evolve while I'm actually doing the job.

SINGER: I believe in preparing a rough draft script in advance that shows how you hope the subject or the idea will shape. It's always interesting to see afterwards how much of this original treatment gets lost in the wash of production. However much change you accept as you go along, I think you must keep to the spirit of your original idea, or the wrong kind of compromise sets in, and then any originality in the initial treatment slips out!

ELLIOT: I think one of the problems in the general rush of television is the extent to which genuine originality can get lost. For example, it can disappear in group work, when a man's individual originality has to be spread too thin.

CAWSTON: Or in magazine production. A new magazine may be original, but then the pattern takes over and there's not often time for originality after that.

SINGER: But you can't just produce in a vacuum, can you? You've got to test the validity of your ideas by talking them out with someone. Surely that's the function of the group system in television, the group producer is there to listen to the ideas of the other producers who are working with him.

ELLIOT: Now that television is so large, do you think it helps us develop originality to have a producer at the head of a group?

CAWSTON: I can't say. I work alone. In any case, I don't think any of us in my particular field is capable of stating initially exactly what we're going to do. Once a subject is approved simply as a subject, I don't want to discuss details of the treatment in advance with anyone.

SINGER: But the group producer should be prepared to discuss developments at any stage along the line of production.

CAWSTON: Well, I still prefer to have discussions of this kind with my editor, which means during the later stages, when there is some film to look at on a screen. But I think originality depends on making it possible to include ideas at whatever stage they may come to you out of the material you're handling. That's why I don't like writing a hard script. Pre-scripting kills originality. I write a script after the job's done. That's why we're more fortunate than the Americans; a sponsor always wants to see a pretty full script in advance.

SINGER: All right. I agree that a group producer must learn to leave his colleagues as free as possible to work out their own destiny. But the group producer is after all a developer of ideas. A go-between linking the management with the producer in the field. A fighter for budgets. And a fighter for the status of the group of which he is in charge, anxious to preserve its originality of approach to the work it does.

ELLIOT: There's another point. We were all film people originally before we went over to television. At first, immediately after the war, we found we were- distinctly limited in what we could achieve technically. Now the range of modern equipment makes television production so much more flexible. How do you think we can use these resources to express our original ideas?

SINGER: Well, television documentary, as opposed to film documentary, normally explores a subject through personality, through people seen in simple close-ups. We have had speaking faces on the television screen *ad nauseam*. My view is that in the future we should use our new resource to achieve the beautiful picture, and not just the talking face.

CAWSTON: I think television is stuck with the human face because of the size of its screen. But I think all of us who work in film on television do try to do something more than just parade faces.

SINGER: Well, Denis Mitchell's *Morning in the Street* and *Chicago*, for example, were both personality programmes in this sense.

CAWSTON: I think *Morning in the Street* was more than that, it was comment through personalities combined with beautiful shots. The use of sound on television is very important. The picture is small and may often be of poor quality on the home receiver, but the sound quality is always very good—exactly the reverse effect from the cinema, where the picture is excellent but the sound has to compete with a large auditorium. This is why the use of sound has been developed so much in television documentaries—such as Denis Mitchell's pre-recorded think-tapes counterpointed with the pictures. I'm all for using synchronized sound, for exploiting natural dialogue between people who are not actors, and for getting rid of commentary. There's probably more scope for originality with the sound track than with the picture.

ELLIOT: When the camera arrived it freed painting from naturalism. Do you think the introduction of the electronic camera frees the film camera from the necessity of being naturalistic? Can film-making, including film-making for television, afford now to spread itself in the direction of a more impressionistic treatment of the subject?

CAWSTON: Well, first of all, we have our audience to reckon with. The electronic camera can never free the *television* film camera from the fact that it all arrives on the same screen. The television audience is huge and relatively undiscriminating; sets are on simply because they are not off. Whatever we do, we cannot afford to confuse people. In the documentary field people still believe what they see— "the camera cannot lie" and so on. Too extreme a form of impressionism or individuality of style in the producer can destroy this faith in the image on the screen, and then the whole documentary currency is devalued. We have to take the audience along with us in whatever we do.

SINGER: I agree there. But some events have a natural lyrical quality which is intrinsic, like ski-jumping. It is curious that any form of lyricism on television tends to come most readily from certain kinds of sporting events. This, of course, is natural lyricism, as distinct from anything contrived by the director. In any case, I believe television is fundamentally a journalistic operation.

CAWSTON: No. I'm not a journalist! There's a division in approach between the originality of the journalist and the originality of the non-journalist. *Television and the World* would have been quite different if I'd made it journalistically; a journalist would have given the subject a hard-hitting, factual quality. A scientific approach would have been different again. The effect I aimed to get was gradual and cumulative, with an appeal to the emotions.

SINGER: I still stick to my point; television is essentially a matter of journalism. It's got to grip.

ELLIOT: Surely no element in television exists entirely on its own. Any programme is like an article or story printed in a magazine; it's not like a book, which is designed to appeal to the reader entirely on its own.

CAWSTON: That's the only reason I welcome commercials; they do act as a buffer between the programmes. But I prefer to work on programmes which one can think of as essays or books rather than articles.

SINGER: That's the essential difference in our viewpoint. For me the height of television is live reporting, the exercise of skill by the opportunist-journalist, the man on the spot who becomes a brilliant interpreter at Ascot on a rainy day. The Cartier-Bresson of television. This skill is still greatly underrated.

CAWSTON: Well, with television film-making too you can try to capture the unexpected on location. But most of the time it's a case of hammering away at it in a back room until you get the effect you want.

22 Foundation of a Film Department*

NORMAN SWALLOW

THOSE of us who work here at Ealing Studios in 1961 are very aware of our inheritance, of the contribution which these studios have made to the art of the film in the days of our own immediate predecessors there under the guidance of Sir Michael Balcon. We are made aware of this, as it happens, whenever we visit the local public house, where the walls of the saloon bar are draped with photographs of Ealing films and of the writers and directors who made them. They look at us as we sit there; sometimes they seem to frown; sometimes they even smile. Then we are very happy.

Regular television began in Britain in 1936, which makes its history about a quarter the length of the history of the cinema. Until about ten years ago, it could not be seen outside of the London area, and in Scotland it could not be seen until 1952. This is very important because it determined to a considerable extent the nature and content of the programmes transmitted. Indeed it is arguable that it held up the development of film in television for quite a long time; for the greatest virtue of a film camera is that you can take it very easily about the country, poking it into this place and that, and thereby reflecting the life of the places you go to. And of course the incentive to go to, say, Edinburgh, increases very greatly when the citizens of

* *SFTA Journal, Summer 1961.*
This article is based on the British Film Academy's Annual Lecture, given at the Edinburgh Film Festival of 1960.

Edinburgh can themselves see the results of your journey. When I came to television at the end of 1949, and incidentally from an area where it could not be seen, I was struck by its failure to get out and about with its cameras and in the first series of programmes that I ever produced myself, I took a film camera on a "social" investigation of Britain from Scotland right down to the Channel, and the odd thing is that it had never been done before—though, of course, there were excellent financial reasons for this, apart from anything else. What I am saying is that the day when television became fully national in terms of coverage was also the day when pressures were put upon it to reflect the daily lives of its new audiences, who also began to increase its revenue by buying television licences. All this meant a great demand for film, and from that day—about 1950 or 1951—the BBC's department grew from two cameramen to twenty-five, and from three editors to nearly forty. From then on we began to ask ourselves the questions "How much film does television need, and what technical facilities must we have in order to answer that need?" And then, later still, the BBC formed film units in Glasgow, Belfast, Manchester, Birmingham, Cardiff and Bristol.

But in 1936 the BBC had no film department of its own. The word "television" really meant "live television" then, except for the occasional news item which was always shot by someone else. Indeed the main use of film cameras in television before the war was to record, for the archives, a cross-section of "live" output.

Television was off the air during the war. It came back in 1946, and it is really from that date that the BBC's Film Department exists. The decision to form a Film Department of its own, to build up its own permanent staff of film technicians, and ten years later to buy the studios at Ealing, was and still remains a very unusual one. Very few television organizations, either in Britain or abroad, have their own film units, and there is none, anywhere in the world, as large as our own. Over 90 per cent of the specially shot film that is seen on BBC Television has come from our own film technicians. Having a Film Department of our own—and here I speak very much from the heart as someone who has used film in his programmes for over a decade—has given us enormous advantages. It has allowed us to possess great varieties of equipment, and given us enormous flexibility in their deployment, so that today we can handle anything from a sudden trip to the Congo for *Panorama** to feature-size work on the largest stage at Ealing. It has allowed us to plan our programmes with considerable accuracy, knowing always just what resources we possess, and not having to wonder whether the outside industry could provide us with what we want when we want it; it has allowed us to tackle urgent assignments at short notice and without reference to anyone else. For instance, we sent four crews to the Middle East in the crisis of 1958 at literally 48 hours' notice, simply because they were our own and we could do what we liked with them. Having a Film Department has also, without doubt, saved us a great deal of money. But above all (and to me this is the really important thing) the existence of a BBC Film Department has inevitably also meant the existence of a group of people, based today at Ealing, whose job it is to think creatively of the role of film in Television. They work full-time in television films, and are making a career of it. Therefore an atmosphere has been created that is receptive to new ideas, and there is a personal incentive, which all of us feel, to push this medium of ours farther forward all the time. We have a permanent team of cameramen, for instance, who realize that they are not just film cameramen, but *television* film cameramen, shooting for a small domestic screen, and always thinking of the physical and psychological conditions under which their work is seen. You do not, I suggest, get this spirit in any other way than ours. You do not get it by sub-contracting, and you do not get it from a changing team of men who are on a hire-and-fire basis. I believe it is significant, I mean artistically significant, for instance, that nearly all the film for the fortnightly magazine programme *Monitor* has been shot by only two cameramen during the past couple of years; and every film in that programme has been edited by the same film editor from the beginning. I am sure that this is reflected in the quality of the final product, and it is my belief that the BBC's ability to work in this way, to create permanent "teams" of creative technicians, is the greatest of all the consequences that followed from that decision, after the war, to form a permanent Film Department.

But between 1946 and 1950 that Film Department was very small. When I first came across it myself nearly eleven years ago, a producer

---

* *Panorama*. A regular weekly programme of comment on current and social affairs, produced by the BBC.

was very lucky to get any film resources for his programme at all. If you wanted twenty minutes-worth of film, you would probably get three days in which to shoot it. There were a couple of cutting rooms in the basement of Alexandra Palace. Nevertheless this was a time when the BBC Television Service began to ask those basic questions; "What is the role of film in television? What do we want it for?" Some of the answers given then have stayed and are still valid. *The use of film to record living history, for example.* To bring into the drawing room significant events and significant people who cannot be brought there in any other way, and which are beyond the range and the scope of a "live" outside broadcast. Significantly therefore, the first continuing film series to be run by the BBC, and in those days produced by its Film Department, was a Newsreel.

There were some people in those days who argued that apart from this very limited use, film had no part to play in television at all. In discussions in the canteen and in other places where television men and women gathered together, there were those who seemed to regard film as outmoded and old-fashioned. Or rather, it was not new, as electronic television was. The great thing, so these people maintained, was to make your programme "live". Not good, but *live*. Now this is all very well for many programmes, and to be quite honest I believe that at a certain stage of television's development it was even a necessary attitude. If television producers had taken the easy way out in those days, and filmed everything, we might never have had any really imaginative *live* television at all. On the other hand there was a tendency, I think, for certain items to be done badly, or at least erratically, in a live studio when they could have been done excitingly on film (and would be done on film today). But, to be fair, this occasional resistance to film never seriously stood in the way of the development of the Film Department. The pace of that development was determined by one factor only—*money*. For film has always been, and always will be, expensive.

When more money became available, when television reception spread across Britain, and as the BBC put more and more of its income into television, its Film Department grew as rapidly as any other—indeed rather more rapidly than some; and the proportion of specially-shot film to the whole of our output is now greater than it has ever been. So, as our film resources expanded, it became possible to answer in a more practical way than before that key question:

"Why does a television service need a film department?" Let me therefore list very briefly the main ways in which the BBC has been using film since those early days a dozen or so years ago. There are four of them.

First (and this I have already mentioned) film is necessary to television for the recording of actual events which cannot, for technical or other reasons, be covered in any other way. This is true of most items of News, and it is true of a great deal of sport. Some twenty of the Film Department's staff work regularly on sports programmes today; one of them holds the rank of Producer. In film work of this sort, of course, the creative element is small. The main function of the camera is merely to record what happens to be taking place in front of it.

Secondly, television drama—I mean "live" drama—has always needed film to give greater flexibility, and very many of our television plays have sequences that are made on film. An obvious example of this would be a car chase in a crime story. In other words we have regarded film as another facility available to the writer and the producer of television drama. This has brought with it many problems, of tempo for instance, and of the technical "matching", quality for quality, between film and live studio.

Thirdly, complete programmes made throughout as films. If a programme idea is a good one, and if to be fully effective it must be made as a film, then it should be made as a film. In the early days it was not possible to do this very often—it was too difficult to tie up a complete unit for the purpose, but in the past six or seven years we have made an increasing number of documentary films, and for the last two or three years we have been completing an average of one a week—which probably makes us, apart from anything else we do, the biggest single documentary film unit.

Fourthly (though this sometimes overlaps point number three), we have developed a form of film journalism that is peculiar to television; I am thinking especially of the film stories in *Panorama* and *Tonight* and *Monitor*,* in which the actual technique is different from that of the cinema, even though the technical equipment is the same.

* *Tonight.* A programme of nightly comment on current matters, sometimes light, sometimes serious, produced by the BBC up to 1965. *Monitor.* A regular programme of comment on the arts produced by the BBC up to 1966.

Now this film "journalism", this use of a film camera as the equivalent to the reporter's note-book and pencil, has arguably been television's main contribution to the development of the documentary film; artistically, that is, and in terms of an individual style. It happened historically because of television's growing need in those early days to reflect the world of which it was itself a part. It was not enough that we should examine a current international or even local problem in terms of a studio interview, with a few maps and still photographs. If it was a part of the BBC's obligation—as it clearly was—and is, to perform a public service by reflecting faithfully the main political and social problems of the day, then it was essential for us to leave our studios and take our film cameras, first across Britain, and then over the world. For the past ten years this has been our main use of film, in terms of time, staff, equipment and money. The first example of our work overseas was a series called, appropriately, *Foreign Correspondent* in 1949. The first examples in Britain were *London Town* and *Special Enquiry*. In those programmes and their successors, the camera no longer merely recorded what took place in front of it. It was beginning to select, and to make a comment—in fact to have a definite point of view. They also introduced for the first time the visible reporter, decidedly a television device, and one that is very much and very rightly despised in the camera. We were already beginning to shoot and edit our film with that small domestic audience in mind. These were not just films; they were pieces of television too.

By 1952 television had already begun to get out and about. Not only that, but it had begun to think seriously and creatively about the relationship between film and television, and about the artistic difference between shooting film for a big screen in a cinema and shooting it for the small domestic screen. For television is a much more personal and intimate medium than the cinema. It is also quieter, and our own film work tends to have a quieter track than the work of film-makers elsewhere. A method like the old *March of Time*, with a strident "shouting" narrator and a fierce orchestral score, is death in the drawing room. For we are addressing a vast audience, far larger than the cinema ever had, but we are addressing it in little domestic groups of three or four. It is a much more personal thing altogether, and this affects our technique. We have always tried to get closer and closer to our subject-matter and to the people we photograph. We very soon found that the old "didactic" form of documentary, for instance, which took a global view of a vast subject, was far less effective than a detailed "intimate" examination of the same subject as it affected a few particular human beings.

By 1954 the BBC's Film Department already existed to do all the things it does now. It was used for sequences in drama productions; it was deployed over the world for current affairs; its technicians had begun to work on complete documentary films. What has happened since has been an increase in size and scope rather than a fundamental change.

There have been technical developments, such as the midget tape-recorder; there have been more mobile 16 mm. cameras that have helped us to travel farther, faster and cheaper; in 1956 we bought the studios at Ealing, with more space, bigger workshops, a "lot" for exteriors. The Film Department has grown in size until it is now over 300 strong, and last year some 1,500 BBC Television programmes had film in them that was shot by our own staff cameramen and edited in our own cutting rooms. The quantity of film we make and show every year is the equivalent of 140 feature films. We are the largest permanent film unit in the world.

It is interesting, I think, that today our Drama Department uses no more film than it did in 1954, though it uses it more ambitiously. The bulk of our work has always been, and will no doubt remain, of a factual or documentary kind. We are primarily a unit making documentary material, and incidentally making it very fast. We expect to shoot a 30-minute film in a couple of weeks, and edit it in three more. An interesting contrast this with documentary units elsewhere, who sometimes take over a year for a single film. I was recently talking to the editor of a very distinguished British documentary film—which has already won a prize at an international festival—and he told me that the film, lasting half an hour, was four months in the cutting room. Four months for him; three weeks for us. No doubt the comparative costs of the two films would show a similar ratio.

I am not defending the speed at which we work. But it is a television speed, and we work in television; moreover, I know from personal experience that some of the best work one does is done in a hurry and against the clock. If you live with a film too long, you cease to be able to look at it objectively. You begin to refine it.

There is no end to the time you can take if you really wish. But it does not automatically get better. Indeed beyond a certain point I really think it gets worse.

Eighty per cent of our work, then, is of a factual kind, and it is made very quickly. And the quickest work of all is the work for the two magazine programmes *Panorama* and *Tonight*. Much of the work for *Panorama* is done abroad and the bulk of it is nowadays shot on 16 mm. The cameraman is sometimes a director-cameraman, and very obviously he has to be something of a journalist as well. For this form of television is journalism rather than art, though art may now and then, if one is lucky, emerge from the journalism. We do not win prizes at Film Festivals with extracts from *Panorama* or *Tonight*, but they are still about the most important thing we do, granted the context of public service broadcasting; and because we are a public service, we do more of it than anyone else.

As my final point, I would like to claim that, in my opinion, the BBC Television Service is probably making by far the most important contribution to the documentary film anywhere in the world. I really believe this. Statistically, of course, that is an easy statement to justify. Our output is greater than that of anyone else in the world, and in terms of film journalism there is obviously a real connection between the amount you do and its ultimate importance. The more you do, the greater your impact—assuming you do it adequately. I can also justify what I say in terms of audience. Our own producers are guaranteed an audience of millions. They are the envy of those non-television documentary men, who still scratch round for non-theatrical audiences and the hope of an occasional screening in a specialized cinema. For both these reasons—the size of our output and the size of our audience—we are certainly important enough. But are we good enough? I mean artistically?

But there's one big reason—and this is the point I want to make as forcefully as I can—why we ought to be both good and important, whether we are or not. That is our independence. I was tempted to say that we are free of both commercial and political pressures, but, of course, that would hardly be true. What is true is that we are in a position to resist them. This is extremely important, because hitherto the documentary film has been a sponsored film—sponsored by a Government Department, or a public body, or an industrial concern. The documentary film-maker in Britain, until the BBC came along, was always a man in search of a sponsor. On the whole, as we know, he has been very lucky—lucky and tenacious, and often personally brilliant. How British documentary films, which were sponsored films, became among the finest in the world is a tremendous credit both to the tenacity and inspiration of the film-makers, and to the public spirit of their sponsors. But despite all this, the fact is that sponsorship, however enlightened, is always liable to be restrictive. For the final decision rests in the hands of men whose prime concern is not necessarily the artistic merit of the film, and who are often not film-makers themselves. This is self-evident. A great deal has been written about it, and every film-maker would agree with me.

But the BBC is different. Its ultimate responsibility is to the public, and its only obligation is to be fair and accurate. The final editorial control is in the hands of men who are themselves television or radio professionals. They have no axe to grind. No doubt, of course, the BBC sometimes fails in this respect, and then it is usually reminded of its failure very forcibly. Now and then it gets praised for its courage. But at least it believes in letting its producers and directors get on with the job. It trusts them. For four years I myself produced programmes that were highly controversial, but at no time during those years did anyone senior to myself ever ask to see the scripts or the rushes. Not once. I say this with all sincerity, because I believe it to be extremely important, and not commonly known.

This state of affairs creates an atmosphere that I believe to be the most important thing that any organization can offer to its creative men, and it is our hope that the spirit which animates our writers and producers also reaches our technicians; our cameramen, editors, recordists. They are encouraged to have ideas of their own. They are given considerable responsibility. One of our cameramen came up with an idea for a 45-minute film a year or so ago, and we accepted it. He directed it, and it was later shown at the Edinburgh Film Festival. One of our dubbing mixers had an idea for a 15-minute film, and he was given the money to make it. He made it, it was liked, and it was accepted for transmission. I believe the spirit that this represents to be extremely important. Technicians are creative men, not machines, and in the BBC they are involved in what they are doing, personally involved in it.

We may shoot our film on a low budget, and we may work too quickly. But what is offered in compensation is, I believe, worth much more than is lost—call it artistic freedom, for want of a better phrase.

23 Presenting Actuality*

CYRIL BENNETT

PETER MORLEY

BENNETT: After ten years and more of current affairs programmes on television, do you think we can at least agree on what television documentary *isn't?* It isn't just cinema in the corner of the living room. It isn't the buggerboo of the early years—the great new "visual medium". What is it then? It's above all an instrument for communicating ideas and information with pictures, but the pictures must *add* to the understanding of the ideas. Pictures for the sake of serving the "visual medium" cliché—picture for its own sake— merely detracts from the communication of ideas.

MORLEY: When ITV started the whole concept of presentation was of course based on the pioneer work of the BBC.

BENNETT: —and, of course, there was the influence of movie.

MORLEY: The overwhelming tendency in the nineteen-fifties was to label television *the* visual medium. Producers were obsessed by the need to present the MOVING PICTURE, to which everything else in the programme becomes secondary. Only slowly did we realize that the fundamental purpose of television is to communicate. This is the real yardstick. The proportion of picture to the spoken word is irrelevant. To cut away from the TV interview in terror that you're not *visualizing* enough, can often destroy the interview. Television,

* *SFTA Journal, Spring 1964.*

we've said, is a means of communication. Very well. And the nineteen-sixties way of thinking is that the only test for the right kind of presentation is to determine what is the most effective way of putting the subject over. This is not achieved by injecting mere bits and pieces of film for their own sake in order to pad out the interest. That, in fact, has been proved the best way to kill the interest by providing too much distraction. Which brings me to the next salient thing—the old prejudice against "talking heads", which were thought to be some kind of evil hangover from sound radio. What's wrong with talking heads when good talk is the best way to put the subject over?

BENNETT: In other words, after ten years, we've found we're dealing with a medium that's different, and much more complex, from what we originally thought it to be. Currently, I believe we're in a kind of mid-period. We've got *some* idea of the medium now, but we're still exploring, and must be aware that a great deal remains to be discovered. I think although we've found out some fundamental things about television, we are falling into what I hope is only a temporary trap—preoccupation with styles and forms. The current obsession with *cinéma-vérité* is a good example.

MORLEY: A moment before we come to that one. There's more to say about the "talking heads". The only standard by which you can judge them is whether the talk is effective. If the talk is good enough, you have a captive audience. This we now know. Currently I'm doing a programme on mixed marriage (*Black Marries White*). At first I feared I could only conceive it in terms of a talking heads presentation; but I soon realized the subject is so strong in itself that talking heads would and could sustain it, and to contrive visual situations as a relief would merely lessen the impact. Of course film inserts and pictures can add to a programme; all that matters is the degree of their relevance. No one should accept a picture merely for the sake of getting rid of a talking head. The old criticism of "too much talk" is based on a completely wrong conception of television. This can be described negatively by saying you can't normally transplant a successful talkie-television show on to sound radio. You simply lose a vital element of character with the loss of the picture. It is very rare indeed for a good television talkie programme to survive satisfactorily on radio—far too much is lost.

BENNETT: Which brings us to the point of what the function of the picture really is. I would put it like this—what you convey with pictures is altogether different from what you convey with words. Pictures at their best convey an impression, emotions as well as images, that can *never* be achieved by words alone. In that sense, pictures become a unique part of any programme.

MORLEY: The test is always—does the picture tell the story most effectively.

BENNETT: I think that nowadays only in the most backward-looking work on television are valueless pictures being added. The point we've been making is pretty generally accepted, and the days of visual padding are virtually over. The journalist has taken his place in television with the film-maker. What matters now is that we all realize that because we're moving into another phase in the work we're in danger of losing certain of the good features of traditional presentation. You might add up to say that we're in danger of losing certain traditional forms of self-discipline. As I've remarked, there's a mad obsession now with *cinéma-vérité*. This often means—don't bother about a storyline. Don't bother about discussion. Don't bother about the traditional disciplines in film-making. There's a tendency now to think that all you need to do is shoot film, without pre-thought, and edit the results without any regard for structure. Picture for its own sake is being replaced by a new danger—technique for its own sake.

MORLEY: Well it's simply a violent reaction against the established ways of directing programmes. And it's going to produce one or two excellent works of art and an enormous load of rubbish. It'll go on, I suppose, until the next phase comes—which I hope will enable us to crystallize our approach in the light of new equipment and how it should be used.

BENNETT: The need now, I think, is to keep some of the lessons of the past well in mind as we move into the future. The critics are often no help. They're only encouraging directors to indulge in an orgy of "technique" at the expense of any true sense of content, style, form and editorial control. Certainly let's make progress—but don't let's throw out the baby with the bath-water! We're still putting over stories.

MORLEY: The critics, having discovered something which, when you think about it, is not all that new, encourage the idea of the runaway camera. Unharness the equipment, they say, and you get the truth. But how can you get at the pure, uncontaminated truth when, right at the beginning there is a subjective selection, not only of the scene being filmed, but also in the composition of the shot, let alone the final selection and juxtaposition of the material in the cutting room. The personal attitude of the team concerned to the subject, is bound to influence the final result. This isn't *cinéma-vérité*—it's *cinéma de bonne-chance*. When you're covering something where a great deal is happening you need a strong element of luck to catch the really revealing stuff. Of course there's room for Richard Leacock with his highly talented capacity for making film-essays unhindered by the old restrictions, but this is not the *only* way in which to do programmes.

BENNETT: We need to be free to choose. Whatever style is best for the subject. But I'm afraid too many directors are going to fall in love with this speeded-up, mobile presentation. I was asked recently by a director if he could do a programme in the West Indies. All right, I said, what's the story? I was told—no story, no point of view; just shoot *cinéma-vérité*, We're in for just a load of junk if this is to be the attitude of programme-makers.

MORLEY: Leacock's great contribution has been to make the equipment ultra mobile and to prove to us, that if used brilliantly, it has got an important place in television. But this doesn't mean we've got to use his techniques in every programme we undertake. It's hopeless if you approach every new subject with a preconceived notion of the style to be used; it obviously *must* be the other way round. It is the subject which dictates the style.

BENNETT: The future, as I see it, lies in the next phase ahead of this temporary set-back of falsified *cinéma-vérité*. Part of this begins with a new evaluation of the viewer and *his* attitudes to television. He's becoming more sophisticated, and the new channel will only intensify his growing sense of selection. The public is getting wised-up to television, and developing gradually a new attitude to viewing. And this, in turn, will mean a new attitude to programming.

MORLEY: The viewing audience has become more sophisticated by now than most broadcasting organizations are willing to grant. The encouraging thing about having a third and later on a fourth television channel, is that we will be forced to recognize the viewer must become far more selective than in the old two channel days. Ratings in the future will reflect this new and enlightened freedom of choice. This, by the way, has nothing to do with the old minority-highbrow argument. I'm referring now to every kind of programme on television.

BENNETT: Would you agree that, so far, we have been making television programmes with an audience in mind that has had the older kind of relationship to the set—as the cinema-screen in the corner of the living-room? This is the armchair, group viewing audience. Surely we've got to revise that image? In the first place, we're going to have receivers in new locations—in the bathroom, the kitchen, later the car, and so on. And that will mean an entirely new concept of television programmes.

MORLEY: Yes. The audience will no longer be the passive onlookers. The future success of television lies in recognizing them as an active force. Active, in the sense of a far more intelligent participation than has been thought possible in the past. In *Black Marries White* I'm relying enormously on this kind of audience-participation. I'm not aiming to give the audience a definitive statement about mixed marriage, even if I could think of one. Certainly I'm not telling them what to think. I aim to present my material in such a way that the viewer is so involved in it that he will spontaneously re-examine his own attitudes to colour.

BENNETT: It's intellectual involvement, participation in making judgments. But there's also another important barrier to overcome and more especially in current affairs. It's true we've already moved out of the old "show-biz" era in television documentary. We've rejected the actor-commentator with his good looks and "television" personality and moved over to the journalist commentator, perhaps with a university education rather than good looks, a man whom the viewer realizes is directly involved in the business of public affairs, who professionally knows what he's talking about. However, television is still orientated in its handling of journalism to a middle-to-upper class viewpoint, whereas the majority of viewers are working-class and must feel a lot of what they hear has nothing to do with them, either individually or as a class. We've got to break through this working-class barrier—not merely in the discussion of current affairs but in drama as well. For instance, we did a programme some time ago on race and colour. I asked a scene-shifter afterwards what he thought about it. He said, "It's all very fine, but it's got nothing to do with me". I found this observation pretty salutary. "It's obvious you chaps have all the theories but you have never had any *experience* of living in a Negro neighbourhood. I do", he added. This stopped me short. I thought back over the programme we'd just finished. Are we communicating at all, I wondered? Has this man ever considered that the middle-class might have a valid point of view, even if quite different from his? Had we examined this important human-social situation in terms that the mass of our viewers have *experienced*—not merely as an intellectual argument? How far, I wondered, can we involve them too? Without involving them no public affairs programme is doing more than a fraction of its job. Far too much television is created by educated, middle-class people without any direct contact with working-class life and experience.

MORLEY: There are many loyal viewers of *This Week** genuinely involved in what goes on in the world, who would not dream of watching *Panorama* on the grounds that the image of the programme, Dimbleby and all, is outside their class. *Panorama*, for them, is solely for the upper class.

BENNETT: Can we really expect anything different in a situation where the expense accounts alone of television reporters sometimes equal the wages of an industrial worker? How can they mix socially? Curiously enough, this links with another problem—that of the failure of women so far in current affairs programmes. The moment a women appears on the screen viewers tend to see her in an entirely different context from that of her male counterpart. In this society, women are still not *really* permitted to be actual thinkers and communicators. This is one area where television can be of immense help in breaking down these prejudices—but first we must break down our own prejudices against women in current-affairs television.

---

* *This Week*. Independent television's principal weekly programme of comment on current affairs.

MORLEY: To sum up then, our part in the future of television (technique aside) is firstly to produce programmes for an audience which we must recognize as being as enlightened and intelligent as we like to think we are, and secondly to break down the class barrier between programme makers and their audience and between sections of the audience itself.

24 Education Through Television*

ROGER MANVELL

I

It has sometimes happened in the past that new opportunities for communication have developed at precisely the time they were needed for the practical application of new thinking. The most obvious example has been the indispensable part played by printing in the development of European thought and education during and since the Renaissance. Printing was there to hand, and the philosophers, educationists and scientists made immediate use of it in the course of creating and disseminating our European culture.

The new opportunity in the twentieth century is broadcasting in sound and vision, combined with recording on film and tape. This form of communication has arrived at a time when the whole pattern of civilization is changing and when the thinking that goes with this needs the widest possible dissemination. The twentieth century represents a new educational era in human history.

One of the problems about education in Britain is the comparatively high standard it has achieved in the service of an over-conservative and traditional form of teaching. Britain is a nation so inbuilt that we believe we are at once the best and of peoples. We are convinced that we have the best ent, the best civil service, the best economy, the best act the best of everything essential to sound living

mmer 1963.

in the world, including, of course, the best educational system. There seems, therefore, no need to reconsider them, to ask if indeed they are still the best of all possible systems. We are loath to change a single thing without taking half a century to do it.

Though the *social climate* in most of our schools, that is, the relationship between teacher and child, has changed radically for the better since the nineteenth century, traditional ideas of what should and should not be taught linger sternly on because of our built-in British conservatism. Don't change anything; you may be throwing away something precious that has been fostered with loving care since the Renaissance itself. The ivy-covered culture suitable for leisured Edwardian gentlemen still has a deep-seated attraction for the over-worked, over-serious, not-too-cultured middle-class of Britain; it is a snob-dream sustained by the most class-conscious nation among modern advanced societies.

If we are as a nation to realize our full potential during the remaining years of this century, we must undertake a thorough re-appraisal of our educational needs. To some extent we are already doing so, casting unwilling but wary eyes on what we regard as the mass-produced, pressurized and over-earnest educational methods of the Soviet Union and the erratic zeal of educational theory and practice in the United States, where every human activity seems to pass for education provided it can have a degree diploma attached to it. Broadly speaking, we realize we are being not so much left behind as deserted tangentially in the educational movement of the modern world. And seeing we have what in our hearts we still regard as a far finer tradition of education than anyone else even if it does still cling to the nineteenth century coat-tails of our more ancient public and grammar schools, we are naturally averse to entering for the cultural rat-race which the great powers of the world seem intent on creating.

This may well be why Britain has seemed almost pathologically slow in adjusting her educational system to her educational needs. To all those with eyes to see, the twentieth century is the greatest century of discovery and of cultural opportunity since human kind became conscious of its ability to progress. The outstanding periods of the past, and especially the European Renaissance, were but preliminaries to this great age of discovery. We need all our stamina, all our cerebral strength, all our intuitive capacity to expand the

meaning behind the ancient concepts of truth and beauty and good-
ness in the light of our expanding knowledge, if we are to prepare
wisely and fully for civilization in the twenty-first century.

This preparation includes re-thinking our concept of education,
the nature of what should be taught to all age-groups and abilities
and the method of teaching it. At the root of all education lies the
idea that we should reveal at an appropriate level of understanding
what is best and most significant in human skill and knowledge to
young and acquisitive minds in such a way that their desire to do
things and know things is excited to its fullest capacity. At the same
time we must equip them to the highest possible standard with certain
basic techniques in speaking, reading, writing and calculation,
including facility in foreign languages.

How can this enormous task be carried out in our tightly-packed
community with its 5,500 "independent" or "public" schools, its
1,600 grammar schools, its 4,000 secondary schools, and its 24,000
primary schools.* Only a small proportion of the large number of
teachers involved have a genius for the job; the rest are fortunate if
at least they manage through application and experience to acquire
a sound professional standard in their work.

There are some six million children in our primary and secondary schools, and classes average 30 in the secondary modern and 40
in the primary schools. The traditional syllabus is tightly controlled
in the primary schools in order to train children for the eleven-plus
examination and in the secondary modern schools to achieve the "O"
level examination. The introduction of change is extremely difficult
without some sort of fundamental revolution, such as the recent
decision by the education authorities in London to rid the primary
schools in their area of the eleven-plus examination by which so much
social and educational damage has been done.

There has also in the past seemed to most teachers and educational administrators to be little time to spare to experiment with
such new-fangled things as sound and television broadcasting in the
schools. Most teachers are fully engaged hurrying from class to class,
from grade to grade, pressing a veneer of their subjects home against
time and, in too many instances, against the grain of either the interest

---

* In addition to this, there are a limited number of comprehensive schools, now
(1967) to become the principal system in Britain.

or the intelligence of their pupils. Our schoolchildren reach puberty earlier than they did, and in their restlessness fail to see the use of much of what they are being taught. They wait anxiously for the time when they will be free to leave and secure jobs in what appears to be the real world outside. For only too many of them the raising of the school-leaving age to 16 will seem a major tragedy. They want to earn money and become, as they believe, independent.

Though there are very many good schools in Britain in each main category—independent, grammar, secondary modern, technical, comprehensive and primary—there are also only too many bad ones, housed in condemned buildings, with both sides losing the age-old battle between weary apathy in the teacher and active rebellion in the pupils.*

Britain cannot afford to squander the potentialities of a single one of its new citizens. The exciting task of the good teacher is to discover these potentialities, but before he can succeed to the full in this great and essential duty he needs all the help the community can give him—a good environment in which to teach, reasonable equipment to enable him to present the modern world to the modern pupil, and time to give his work the full professional attention that it requires. If the teacher himself is living a life of constant strain and defeat, he can hardly be expected to stimulate creative interests in others.

The position seems, therefore, to be something like this. The competitive demands of world technology and culture are forcing us to overhaul our out-of-date educational system rather against the grain of our traditions. The essential practicality of the British people, in whom laziness about thinking is always counterbalanced by an intuitive common sense about what we ought to do in our national interest, is creating a healthy climate of opinion in which sensible changes will probably be accepted by those in authority to accept them, if only because we want to keep up with the Americans and the Russians. For example, you have not got to be a reader of the educational journals to know that new, mechanized systems of language teaching are being tried out, that entirely new approaches

---

* The films *Blackboard Jungle* and *Spare the Rod* may both have been sensationalized, but the conditions they presented so melodramatically are a dark aspect of the truth about the lower depths of the educational systems of America and Britain from which we have in the past turned a blind eye.

to the teaching of science and mathematics are being actively studied, or that certain education authorities are experimenting with the so-called teaching machines programmed for individual use and already popular in the United States.

Part of the change taking place is the introduction to the classroom of practising teachers of genius or high skill through sound radio, film and television, and the consequent release to some degree of the large numbers of competent, professional teachers from repetitive forms of group teaching that gradually wear them out and kill their enthusiasm. These teachers will be able to recuperate their strength and interest in their work and give better attention to the essential business of developing the individual skills and understanding of their pupils.

In the education of the future, the teacher should regard the gramophone, the tape recorder, the sound radio and television receiver, and the film projector—especially in its modern form which is cartridge or cassette-loaded and ready for instant use with inexpensive 8 mm films from the school library—as assets and not intrusions on his teaching routine that are a nuisance to set up and only excite his pupils to ask questions he may feel competent to answer. At the same time, though carrying out the established national requirements in terms of syllabus, the teacher should feel freer than he is at present to create his own individual approach to the subject in which he specializes, adding his own personal perspective to those presented by the other teachers who enter his classroom through the loudspeaker and the screen. The impact of more than one mind on a subject should help to inspire a genuine interest in pupils whose curiosity is roused by discussing the programmes they view with a teacher whose opinion they respect.

II

Educational television in this country is very new indeed. It is, in fact, just over six years old, beginning in 1957. Its only parallel has been in the medium of sound radio, though the overall costs of programmes in vision are in general some ten times as great as they are for sound alone.

The BBC has been careful to develop educational television alongside equivalent services in sound; the work in the two media is now complementary. Educational television has been very restricted so far largely because of its newness; in 1962 some 3,000 schools made use of the transmissions, including about 600 primary schools.* The age range served was from seven years to the sixth form age groups.

The development of BBC educational television during its first five years was given in a Report published in September 1962:

First, those series which by 1959 had already demonstrated that they filled needs in schools for which television was peculiarly fitted—e.g. *Spotlight* (Current Affairs) and *Going to Work* (Careers), *People of Many Lands* and *Science and Life*.

Secondly, series which have come into being since 1959; and which have similarly established themselves as regularly expected contributions—e.g. the series for backward children, *Television Club*, the series *For Sixth Forms*, *Discovering Science*, and *Signpost*.

Thirdly, series which have from time to time appeared as units or termly contributions. Some of these point to future round-the-year contributions; others may obviously perform a more useful function as occasional supplements, or as "shots in the arm" for the teacher's work. These series include broadcasts in the fields of history, mathematics, geography, the visual arts, and music; and on such themes as teenage leisure interests and social problems, the cinema, and drama. One problem facing the planning of school television today is to strike the best balance between series of this kind and series offering a regular and forecastable contribution to school life and work.

Independent Television has also developed school broadcasting over a similar period. The number of schools receiving the programmes was equivalent to those served by the BBC. Associated-Rediffusion, for example, began transmissions in May 1957, actually

---

* The Pilkington Committee in 1962 gave the number of schools equipped with television as "rather fewer than 4,500". The Ministry of Education had made it clear in the early stages to Local Authorities that only very limited expenditure on sets would be recognized for grant-in-aid. In the United States and Canada, television in schools was by 1963 universal: in Japan some 28,000 schools used television. In France and Italy the number of schools equipped was comparable with Britain. (By 1965 the number of British schools equipped with television had risen to 11,000.)

a school term before the BBC,* and in a Report published in 1961 the company summarized the experience of their education department as follows:

Any educationist contemplating the introduction of television into a school or assessing the advisability of keeping an existing receiver may by the evidence of reports on Associated-Rediffusion's programmes from schools, be assured of the value of its contribution to the teaching of a number of subjects. For example:

(a) The interpretation of Drama, using resources beyond the scope of any classroom, and the dramatization of book talks to encourage reluctant readers in English.

(b) Vicarious experience of the flavour of life in France shown with gusto and humour and presented in simple but accurate French.

(c) Independence of time and place and a "knocking down" of the walls of the classroom in the treatment of science and geography, and background series such as *The Farming Year* and *The World Around Us* (People at Work).

(d) Selection of material and research in wide fields of knowledge presented in easily comprehended and retained visual terms, such as moving diagrams, models and maps, which are easily understood and remembered.

(e) The value of simultaneous appeal to eye and ear in providing common experience for discussion between teacher and children and for stimulating the imagination and widening the horizons of young viewers, including backward children.

(f) The provision of examples of excellence in biography, drama and art by means of interviews with experts in many fields of knowledge.

Both Granada in 1959 and ATV in 1961 began their own schools television service, while Scottish Television have since 1958 been transmitting programmes to schools in Scotland in collaboration with Associated-Rediffusion.

Educational television has many problems to overcome. The first and most obvious one is that only some 4,500 out of some 40,000

---

* The BBC conducted a pilot experiment in educational television during May 1952, with transmissions from Alexandra Palace to selected schools. A Report on the broadcasts and the reaction to them in the schools appeared in 1953.

schools in Britain are equipped with television receivers,* whereas by now some 30,000 have sound radio equipment. Getting money to equip our schools with television has not been easy, as the Director of Education for Nottinghamshire pointed out at a Conference on Educational Television organized by the Authority in association with ATV in November 1961:

> I don't think Nottinghamshire can claim to be more venturesome than anyone else. Nottinghamshire has over 450 schools, over 90,000 pupils, 4,000 teachers, but the Authority as yet has no more than about twenty-two television sets in operation. They have come from a variety of sources: the limited ration which the Ministry of Education in the first place approved of; gifts from ITV services; those which the Authority has begun to put in its new schools; and perhaps, too, a field for personal adventure, as when Parent-Teacher Associations and other voluntary bodies wonder how best to help schools.

Another obvious problem has been the adaptation of the intricate school timetable to allow for the reception of the programmes or their repeats regularly each week during the school term; this is specially true in the case of schools up against a tough examination schedule. Then again, the teacher may not like the treatment and continuity of the course offered in his subject, which may well prove different in approach from that in his own syllabus. However, it is a narrow-minded teacher who is not prepared to learn from another teacher's methods of presentation and adapt his syllabus (possibly a little dog-eared by now) to match the structure of the television course. It has to be realized there is an increasing shortage of skilled teachers in the sciences and in mathematics, subjects which collectively represent a considerable cross-section of the school syllabus and which are growing considerably in importance. Whereas the skilled teacher can turn fruitful differences of approach between his own methods and those of another skilled teacher to his personal advantage in building up interest in his pupils, the less skilled can

---

* According to the BBC in September 1962, only one secondary school in six had a television set; even after the abolition of the Ministry's strict quota system, the response of Local Authorities to the equipment of schools is described as "patchy". Authorities differ widely in policy over such matters as equipment for schools.

to a major extent lean on the experience of the teacher on the screen and so learn his profession in the process.

At the Nottinghamshire ATV Conference, some of the great values of educational television to the teacher were expressed by teachers themselves. John S. Flavell, a former Primary School Headmaster and teacher of mathematics, put it this way:

> How shall we get the child to reason? I would suggest that at this early level we do it by encouraging the child to ask why and when and how, and encouraging him to ask questions. Now the good teacher—and let us bear in mind there always have been first-class teachers of mathematics—the good teacher does that by the stimulation of the touch of his personality. But even a good teacher can be helped. He can be helped, I would suggest, in two main ways. First, by putting the child into situations chosen with care as being loaded, saturated with numerical and quantitative significance, giving him simple experimental work in those situations, challenging him to experiment and to discover.
>
> That is the ideal behind a number of the programmes in this series *Summing it Up*—putting the child, through the screen, into an experimental situation, maybe a traffic census, the fitting up of a weather station, and getting the child to experiment. He is then most likely to ask questions, and once a child begins to ask questions he begins to reason, he begins to understand a little of mathematics.

Television at its richest is always a meeting-point of people. Through television children can meet the enthusiasts, the specialists, the men and women of some note who are doing interesting things. Nothing is more stimulating to a child's imagination; human personality counts on every level of instruction, from the hardest utilitarian teaching to the presentation of the so-called subjects of "enrichment". People seen to be actively engaged in jobs in which they are keenly interested come by means of the screen to the classroom, and the old window-on-the-world cliché takes on its true and perpetual significance. Children meet real MPs, real explorers, real zoologists, real builders, and so on; this would seem to be obvious—except to the large percentage of head teachers and their assistants who simply do not make the effort to organize the purchase of a television set and adapt their work to allow for its use.

As the BBC puts it:

The national function of School Television Broadcasting is likely to remain, as that of sound has always been, to supplement the teacher's work and enrich it with resources beyond the scope of the classroom. This is, however, a very wide and elastic definition, fully compatible with broadcasting being for some purposes the most effective teaching media. Indeed, it is a false dichotomy that is sometimes maintained between "enrichment" and "direct instruction". Obviously there will be degrees of variation between a series which does a "tool" job in science and one which offers a new insight into poetry or painting: between the number of broadcasts closely arranged as a "teaching" unit and broadcasts which can be selected individually as they appear to be relevant to the teacher's other work. The one type of series will lean more heavily towards inculcating discipline in the use of mental or physical skills, will lead children towards precisely defined areas of exploration, and will relate to and march in step with, or even point directions for, the teacher's over-all organization of work. The other will excite, inspire, have the force of novelty, and in these capacities will be acceptable to the teacher as a springboard for original ventures, or as a unique stand in the existing pattern of his work.

Once television is accepted in education and no longer regarded as a changeling like sound radio once was (and still is in some schools), the fascinating problem of finding the right teachers to work for the screen and experimenting with fruitful techniques of presentation faces the educational television producer during the present pioneer period. With production costs amounting to some ten times those of sound broadcasting, it is important not to use television where sound alone will do as well or even better. The BBC has therefore integrated its sound and television educational service as a whole, as the Report already quoted explains:

It still seems to be as true as it was in 1959 that sound is "likely always to remain the major contributor in music, in story-telling and the dissemination of our literary heritage, in the imaginative evocation of the past, in astringent discussion in the realm of ideas". Television, on the other hand, can demonstrate—in many ways quite outstandingly well—it can show things happening, it can introduce its viewers to interesting people of all kinds, it can be "a window on the world", it can give a sense of reality. It is the familiar medium of the children's homes. Often, as a recent reviewer has said "It is like life and thereby sparks off hidden sources of expression". We are fortunate in being able through the BBC to plan the future of school broadcasting in both media as a co-ordinated whole.

Whether sound broadcasting or television is used, the personality coming in from outside the classroom must behave as a visitor should. If he is a teacher, his principal function is to use his particular expertise and the resources of demonstration at his disposal (including telecine) to support and supplement the teaching that will (we hope) already be taking place in the school. He brings added perspective, clarification, and, where relevant, the link of the subject with practical activities going on in the world outside. If he is not a teacher but what the 1961 Report from Associated-Rediffusion* calls the "anchor-man", the compère in an educational television series, then he must have a quiet, friendly but authoritative manner and know how to steer a subject, or the knowledge of a visiting expert, into the heart of a child's interest. He must know how to be unobtrusive without losing face. He is the friend of the teacher as well as of the children, their joint servant, a professional editorial commentator on the subject they are studying together. The last thing he must do is try to steal the show from the teacher sitting there with the class.

It is easy to specify such qualifications as these, but supremely difficult to nurture them during the process of practical programming on limited budgets with limited rehearsal time. The best thing seems to be to plunge in and do the work, with provision for adequate "feed-back". Feed-back means keeping constant liaison with the user, both the teachers and the taught. This can be done by organizing regular reports and questionnaires on the programmes, and best of all by constant meetings with teachers and visits to the schools using television by the staff responsible for the programmes or their close colleagues. As the ATV Report puts it:

The Maximum collaboration between the producer and schools must be maintained. It is the practising teacher who can give

---

* Now called Rediffusion Television.

advice, encouragement and guidance and so cultivate a real sense of unity among all who work in this new venture. Periodic visits by Education Liaison Officers and Programme Producers will do much to strengthen this link. A thrill was experienced when Mr. A. Royds recently visited our school and sat down with the children to watch a lesson in the *World Around Us* series, written by him. To see his name on the screen and to know he was sitting in the room meant a great deal to the children. They were very eager to write answers to a number of questions he set for them after the lesson.*

A magnificent and well-known example of elementary adult education promoted through television is provided by RAI—Radiotelevisione Italiana; it was no accident that Richard Cawston made this remarkable and strangely moving experiment the climax to his film for the BBC, *Television and the World.*† A brilliant and sympathetic teacher was chosen to help break down the mass-illiteracy which holds back the development of Italians in the centre and south of Italy and of Sicilians; there were 5,000,000 illiterate in 1951, who by various means were reduced to 2,000,000 in 1961. This final hard core of illiteracy was tackled in a programme series called *It's Never Too Late*; during the first session in 1960 some 40,000 illiterates were taught to read and write at special viewing-centres throughout Italy.

In its educational work television can as a matter of policy either follow tradition in educational thought and presentation or play a leading part in developing a new approach to teaching. Is it too much to expect that as it establishes itself increasingly in the schools, it will increasingly challenge accepted educational practice, demonstrate new approaches to teaching and present subjects of importance not usually given time in the schools? This would reflect too much, no doubt, of the initiative and imagination so often shown in America, where competitive urges between educationalists and educational institutes sometimes lead to forms of experiment rare in Britain.

---

* The BBC's Report concludes with a detailed survey of how the reactions of schools using the service is tested, and Associated-Rediffusion's "School Report" has an Appendix giving a statistical summary of user reactions to the French language teaching series *Chez Les Duprez* following its transmissions for adults in the evening.

† A full account of the experiment is given by Italo Neri, head of RAI's Telescuola Centre which originates regular television programmes for schools, in the European Broadcasting Union Journal, September 1961, pp. 16–17.

America, no doubt, sets too fast a pace for us with its local short-range stations based on Universities, with its use of closed circuit for giving instruction in rural areas, and with over a hundred colleges and universities handing out degrees and diplomas to those qualifying by means of television correspondence courses. It is easy to be critical about educational standards or the over-academic palaver that exists in the expression of American theory, but what vitality and enthusiasm all this activity in educational television actually represents.

There are fifty non-commercial television stations in the States which regard their entire output as educational. American educational television is decentralized; it is very much the creation of individual academic centres, designed to meet local educational needs and supported by grants from foundations. It is essentially non-profit-making. The stations are either wholly local and promoted by single educational institutions or by a community, or they cover a State and are promoted by a State educational authority. However they originate, the stations are all affiliated to a National Educational Center which helps to co-ordinate their work by commissioning numerous programmes on tape or film for use by individual stations. The Center has initiated several thousands of programmes all of which are available for use by its affiliates. Burton Paulu, Director of Radio and Television Broadcasting, University of Minnesota, summarized American educational television in the European Broadcasting Union Review (September 1961) as follows:

At present 55 non-commercial educational stations are on the air, most of them thriving. Some are built around single schools or educational institutions, as are most of America's educational radio stations; others are "community stations", operated jointly by educational and public service groups; while still others are run by state educational agencies. Their money comes directly and indirectly from tax sources, national and local foundations, local industries, wealthy private donors, public fund drives, and the organizations which provide the programme. Although in a few instances commercial broadcasters have opposed such stations, in more cases they have helped them through gifts of funds and equipment.

In 1961 the Ford Foundation had already given over $50 million in grants to educational television.

In the same article, Burton Paulu describes an Airborne Television Instruction Service:

Unique is the American Midwest Programme on Airborne Television Instruction, another responsibility of the Learning Resources Institute, scheduled to get under way in the fall of 1961. This will broadcast programmes on two UHF channels (Band V) from high-flying airplanes, covering schools within a circle from 300 to 400 miles in diameter, extending from Milwaukee and Detroit to Cincinnati and Louisville, including portions of six states. It is hoped in this way, at relatively low cost per school, to reach children in small towns and rural areas beyond the range of regular educational television stations.

"Airborne", as it is called, will cost some $7,000,000 in its planning stage and first year, with funds coming from a $4,500,000 Ford Foundation appropriation, plus other contributions from industry. At the outset it will offer up to 24 half-hour lessons, six hours a day, four days a week, with later as many as 72 half-hour lessons each school day. Initially these will be videotaped for transmission from the two airplanes alternating as transmission points, although later there will be relays of live programmes from ground studios.

The whole business of instruction by means of closed circuit television is in its infancy in this country. Two examples given by Burton Paulu from America, where the educational problems differ from ours only in so far as there is vastly more space to cover and many more people to serve, will show what closed circuit can mean in education:

One outstanding example of close-circuit instruction on the college level is found at Pennsylvania State University, where courses in chemistry, psychology, music, speech and German, among others, have been taught that way. The nation's first closed-circuit television network covering a number of college campuses was initiated in 1961 when three campuses of the University of Texas were linked by microwave. By fall of 1961 this network is expected to include eight other colleges and universities in the state. In Texas, basic courses in chemistry, German, history, mathematics, music, psychology and science are presented live or videotaped by outstanding authorities for reception in all the institutions taking part in the experiment.

The other example is from Maryland:

What Airborne does for thousands of schools by stratovision, the five-year experiment in Hagerstown does by coaxial cable for public school students in Washington County, Maryland. Almost 75 miles of cable, with a potential of six programme channels, connects some 40 schools. Each of the 16,500 students in those schools receives at least one period of television instruction daily, and the system offers a total of 125 lessons weekly in all major subjects to all twelve grades. To originate these programmes, a television headquarters has been created with five studios and offices for 26 television teachers. This project has received over $1,000,000 from the Ford Foundation and the Fund for the Advancement of Education, with television and telephone companies contributing more than $300,000 worth of equipment.

The "twenty-one inch teacher" is hard at work in the States.

The BBC has its own views on this subject:

Schools are faced during the next few years with a great shortage of teachers and especially of specialist teachers in science and mathematics. How far can television help to fill this gap? Not we think in the main by courses of instruction of a kind for which high claims have been made in America. In practice the air space of four channels, or even six, would hardly suffice for television to take over the direct instruction of more than a very few syllabuses in a single major subject. If the medium has a future in this direction it seems rather to be on closed-circuit television.

The Pilkington Committee rejected the idea put forward principally by the ITA of founding an educational channel in the public television service; the Committee accepted the view that "the segregation of educational from general broadcasting would be harmful". However, some educationists still advocate a separate channel, particularly for specialized and general adult education. For example, in a letter published in *New Society* (22nd August 1963), H. C. Wiltshire of Nottingham University wrote: "We need a real, avowed educational channel on television (not education-by-stealth). And we must make this a real teaching (not a give-them-culture) service—which it could be if it were built into a network of correspondence-course and face-to-face tutoring. We have in Nottingham a pilot scheme of this sort, fully worked out and quite practical, by which we could teach basic economics to a class of 2,000 students instead of our usual 20. All we want is a research grant!"

Whatever form or forms it finally takes, British educational television will have a large and responsible part to play in developing the resources of education for future generations. Technical skill and scientific knowledge combined with a far wider range of general understanding and response to the humanities and the arts are what we all desire for the next generation and their successors. It could well be that the slower, deeper approach to cultural innovations which is characteristic of the British may, provided the adjustment does not take us too long, make Britain a world centre for imaginative education through film and television during the nineteen sixties and seventies. Our creative workers in film and television possess a particular kind of academic thoroughness and dedication which, if fostered with imagination, might well establish us in the forefront of visual education. But it will need the combined vision of both teachers and creative workers in the studios to develop educational television so that its national or international contribution is both widespread and deep.

25 The Outlook for ETV*

KENNETH FAWDRY

THE one certain thing about educational television in the next decade
is that it will expand, and substantially. There is no lack of possible
avenues of development: the problems are all concerned with
deciding where the priorities lie. Let us begin with school broadcasting, which is at present the sturdiest plant in the field of systematic education on the air.

---

* SFTA Journal, Summer 1963.
The article above, though written only just over two years ago, already has the
flavour of the archival. Let me try to up-date it a little.

In School Television, the 96-programme mathematics series referred to has
been discontinued, not because it was not useful, but because we felt it wrong to
use television's support for a syllabus which contemporary thinking is making
obsolescent. It has been replaced by a series which deals in some depth with
three discrete aspects of mathematics: Statistics, Logic and the Computer, and
Mathematics Applied, which are growing points in the development of new
syllabuses. It thus parallels at a higher level the third-form series referred to later
in the article, in that it is helping teachers bring their own specialist qualifications
up-to-date as well as providing stimulating material for pupils. Indeed, it is also
transmitted in the evenings for the benefit of teachers and other adult students,
with associated discussion programmes and a correspondence course run by the
National Extension College.

This is only one of the many series for schools which reinforce my statement
that BBC School Television is becoming progressively more involved with the
teacher. Other illustrations are the programmes we now offer to help
problem of backward readers in the Primary School; and the new series
ool Physics", which has been worked out in co-operation with leaders
d Science Teaching Project and is designed to help teachers trying
arning of physics a process of discovery.
and Adult Education recent developments are still more signifi-

The feature of BBC School Television's development in the last two years has been its progressively greater involvement with the task of the teacher. In its extreme form, a television teacher simply takes over the class teacher's role completely: this is exceptional, but we have currently four transmissions weekly which exemplify it. They are part of a series of 96 20-minute programmes spread over two years and designed to help the mathematician on his way from "O" level to "A" level. The incentive to provide the series was, of course, the known shortage of good, even competent, maths teachers at this level. The programmes are austere stuff, but though using minimal resources they are genuinely "televisual". The main problems can easily be imagined, and are not to be lightly dismissed. The pace is almost certain to be too fast for some and too slow for others. Schools are taking a little time to find the right audience for it, and only a minority are trying it out with no teacher present at all. But Grammar Schools have shown a great deal of interest, and we find even quite experienced teachers are delighted to have the opportunity to see another teacher at work. They can get ideas from him which will affect their own approach to their exposition. And for pupils at this stage, the very remorselessness of the medium can be an incentive

---

cant; and the BBC has created a new and substantial Department to take charge of them, with appropriate machinery for guidance by the educational world. It controls an output of five hours programming weekly (excluding repeats) on our two channels, and is certain to expand whether or no the government's "University of the Air" project materializes. This development has given the lie to the view expressed below that programmes specially designed for teachers would probably be developed mainly on closed-circuit. Already the BBC has broadcast in this field, besides the Mathematics series referred to above, short courses on physics teaching, programmed learning, and aural and visual aids in education; it will continue to make the provision of in-service courses for teachers a main feature of its work in Further Education.

At the same time there has been an adjustment in the balance of attention given to the claims of liberal adult education for the population at large, designed to foster the constructive use of leisure time, and to the needs of discrete and often small minority audiences. It is in the latter sphere that the main development has taken place: computer appreciation, management studies, labour relations, and several aspects of technological development are examples of the fields in which broadcast series have been or are being provided. The main criterion applied to the choice of course topics is that of national need.

Meanwhile, closed-circuit educational television enterprises are mushrooming, some within individual schools and colleges, some as L.E.A.- or university-based complexes. Their part in the total pattern is bound to grow, but for the next ten years at least the national organizations will continue, in this country, to carry the main burden.

to stretch their powers of assimilation to the maximum during the 20 minutes the broadcast lasts. I remember an American student telling me after a television lesson that she preferred television to the live lecturer because it didn't give other students the opportunity to flaunt their egos by interrupting with unnecessary questions.

Another recent development in relatively "direct" teaching has been the series *Engineering Science*, designed for younger students in Technical Colleges—former Secondary Modern pupils who are released from their firms for a day a week to study for the national "G" courses leading to qualifications in Engineering. In this case, of course, we do not visualize students watching on their own, so the programmes are really a supplement to the work of the College lecturer. The idea is to show applications of the theory they are taught; but you cannot show applications without relating them to the theory, so in effect this too is a teaching course. We reckon that even in purely didactic terms we can often save the time of the lecturer by making points with greater economy and precision than he could do with the means at his disposal and we use considerably more sophisticated techniques here than in the mathematics series.

Alongside these developments in didactic programming have been, of course, others which are much more in the tradition of memorable interruptions of school routine, and in scope (whether documentary or dramatized) often more akin to general than to teaching programmes—plays, documentaries about careers, specially shot films about modern art, and so on. These are, and will remain, an exciting and essential element in television's contribution to schools. But in their different way the more didactic programmes are at least as significant for educational development, not so much in themselves or even in their direct impact on viewing students, but for the new ideas they can offer the *teachers* at the receiving end. Indeed, one of the most important functions of television in education may turn out to be its capacity to disseminate so rapidly new ideas about both teaching techniques and the content of school syllabuses. That television should back the right horse is, of course, desirable. But convervatism and natural lethargy have always been greater dangers to the teaching profession than excessive susceptibility to new fashions which may prove ephemeral.

The world of mathematics teaching is in considerable ferment at the present time, and at every stage syllabus reforms are being discussed or put into practice. This year a new BBC series for third forms in Secondary Schools is on the air: with topics such as binary number, motion geometry and statistics, it is designed to encourage any teacher inclined to be adventurous and to give pupils a new sense of purpose in their studies. At present, our teacher training on the air is, as it were, surreptitious and ostensibly we are speaking to children only. Programmes specifically for teachers will no doubt come, but logically the place for them is on a closed-circuit system. For closed-circuit television as well as local and regional broadcasting will, of course, inevitably develop rapidly in the next decade. So far there are small pockets of enterprise only, but almost monthly one can read of new ones in operation or projected, of which the "Cambridge week" is at once the most recent and most eye-catching example. This is a healthy sign; hitherto we have been inhibited by a tendency to regard large national organizations as the sole purveyors of television. They will, in fact, have much to learn from closed-circuit operations, even those conducted on very modest lines—quite apart, of course, from what they stand to gain in their talent scouting from the increase in the numbers of those with experience in front of cameras. Closed-circuit operations have certain great advantages: they are free from the pressures of restricted airtime, they can afford to be more thoroughly experimental, and they can achieve a closer liaison between provider and consumer than is possible in nation-wide broadcasting.

Closed-circuit broadcasting is obviously only suitable for audiences institutionally based; it cannot reach those who, of necessity or by choice, want educational opportunity brought into their homes. But within that limitation, it can not only serve to make first-class teaching available to larger numbers, it can also stimulate thought about the teaching process itself. It can at least break down the notion that good teaching of any kind can really take place only in a room inhabited by one teacher and up to forty-odd pupils; and here America, with its larger concepts of educational opportunity, has been bolder to experiment than we have. She is adapting herself to a situation in which conventional methods alone can no longer measure up to the demand for teaching.

With the opening up of new UHF channels, there are already a bewildering number of claimants to airtime for specialized needs on open-circuit broadcasting, and the case for a new national network will eventually prove overwhelming, for most of these needs are in areas where neither the subject matter, say Accountancy or Intermediate Russian, nor the likely audience is in any way localized. If the BBC runs the network, I think we shall need to think carefully about what good television is in this sort of context. We can assume an audience anxious to learn and not needing titillation, or dressing up of the material to make it overtly attractive. Relatively few and simple visuals, carefully prepared and used to the full to extract the maximum teaching value from them, may sometimes be a better prescription than one in which, in the interests of "good television", the eye is fed with a succession of images which would make a clear recall of the main teaching points more difficult to ensure. Television is after all only "good" if it serves its primary purpose, and this purpose may be one which requires pictures here and there to clarify thought expressed in words, rather than a theme which is essentially visual and is supported by a minimum of verbal comment.

These specialist groups have their legitimate claims, and the BBC's Second Channel will provide an opportunity to meet some of them. But equally important, for nation-wide television is the need to extend the range of interests of wider sections of the population at large, to encourage them to acquire new skills, and to deepen their understanding of the contemporary world.

Much general programming helps to serve these ends incidentally, but without directly encouraging any systematic study, and without giving people much conscious or sustained feeling that they have made perceptible progress and acquired something of more than ephemeral value. The task of programme planners in this field is to aim at significant minorities among the broad middle mass of viewers and to try and make these minorities larger—to help people to realize their own potential. They therefore need to woo the public— to present their programmes as attractively as those which now engage the attention of millions. The job cannot be done on the cheap.

The field of potential subject matter is vast. More people want to enlarge their appreciation of art than those who have the kind of background which a programme like Monitor tacitly assumes. More people want to acquire the elements of a foreign language, perhaps because they are going abroad for the first time. More people would like to understand about money than their daily life has hitherto required them to—it may be because they have never used a bank before, or because they are considering making small investments, or because they are tired of hearing phrases like the balance of payments or the bank rate bandied about in the News, without really understanding them. More people, better educated than they were ten or twenty years ago, are working in jobs which do not fully stretch them; and they have more leisure time which they could, and would with encouragement, use more creatively—perhaps to master the skills of dressmaking, perhaps to acquire a new interest in archaeology.

These are the kinds of ideas on which the BBC's Adult Education programmes are currently based, and I believe that this kind of programming will continue to form the core of our provision for adults for some years to come. They require of the producers a sensitivity to audience needs—and this implies continuous consultation with those working in the adult educational field, just as we have with the schools; a belief that people want to learn; and a recognition—to come back to a point I made earlier—that learning is bound up with feeling, that programmes for learners must therefore be as imaginative as any others, and that this is likely to call for the full resources of television.

26 ETV in Transition*

JOSEPH WELTMAN

THE preliminary figures of British schools which have expressed an intention to view Independent Television school programmes in the new school year, are very encouraging. There has been a sharp increase during 1963 which may well take the total audience up to the 6,000 schools mark. Last year it was little more than 5,000.† Obviously teachers and local education authorities generally are now taking schools television seriously as a very valuable addition to their educational resources. If so many more schools are now prepared to view, they must have been equipped with television sets. In most cases this provision will have come from the local education authorities, who are now finding welcome encouragement for their progressive policies, not only in the changed climate of opinion in the educational world at large, but also by a much more positive attitude on the part of the Ministry of Education.

The range of programmes offered by Independent Television in the new school year, extends from a miscellany series *Story Box* for primary schools (8–10 years) to the advanced sixth form science programmes of the *Discovery* series. In between there are also foreign language programmes for sixth formers and middle school; drama (*Hamlet*, *She stoops to Conquer* and *Playboy of the Western World*) for 13 years and over; and general science programmes for

---

* *SFTA Journal, Summer 1963.*
† The rate of increase has been maintained. Corresponding figure for October 1965 was over 11,000.

14-year olds. New departures include the current affairs series *Afternoon Edition* (14 years and over) in which classes will hear informed commentary on the most important events in the past week's news: the Railway Age social and economic history for grammar school sixth formers; and series offering religious education and some planned for less-able children. The last two are planned for the Summer Term, 1964. In the case of *Afternoon Edition*, an attempt will be made to achieve audience participation by encouraging schools to telephone questions to the studio during the course of transmission.

All these programmes are planned with the advice and guidance of practising teachers and educationists. The emphasis throughout is on supplementing the work of the teacher, not supplanting him. In other words the programmes are designed to fit in with the existing patterns of instruction in our schools. Now this may seem an over-cautious, not to say backward-looking attitude to those who feel the times are ripe for profound and far-reaching educational change. It is easy enough to express dissatisfaction with established methods, to foresee an educational revolution, and to think of television as the main cause of this revolution. There are some enthusiasts who seem to think that our educational system needs to be completely transformed in order to make it easier for educational television to do its job. It would be nearer the truth to say that the natural evolution of the system has created a situation in which the use of a "mass medium" for educational ends seems a logical next step. The educational "revolution" has been going on for a long time in Britain, at least since 1870, probably longer. Educationists are by their nature always two-faced. They are both traditionalists and potential revolutionaries: they are agents of social and cultural continuity, but it is also their task to think out afresh the very bases of inherited knowledge and attitudes for the benefit of each new generation. None of the political, social and technical changes which have made our century a truly revolutionary one would have been possible without "educating our masters". The main impetus for educational change comes from within the educational world itself. It is not putting too fine a point on this idea to suggest that a public which is dissatisfied with what the educational system offers its children, is already showing in itself the benefits of education. Inevitably as more and more children have been given access to full-time education to 18 and beyond, curricula and teaching methods have changed. When education ceases to be something bought and becomes instead a compulsory gift, one has to look more closely at the way of making the gift acceptable and worth having. A great deal of such thinking has been done since 1947.

There have been other pressures too. The passage of the "bulge" created a sense of crisis, aggravated by the continuing shortage of teachers. Another bulge is now on the way.* Even the economists have begun to speak of education in terms of national investment. As our outmoded nineteenth-century industry wakes up to the twentieth century, and the old empirical methods of training disappear, technical education increases in importance, and the old irrational divisions between vocational and non-vocational education are beginning to fade away. Education is no longer just seen as "all right for those who can afford it" and have the leisure to enjoy its fruits. It is increasingly recognized that right thinking and efficient doing are connected. Over the last decades there has been a steady trend away from the academic bookbound approach to teaching. The more education becomes practically orientated, the more readily are effective visual methods looked for and accepted.

All these changes are taking place now. And, because the pace of change in the world at large is greater today than ever before, the stresses and strains in the educational system are many and conflicting. No doubt in the course of the next generation a very different pattern of education will emerge in Britain. And I have no doubt that television, one of the most successful of all means of communications so far devised, will then be seen to have played a major role as an instrument in the policies of educational change. It may well be that we shall then look back at our present, relatively successful, efforts and see them as very tentative, experimental, first steps. Of course, they are still experimental and, of course, they will change as the educational system they serve changes. By keeping in close touch with the best educational advice and the best teaching practice we shall continue to experiment under their stimulus and inspiration.

We have in this country a decentralized educational system which has created a favourable setting for experiment. Independent Television is also decentralized, and the regional companies are very

---

* The bulge has now (1965) hit the universities. And by the logic of history this year has also seen the appearance of the Report of the Brynmor Jones Committee on the Use of Audiovisual Aids in Higher Education.

much in touch with their areas. If local educationists have an idea they think television would help to materialize, they can go to their regional company and put forward their scheme. They can and do. There have been examples of this recently particularly in adult education. Ulster Television, with the co-operation of Queen's University, Belfast, transmitted last year a series called *Midnight Oil*, an adult education programme on about the same level as W.E.A. classes. This was highly successful. It proved a substantial local audience existed. It was followed up this year with a similar series called *The Enquiring Mind*.

Scottish Television, in co-operation with the Glasgow Post-Graduate Medical School, are transmitting a more specialized series for general practitioners and doctors in hospitals, helping them to keep up to date with the latest advances in medical research. This is a new field for educational television in this country, but obviously one of great importance.

In the South-West, Westward Television and University of Exeter Institute of Education are co-operating in a similar venture for the "in service" training of teachers.

Another specially interesting experiment arising from regional initiative is *Dawn University*, a series of six early morning lectures given by Cambridge dons like Professor Fred Hoyle on "The Mathematics of Violence", Nobel prize-winner Dr. J. C. Kendrew, on the "Molecules of Life", and Raymond Williams on "The Changing Vision of the Future". These programmes have been made possible through the co-operation of Anglia Television, Cambridge University, and the Independent Television Authority. Early morning educational transmissions at undergraduate level, are familiar enough in the United States and it will be interesting to note the response in this country.*

The Cambridge experiment will also concern itself with closed circuit. A two-way vision link is being set up between Cambridge University and Imperial College in London for an interchange between post-graduate researchers, a sort of research colloquium. A link is also being set up between Norwich University and Cambridge University so that undergraduates at both, in their respective lecture rooms, can share the same lectures.

---

* A T.A.M. (1965) estimate put the total audience for all six broadcasts at 200,000.

Another example of local experiment comes from N.E. Scotland, in primary education this time. The Chief Education Officer of Aberdeen hopes to be able to stimulate improvement in the primary school curriculum. He approached Grampian Television and a new series of programmes for primary schools is being transmitted in the current school year as an addition to the nationally net-worked schools programmes on Independent Television. We hope to see more of this kind of experiment.*

One final word to those who talk about "revolution".

Teaching children through the medium of television means that we are teaching them through a medium which is well-known to them. The children in schools today have never known life without television. They do not regard it as we older folks tend to do, as a disturbing modern phenomenon like the aeroplane or the atom bomb. For them it is something which is alive, which is part of their everyday life. They associate it with delight and interest. And that is something that every good teacher at all times has tried to give.

---

* The hope was not vain. Grampian has continued with a regular additional local primary school series. Scottish Television and Ulster have also since produced local programmes for secondary schools. Perhaps the most important of such regional experiments has been the elementary economics course produced in 1964 in co-operation between the Midlands weekday company, ATV, and the Adult Education Department of Nottingham University. This course linked television with correspondence course methods and some face to face group teaching. In a sense, it can be regarded as a successful pilot for a future "University of the Air" (1965).

27 A Teacher Faces Camera*

MINNA K. BARNETT

A TEACHER faces television cameras—and learns that cameras are not students and the studio is not a classroom. The skeptics and the daydreamers, the bored and the anxious, are as missing as the receptive. But somehow, in the empty lens of the camera, the television teacher must find them all. She must talk with them, tease them, cajole them, enchant them, beguile them. She must never bore the quick or rush the slow. She must anticipate every question, gesture, or whim before she faces the camera. There is never the reward of the answering gleam. What are her chances for success?

I can only place such questions and challenges within the framework of hard experience, and draw therefrom what rules and reflections I can. The "hard experience" came out of my association with *Transition*—a series of 30 half-hour programs for in-school viewing I prepared and presented under the aegis of the Regents Educational Television Project of the New York Board of Regents. The series' stated objective was to enrich the social studies curriculum for the eleventh and twelfth year pupils in the metropolitan area's secondary schools. In a community surfeited with excellent television coverage of current affairs, what and how much more could the television teacher do with this exacting medium?

Educational television could present new scholarship and at the same time subject this scholarship to critical analysis. It could bring

* *Television Quarterly, Fall 1962.*

the leaders of our time, both theoreticians and practitioners, directly into the classroom. It could reduce the "cultural lag" of the over-burdened, chore-beset high school teacher. One half-hour a week could perhaps inspire new reading, and stimulate discussion along new and untrod paths. Television, the mass medium of the inter-planetary age, could make the classroom a meaningful experience in the present, not a training ground for the problems of the past. Our yardstick for success was:

> *Educational television for in-school viewing measures its success by how much it has added to the learning process not otherwise possible.*

The small group of social studies teachers and curriculum specialists who were assembled to plan *Transition* for the 1960–61 school year chose three subject areas now featured to varying extent in all the courses of study in the metropolitan area: *The Presidency and the Voter*, *New Nationalism in Asia and Africa*, and *The Civil War—100 Years Later*. Since there were no curriculum imperatives, popular interest and the opportunities of the television medium determined the extent of coverage and the timing of the programs.

Ten programs on the Presidency were offered in ten weeks during the fall of 1960, even though the most politically-oriented teacher may find five consecutive lessons on the Presidency excessive in a one-year survey course in American history. In view of the Congo crisis in 1961, twelve weeks was allowed for a study of the new nationalism in Asia and Africa—more time than would be devoted to the subject even in world history classes.

It should be noted that only by prearrangement, and under experimental conditions, would any two schools have agreed to pre-sent these units in the same way, or have permitted a series of television programs, however scholarly, interesting, or original in organization and presentation, to determine the sequence of lessons. Although the subject areas chosen did not parallel any courses of study in these areas except by chance, no change in traditional procedures was suggested or contemplated.

But what would induce teachers with overburdened curricula to set aside—voluntarily—a half-hour each week for in-school viewing of a television program? It was hoped that the presentation of special scholarship in the subject of the day (preferably the author of a distinguished book or one whose viewpoint challenged earlier findings) would set new standards of excellence and thereby overcome this problem.

Of the 46 guests who appeared in the series, then, 14 were college professors or scholars associated with institutions or organizations sponsoring research. These specialists offered new interpretations of the nature of the Presidency and of the American electorate, the causes and results of the Civil War, and the role of Lincoln in that conflict. The series on *New Nationalism in Asia and Africa* suggested the use of specialists in those social sciences not usually taught as separate disciplines in the secondary schools—anthropology and sociology.

In the treatment of controversial subjects, proponents of several prevailing views challenged each other's choice of facts, reasoning, or motives to help develop criteria for forming judgments. Two United States Senators from both sides of the aisle discussed *Platforms and Issues.* Three members of cabinets or advisers to Presidents analyzed the extent of the differences among political parties; four foreign correspondents from as many countries in as many continents did a *post mortem* on the 1960 Presidential election. A former district attorney, a leading American journalist, and a political scientist described, from different vantage points, patronage and party influence as they affect the President. Ambassadors from Asia and Africa appraised the future role of the President as leader of the Free World. Authorities on nationalism in Europe, Asia, and Africa analyzed the entire concept of nationalism. Ambassadors from a new nation and from that nation's metropolitan power, in a discussion entitled *The Future of Nationalism,* clarified their differences and indicated areas of agreement.

It must be said that distinct educational attainments had been reached. The series brought into the classroom men who were making decisions affecting war and peace and the future role of government in the social and economic development of their countries. It introduced to students the representatives of the many different groups which seek to influence governmental action. It introduced the intellectual leaders of our time, men and women who could transport young people, *and their teachers,* into a real world of affairs by offering insights acquired neither from a printed page nor by isolation in an academic "ivory tower". Could any one school or school system bring to its social studies classes in any one year ten diplomats of whom seven were of ambassadorial rank? Or eight leading spokes-men for influential groups in this country? Certainly the achieve-ments of these guests established excellence as a realistic goal instead of an illusory ideal.

Although the resources of the New York metropolitan area are perhaps the most favorable in the world, they remain largely un-explored or unknown to most of its residents. For one lesson on the Civil War the average teacher could not, in search of original docu-ments, comb the files of the New York Public Library, the New York Historical Society, and private collections. This we could do, and the search yielded meaningful realia: a receipt received in payment for the sale of a slave; a poster announcing the sale of raffle tickets (price one dollar) for the possible prize of a Negro female slave, age twenty, or for a mare in good condition; an early paper-back edition of *Uncle Tom's Cabin;* a warning to fugitive slaves published by the aboli-tionists in Boston; contemporary copies of *Harper's Weekly* and *Leslie's Illustrated.*

Nor could a classroom teacher present a map showing the changes in the extent of cotton culture in the United States up to 1860, trace the changing prices of cotton, or collect statistics of taxes paid by Southerners. We could offer these, as well as lists of benefits received from the federal government, the special benefits the South considered the North received from the central government, and other documents which illustrated the Southern view of its relationship to the Union.

In two programs, *Ancient Civilizations in Modern Times* and *The Peoples of the New Nations,* an African ethnologist from the Ameri-can Museum of Natural History illustrated his analyses by using artifacts and art objects of several African tribes in addition to many objects associated with the different religious groups of India—all borrowed from the Museum and the legations. Ghanaian drummers with their own instruments, a missionary renowned for his work in the Congo, and pictures taken from the study of Tropical Africa sponsored by the Twentieth Century Fund gave a *You Are There* quality to the portrayal of conditions in Africa.

A sample voting machine was used to make the Electoral College more meaningful. The assembling of new or little-known data, maps used in different ways or unknown to most classrooms, motion pic-ture material otherwise unavailable to the teacher, charts in as many forms as possible—all of these, we hoped, would inspire a search for those new approaches in the learning process which would add dimension to conventional procedures.

The problem of proper classroom scheduling created a major obstacle. In order to view the program from 2.30 to 3.00 p.m. one teacher and her students had to march around the school building for fifteen minutes of the half-hour to await the end of the preceding period. In another school the day ended ten minutes after the beginning of the program; but the teacher and students could not, even if they cared to, linger for the remaining time because other students must either pick up their clothing in the rear closets or the entire school's closing procedures would be disrupted. Where the longer school day did exist, more often than not the program time straddled two periods. In no school did all the social studies classes for whom the program was intended meet for social studies at that time. Teachers with two or three classes in the grade found it inconvenient to expose one class but not the others. In one Long Island high school only representatives from each social studies class could be regularly detailed to view the programs and report back the next day. Although this was not as desirable as direct and continuous viewing, it did introduce students and teachers to the potential of television in the social studies classroom.

Most schools are not built to facilitate in-school viewing of television. Reception too often is uncertain, and repairs are costly and long delayed. Sets cannot be moved from room to room without upsetting regular instruction. As long as the values of the particular program, or of television as a medium of instruction, remain unknown quantities the teacher hesitates before tangling with complicated administrative procedures. That teachers did take time from a well-planned series of sequential lessons to introduce, under these circumstances, even a few of the programs on *Transition* is indicative of the flexibility and professional awareness of many social studies teachers in this area.

Transition was designed to meet the challenge of the above-average and college-bound student. With the teacher present, students were exposed to new standards of scholarship and to new approaches, to the unresolved or abstruse idea which provoked questions. Reading beyond the text now seemed essential to the student, and the discussion more pointed.

But no such audience had been alerted or prepared. Indeed, some teachers argued that what was educationally desirable for the best students should not be denied to the others. For the average, they complained, the pace was too fast, the materials too scholarly, the guests too philosophical, the lessons too detailed for students lacking enough background. If the able students found these same programs interesting and, once exposed, sought the opportunity to see others, teachers could not so "discriminate". After all, they indicated, one of the great advantages of television is its ability to reach a "mass" audience at any time. The use of television as a medium, even for in-school viewing, has little justification otherwise in their opinion.

The unfamiliar tends to be uncomfortable. Teachers, as well as students, can be reluctant learners, even as they may be fearful of feeling insecure in their mastery of subject matter. The new nations of Asia and Africa, emerging so recently from colonial tutelage, remain in the minds of most adults, including busy teachers of social studies, as large geographical areas important to us only for their raw materials. Given the new pace of events, the mere facts of change are complicated enough to master: new place names, new leaders, new political parties, new participants in international politics. Teachers *may* vaguely sense that none of the problems relating to these new nations will be completely comprehensible and that no responsible public opinion can be developed just by the acquiring of facts. But anthropologists, sociologists, missionaries, economic advisers to American business interests, journalists and diplomats with varying countries of origin and representative of all races, spokesmen for the many interested organizations and foundations, and United Nations officials—to mention only some of these presented on *Transition*—offered different interpretations.

"Aren't the facts complicated enough?" one teacher plaintively argued. "Even I can't get them straight. These varying interpretations are just confusing." And it is this which draws our attention to the fact that it is a teacher, not a student, who turns on the television set for in-class viewing. How receptive are teachers to new ideas and interpretations? How willing are they to acknowledge to themselves and to their students that learning cannot be limited to those on one side of the desk? After all, a television program, unlike a book or a motion picture, cannot be previewed and digested.

Television may be a new force in education but rigidities already prevail at both the production and receiving ends.

The techniques used in subject areas at grade levels at each end of the educational spectrum in which the medium was pioneered now set patterns for new areas and different grade levels. In the elementary grades the attention span is short, and the visual appeal transcends the verbal. A vigorous pace is therefore equated with the amount of motion on the set and the number of time segments—each with a different activity, and the greater the variety the better.

In the social studies, where vocabularly and concepts are presumably common parlance, erudition and subtlety of interpretation to the layman are at best disturbing and at worst confusing. To production specialists untrained in the social sciences, mere maps and statistics are the tools of the pedant and the bore. An extended exchange of ideas, regardless of what is being discussed, without the interjection of a movie clip or a "still" at appropriate intervals, fails, in their view, to make "optimum use of the medium". Instead of exploiting the medium's ability to use visual material to illuminate a concept, the visuals *available* tend to determine the concepts taught, the method of development and the points of emphasis. In programs on science, mathematics and art, among others, a critique without a demonstration would be unnatural both to the subject at hand and to the guest or television teacher.

Although the presentation or demonstration is possible and frequently desirable in the social sciences, more often the tools are words, with reference to visual materials not always necessary, possible, or sufficiently illuminating to be worth the time. Dramatic effect in a discussion among experts may be achieved by developing differences of opinion, shades of meaning or new interpretations in which the visual may only strait-jacket thought, not probe its meaning. *"Talk" may not be "good" television, but it can sometimes be great television teaching.*

Production consultants, aware of themselves as professionals in the art of visualization and sensitive to the stern demands of the medium, mysteriously manipulate and coordinate cameras, microphones, sets and cues. To how many of them does the "ideal" subject specialist remain a novitiate in the use of the medium, dependent, preferably helpless? For the educator, adaptation and resignation, not experimentation, once again become worthy, and necessary, attributes.

On the other hand, the classroom teacher, burdened with an overloaded curriculum, has over the years developed practices he considers indispensable. He is a ritualist by necessity and choice. The textbook, or the curriculum, too often spells out finite limits to the course of study. Memorized learning, with extensive note taking and repetition, becomes a *sine qua non*. Others who stress understanding use skillful questioning to elicit the "why, how, and so what". Where subject-matter specialists of either variety in the high schools are in short supply, the televised lesson is intended to replace the skilled teacher for part of the class time.

Television is not the path to education at a bargain price. It is no substitute for competent teachers, adequate schools, well-stocked libraries, or other appurtenances of instruction. Viewed as the twentieth century's contribution toward attuning the educational process to the accelerated rate of change in science and technology, the economy and international politics, television offers a vast unexplored frontier. Untutored in the intricacies of the new medium, inadequately prepared for the rigors of a new regimen, denied assistance with the unending and unfamiliar series of chores, and starved for funds to ensure the best possible presentation, the teacher-pioneer is forced to choose between his ideals and his exposed position.

Classroom teachers who have helped to plan the series of TV lessons, from the subject matter and the realia to the guest list, will more readily adapt their course of study to the new offering. Continuous and direct contact with the classroom teacher may serve to adjust the pace to the needs of the live audience and heighten interest and establish contact between the TV teacher and his unseen students. This new relationship between the television teacher and the teachers in the classroom may encourage added preparation by the classroom teacher, suggest new classroom techniques, and raise standards of performance required of students, but this time by joint design and without disturbing the self-confidence of the teacher.

Important as it may be to maximize on the potential of the television medium, in-school programs in the secondary schools must first meet the special requirements of the subject specialist. The television lesson, like the lesson in the classroom, must be planned for a specific audience and that audience must be prepared to receive and respond to the lesson. What is *educationally desirable* for the television lesson should be made *financially possible*. If three cameras instead of two, an honorarium for a consultant, a fee for newsreel footage, additional rehearsal time, or other items will teach the lesson more effectively, should not these be made available? Is not the purpose of the television lesson to make an otherwise impossible but valued addition to the classroom lesson? *If the television lesson was worth the time of the teacher, production and technical personnel, not to mention distinguished guests, should not its use by the widest possible audience be facilitated, even if that means kinescoping or taping?* To offer a series of programs for in-school viewing without close attention to the requirements of the school audience either as to timing or subject matter is a futile gesture and productive only of frustration and cynicism.

To a teacher facing television cameras the studio does not offer sanctuary within which to build the usual system of communication with his students. Cameras are curiously unresponsive, even though cameramen often ask better questions than the high school student. Teachers on television not only do not see their audience, they cannot assume the usual "captive audience". They must attract one.

The television medium is indeed an exposed frontier for the educator. Removed from the public's scrutiny in his classroom, the classroom teacher is judged primarily by his students. As a television teacher, his values, his judgment, his wisdom, his cultural background, not to mention his scholarship, are on view for evaluation by all—his colleagues and the general public, as well as his students. The teacher so exposed will provide a new image for an ancient, and now often tarnished, role. His is the task of restoring its honor even as he sets new standards of achievement to help his students grapple with the complexities and uncertainties of an ever-changing world.

28 Screen Science*

JAMES McCLOY

THE glittering cascade of glass marbles tumbled and rattled, and as Sir Lawrence Bragg took away his steadying hand over four million viewers could see the perfect pyramid into which they had fallen, a model of a crystal. And they saw this demonstration in the comfort of their sitting rooms far more clearly than any member of the audience present that night in the famous lecture theatre of the Royal Institution. Moreover, it has been estimated that Sir Lawrence would have needed to be able to repeat his lecture to a full house every night until the end of the century to reach the same sized audience that he had for that single television programme. These are only two aspects of the power of television in the communication of science. Of course, in many ways, science is a natural for television; and in this election year we are not likely to be left in any doubt about the vital importance of science to the community at this point in time. But what kind of science? How should it be presented on television? And at what level?

A lecture, such as those given by Sir Lawrence Bragg or, more recently, Professor Hermann Bondi and Dr. John Kendrew in the adult education series on Saturday, is one way. A distinguished scientist who is a skilful expositor lectures to an invited audience with the television cameras, however favoured, in what is essentially an eavesdropping situation. Psychologically the viewer has been taken from

---

* *SFTA Journal, Winter 1963.*

his sitting room to the lecture theatre and it is hoped that he has the illusion of being a member of the audience there without all the trouble of going out on a cold evening. Here television quite legitimately takes over, almost ready made, one of the oldest techniques for the communication of science. And as with all lectures success or failure depends ultimately on the personality and skill of the lecturer.

At the opposite extreme television can eliminate all personality and borrowing the traditional scientific film technique, present its subject in pictures, diagrams and demonstrations with only the voice of an unseen commentator. This is possible because the bulk of science is concerned with physical objects and their behaviour and not at all with people. Between these two didactic extremes are all the presentation techniques evolved by television itself in documentary and feature programmes, techniques which can enrich a programme with all the intimacy and informality so peculiar to this medium. But there is space here only to draw attention to one special quality of the electronic cameras in presenting science in comparison with film technique. A scientist talking about his subject naturally wants, and for effective communication needs to show, various bits and pieces—the materials he works on, his apparatus, photographs, models and so on. These demonstrations in fact should be closely woven into the exposition. To present this on film involves a long series of individually prepared and separately taken shots which are later edited to give the illusion of continuous action. In contrast, using three or more television cameras, we have continuous action and the programme can be recorded without any interference to the flow of the argument. With an amateur speaker the gain in naturalness and sense of communication achieved by this technique adds almost another dimension.

So television is uniquely equipped for the communication of science, but what kind of science? Sir Cyril Hinshelwood, when he was President of the Royal Society, wrote: "It is very difficult for any but experts to understand what is going on, not as so many non-scientific people are fond of asserting, because men of science are incapable of expressing themselves clearly, or are unwilling to try, but for the simple reason that many aspects of the subject are of very great inherent difficulty. They are based upon unfamiliar conceptions, often developed by advanced mathematical reasoning and sometimes expressed in a complex and abstract symbolism." Clearly there has to be a careful selection of science subjects, particularly in physics, for large audience programmes. But by aiming at a more restricted audience composed of those with some background of science who are prepared to make a sustained effort, as we have in some of the off-peak adult education programmes, it is possible successfully to present series of ten programmes such as those by Professor Bondi on relativity. Here a real attempt was made at the vulgarization of a subject which was not long ago considered to be understandable only in terms of advanced mathematics.

All this does not mean that the difficult but exciting adventures in current scientific research are excluded from the mass audience. It is possible to talk about them and to show the kind of thing the scientists are doing without attempting to go very deeply into the scientific principles involved. The peak hour science feature such as *Man Tomorrow*, *Challenge* and *The Virus* try to do this. Some of these programmes have been described as using the "Gee Whizz" technique, but regarded as one aspect only of television science it serves the purpose of presenting science in an entertaining setting and making a large audience aware of the kind of thing scientists are up to. In an atmosphere where talk of two cultures prevails this could be an important function of television: to show the scientist as a person, the kind of question he asks and the kind of experiments he performs to get at the answers.

Currently the BBC is regularly producing some programmes with the specific aim of showing scientists simply as people. Among these have been *The Prizewinners* (the molecular biologists who were jointly awarded the Nobel prize), *The Cosmologists*, *The Particle Physicists*, and so on. The programmes have tried to reveal not only the scientists' attitudes to science and the act of discovery but also to life in general.

Scientists themselves are particularly anxious to communicate the scientific method and attitude. They see science as more than an organized body of knowledge about ourselves and our environment. The scientific attitude has for some the status of a whole philosophy of life. This aspect of science is probably the most difficult of all to communicate by television and some consider it impossible. However, it is inherent, if not always explicit in very many programmes, and it illuminates and enriches programmes whose main interest and appeal for many of the audience is their account of the knowledge that science has built up.

Much if not all of the success of a science programme depends on the skill in exposition of the speaker. Up to now the universal science popularizer has not gained a strong position in television and at his best a scientist talking about his own work and experience has a quality which no interpreter could achieve. But the narrow specialism of modern research greatly limits the range on which scientists are prepared to speak. So on a programme which surveys a wide field a scientifically qualified anchorman may be needed to introduce the various specialists, and present an overall picture. Similarly good scientific scriptwriters are needed who can construct a coherent story from the isolated branches of specialized research. And such people are in very short supply.

For the large audience the simplification of science without distortion presents a constant problem. Reducing the subject to words of one syllable and eliminating the jargon is not a reliable solution since the concept itself may be too difficult or demand a background of scientific knowledge that the audience does not possess. In any case it is never possible to tell the whole story and after selecting the topics to be treated it is necessary to decide which of these can be explained relatively fully at the level of the audience and which are just to be shown and talked about. For example, one may show a computer recognizing and learning visual shapes, and the kind of mistakes it makes, but how the computer actually does this may have to be omitted completely. Much of science on television presents the descriptive or observational aspects as in natural history and many biological subjects. Scientific principles are less easy to communicate.

In all exposition of science, showmanship is as important as it is elsewhere in television. The creation of suspense may however take a quite different form in which intellectual tension substitutes for emotional tension as in many detective stories. This engagement of the curiosity of the audience so that they are led step by step through the unravelling of a scientific argument adopts a kind of detective story technique. Controversy is unfortunately rarely possible as a component to involve the attention of the large audience. For one thing there is little of it in the scientific knowledge at the level of the audience. Where it is present it is usually at the frontier of knowledge and scientists arguing it out in a natural manner in front of cameras would be unintelligible to an audience with no background of science. To take an admittedly extreme case, it is difficult to imagine Hoyle and Royle arguing out the rival merits of their theories of cosmology for the entertainment of a peak-hour audience.

High quality visual aids of all kinds have become such a natural part of scientific exposition on television that they are taken for granted but even quite simple models can be helpful in providing a focus for the speakers' explanations and freeing the imaginative effort of the viewer to cope with the strange ideas he may be meeting for the first time. But with all the visual aids, the films, the models, the animated diagrams, the demonstrations and experiments, how far the viewer is prepared to go, and how the subject is to be presented are governed by his starting point of natural curiosity. The level of difficulty and the poverty or richness of illustration required to hold a large audience might be quite different in a programme on the scientific basis of contraceptive techniques and one on particle physics.

There are so many different points of entry of science into television schedules, from news and current affairs (*Tonight* and *Panorama*), through popular science, and the feature or documentary to the more directly educational programmes that it is impossible to talk about a best way to communicate science by television. In an industrial society such as ours where science impinges so much on everyday life it would be as pointless to talk about a single technique of presenting science as it would be to talk about the one way to present politics.

What is surprising is that technology, with its even more obvious impact on society, has featured so little on television. Television has in fact tended to lump together technology and engineering in the same bracket as science. A new kind of satellite is launched, and it is described on television as a triumph for science. In fact very many of these so-called scientific "triumphs" belong properly to engineering and not to science. It is difficult to understand why engineering has had such a small share of television time. Perhaps television is here simply reflecting the attitudes of the country in this neglect. The creative engineer was once a national hero, and although our great engineers are playing just as vital a role in the community today, television has not made household names of our modern Stevensons and Brunels. Their work is certainly more exciting and much more dramatic than the quite often tedious round of the pure science research laboratory. Moreover the British are supposed to have great mechanical interests and certainly many people are interested in how things work and how they are made. These again are just the things which television is so well equipped to show. This is the area where there is greater need for experiment and beginning on BBC-2 there is likely to be a new trend to exploit this rich programme vein of creative engineering. Perhaps we may see a new television fashion which will do for technology what *Animal, Vegetable and Mineral* once did for archaeology. Many have said that television has had a great effect in raising the status of the scientist in the community and has played an important part in the recruitment of young scientists; few would dispute the national need for a similar treatment of the engineers.

29 Television in Pursuit of Wonder*

JULES BERGMAN

SCIENCE reporting, on television, is closely akin to hurling a space-craft into orbit: The booster must give just the right amount of power to the spacecraft at exactly the right instant and place or miss achieving orbit. Astronaut John Glenn likened the process to "threading a needle 100 miles over the Earth". In television's terms, the science reporter faces the terrifying dilemma of either under- or over-rating his audience, of either going over their heads or drilling home the commonplace.

In an industry concerned with common denominators, this is obviously no small problem. To find the right level—to "thread the needle" with consistent accuracy, and yet maintain a high level of interest—is an 18-hour-a-day challenge. When you add to these initial requirements the need to tell the story *visually*, especially when dealing with esoteric scientific concepts, the job can be mad-dening. More stories than I care to admit have missed orbit because words alone were not enough, because the *pi meson* means very little spoken, yet springs home with the ring of fresh knowledge when it can be seen as well.

Topping all the other problems is the stringent one of time: what could be told easily, and with loving care, in a half-hour documentary is a ruthless struggle against time in the one- to three-minute confines of the 15-minute network nightly news telecast.

---

* *Television Quarterly, Spring 1963.*

And yet, that very struggle is a harsh discipline. What is worth telling, and what has been worth telling through the centuries, has most often been that which can be told crisply, briefly, succinctly— with an immediate and penetrating clarity. Though there are arbitrary differences of opinion in the make-up of a news show, the report of a new scientific development will mean the most to the viewer when it is pared down to its lean and major components. Not the average viewer, for I maintain that there is no such creature. Not all the viewers may write in their reactions, but an amazing number *do*—with startlingly observant comments. He wants to know why more detail wasn't supplied on a new laser light ray device that has no immediate, ringing importance, yet stirs his curiosity and desire to know.

Sorting, scanning, seeking to emerge from the pile of scientific journals, releases, and data that cascades in with the mail every morning, the TV science editor tries to seek out the new, the fresh, and the stimulating. By such elimination, I'm down to a few hundred items. I then try to ask myself which of these is really important, since our two nightly network TV newscasts can only treat so much. Getting to the story (after convincing frequently skeptical assignment desks that it *should* be gotten to) is the next problem. Space, aviation, rocketry, nuclear power, and medicine stories—with these I am primarily concerned—have a nasty habit of happening in different parts of the nation at the same time.

Not everything can be covered. Or is worth covering. So the agonizing selection process continues. It ends with a final step, as I ask myself—before deciding between two or more choices—what does this *mean* to people? Does it or will it change their lives, their habits, their thinking?

That's the end step in the selection process. After it, covering the story seems almost simple by comparison. And it is relatively simple when it happens at Cape Canaveral. For a major manned space-shot, we're armed with videotape machines, production crews, and switching facilities.

But for every such well-oiled event, there are a dozen back-breakers. Some are just physically trying. The classic case in recent years took place in December of 1961 at America's first underground nuclear blast, testing the peaceful uses of atomic energy. It was before dawn, about 5.30 a.m., on the New Mexico desert, some

35 miles from Carlsbad. The event was called Project Gnome, and it was the first shot in Project Plowshare. A raw wind was pumping 10° air through the thin raincoat I was wearing. (Someone had told me it was warm and sunny in New Mexico!) I'd just finished a film interview with one of America's most famous physicists who assured me that only a slight shock wave would be felt and that no radiation could possibly reach the surface.

Ground Zero was some two miles away, and as the countdown reached zero nothing at all seemed to happen. The famed physicist was in a helicopter orbiting the blast area. The chopper turned tail at about the moment the shock wave lifted me, the camera, and the ground about 12 inches into the air. Through my field glasses, I watched the desert floor at Ground Zero heave some four feet into the air, then fall back abruptly. Just as I was about to tell the cameraman to stop the camera, another physicist (somewhat less famous) tapped me on the shoulder.

"Leave the camera running", he muttered quietly. "You'll get some interesting film." As I turned back to the blast site, a thin plume of steam thickened into a geyser-like flow out of the ground. "It's venting!" somebody shouted. As usual, no official had any explanation, but many phones were picked up by many officials, and suddenly there were warnings that we would have to move out of there like lightning or not be allowed to leave at all.

The radioactive cloud (of low order, it later turned out) moved in our general direction, then veered off to the side. Just as I was about to pick up my film, state troopers closed-in from all directions. "No one leaves", the order went out. And there wasn't even a working phone to call in the story for the ABC radio network. I made a few experimental sallies at the roadblocks, but the troopers heavily outnumbered me. I did glean, however, that I could leave by the road to the north—it was only 100 miles back to Carlsbad that way. I also found out that if I were daring, there was a dirt road across the desert.

So off I went, with another reporter, one eye on the dirt road, the other on the radioactive cloud as it pushed steadily toward us. After two hours, we had gotten completely lost; a few Mexican farmers offered no help; and we were running out of gasoline. Desperately, I took the less likely of two dry-gulch trails and ended up at an old potash mine shaft. It even had a phone, though no one in New York believed me when I called in. After borrowing some gas, I headed off toward Carlsbad, clutching the can of "hot" film (hot indeed, possibly). We passed two more roadblocks, and the troopers waved us on when we told them we were merely lost tourists. "Who me? A reporter? Not a chance. . . . "

Reaching Carlsbad, I found I had a "hot" car; we both got a quick radioactivity count and passed. I had driven through the radioactive cloud, but it had dissipated by then. After battling a snowstorm through the mountains to get out (I had hit a dust storm flying myself in), I reached a jet at El Paso at 4 a.m. and got the film to New York. Meanwhile, back at the press site, everyone else was still trapped.

The moral of this story, other than to always carry a Geiger counter, warm clothes, spare gas, and a good compass, is somewhat vague. But it is roughly this: Scientists can be wrong, too, and part of the adventure of my job is being there when experimental tests do go awry. And even with the degree of failure, the shot—to determine if nuclear blasts deep in salt caverns could be harnessed to produce heat and thus useful energy—was largely successful, though there are a lot of newsmen who remain unconvinced.

For all those storybook launches that take place roughly on time at Cape Canaveral, there are a dozen anti-climaxes when, after waiting-out the soggy night and dripping dawn, the clouds roll in over the Cape and ruin a perfect countdown. Or when the countdown dies at an embarrassing T—6 minutes in a stuck valve or temperamental transistor. It ends then with a tired voice anonymously intoning over the loudspeakers: "Test 6510 is scrubbed."

I've watched them blow, I've watched them go, but the all-time end-all was a test three years ago when I watched the count go beautifully right down to T—0. The firing button was pressed. Nothing happened. The bird just refused to fire up and take off. The only thing lacking was the cartoon ending, where the Test Conductor runs out and kicks the darn thing to get it off the ground.

Many of us still think of a scientist, as differentiated from the space engineer, as being a wild-eyed, wooly-haired character who views with deep alarm anyone calling himself a reporter. I've met only one scientist even faintly resembling that description and, after a brief and bitter struggle, converted him. More often than not, the scientist is a harried, over-worked character, just like yourself, who is eager to tell his story and delighted that somebody thinks it may be of interest to a broader audience than the scientific community.

The "third revolution", as Dr. Glenn Seaborg, Chairman of the Atomic Energy Commission, has so aptly characterized the scientific revolution that is changing both our world and ourselves, has made science itself so complex, with so many different disciplines, that the average scientist himself generally isn't familiar with developments outside of his own speciality. Thus, when asked to reduce his story to its essentials, in language the layman (whatever and whoever *that* may be) can understand, he is generally most understanding and cooperative.

Though I wouldn't have believed it two years ago when I embarked on this mission as ABC's Science Editor, I've since succeeded in getting DNA, the protein building block we're now tracing to our beginnings, explained for a one minute and thirty-second newsfilm spot. In a similar manner, we've managed to treat viruses, and complex aerodynamic principles for new types of aircraft, as well as the far simpler technological developments of our lunar landing technique.

Despite all the frustrations, all the fatigue of running for airplanes, and all the exhaustion of emerging at dawn on too many stories, science coverage can afford moments of rare satisfaction and human drama. Moments that often go unreported, because the television news medium functions far differently than the printed word; our 15-minute nightly news show, in effect, has no page two—only a fast-moving front page.

Of all the moments of satisfaction, probably the most satisfying single event came when I watched a woman regain her hearing in a stapedectomy performed at Polyclinic Hospital in New York. The operation wasn't brand new—the technique of using a miniature TV camera to show it and instruct other surgeons was. We shot our film story, and, as the brief surgical procedure concluded, the chief surgeon leaned over his patient, testing to be sure the tiny tube he'd placed in the ear to conduct sound waves had been properly positioned.

"Can you hear me?" he asked, in a voice hardly above a whisper. The woman on the table, who had been deaf for 20 years, grimaced in pain and then declared, "Please, not so *loud*".

Without question, the biggest reward I've gotten while covering a story—especially since I fly small planes and occasionally bigger ones—was going through the physical qualification tests undergone by our first seven astronauts. Administered at Wright-Patterson Air Force Base in Dayton, Ohio, these consisted, after a rigorous general physical exam, of being whirled at up to 5 g's on a centrifuge; flying weightless in a transport plane and then in an F-100 jet fighter; enduring three hours in a 130° heat room as a test of mental and physical stamina; the cold pressor test—in which your feet, up to the ankles, are immersed in ice cubes; running for ten minutes on a treadmill; and flying "blind" on a violently oscillating "shake" table—a pilot's seat mounted on a gyroscopic motor. The finale was being tossed into a dark isolation chamber for several hours of meditation and then being exposed to head-rocking screeching sound-levels in a noise room.

Not once did I reach for the "chicken switch"—the button to signal that I'd had it, that I couldn't take that particular test a single moment longer. And the tests—as well as working-out later on the training devices used by the astronauts—have, I believe, enabled me to understand the problems of my field the way they should be understood.

In the same way, since I am a pilot, I've tried to ride up front in every current military and commercial jet, and handle the controls for as long as I can. That, as well as spending time with the pilots, enables me to grasp the problems of supersonic flight and stay ahead of the field. If you happen to be devoted to airplanes, what could be better?

It has been claimed by Stuart Hood, Director of Programmes for BBC-TV, that television lacks the ability to convey "higher thought". Hood points out that a newsfilm sequence, for example, may play tricks with "a viewer's visual memory" so that he "retains some striking but irrelevant detail . . . some distracting element".

"There is the danger", he continues, "that by appealing too often and too strongly to the viewer's sense of wonder we may blunt his perception and his ability to marvel at all. Everything has been seen. . . . There are some topics involving logical argument at a very high level which do not lend themselves to the simplifying process basic to mass communications. . . . "

I cannot agree. I believe that the appeal of science—and of

the written, as well as the visual, image in our time—is the constant appeal to the sense of wonder. If we can *perceptively* tell how life is being created artificially, if we can *forthrightly* document man's march into space and under the seas, certainly television will never lack the ability to convey "higher thought". We may not be able to trigger the exact and individual emotional-aesthetic response to be found in the solitary experience of a Beethoven quartet (and where can the "sense of wonder" more often be stimulated?), but we can unquestionably get more people to listen to more Beethoven quartets. Or, having been stimulated by a given event that stirs them alone, encourage people to delve more deeply into it by themselves.

If any of us seriously believe that television lacks the ability to convey "higher thought", then perhaps we'd better examine ourselves and the communications methods and techniques we're using to convey these thoughts. For it is clear that the sense of wonder walks with the spirit of inquiry. Dr. Melvin Calvin, the Nobel Prize winning chemist, as we talked in his laboratory in California where he searches for the roots of human life, expressed it better than I can.

"Why?" I asked, as our cameras rolled in the background, "are you doing this?" Without even pausing, he said quietly:

"I just want to *know*."

And so, I submit, do television's viewers.

30 Science on Television*

GEORGE NOORDHOF

GEORGE NOORDHOF is a free-lance producer of popular science programmes, mostly on ITV. He was responsible for the Dawn University programmes on Anglia Television.†

The part played by television in presenting science to the general public has always been somewhat uncertain. In TV schools and other educational programmes it appears in full flourish. However in evening programmes the amount of science has often been disappointingly small or non-existent if we take Independent Television.

Television's treatment of science—and I exclude medicine from this consideration—has had a long series of ups and downs. In the past it was coloured by a vague feeling in the minds of some programme planners that science, apart from natural history, was too much "nuts and bolts", or at any rate, too complex, too far removed, from ordinary life to be acceptable to the average viewer.

On the strictly presentational level, the typical science programme on television ranges from the talk by the university professor or "expert" with the usual illustrative and demonstrational material, to the situation where an anchor man interviews scientists in the studio or in the laboratory, again with demonstrations, film, captions, etc. Use has also been made of the scientist cum television

---

* SFTA Journal, Winter 1963.
† See article by Joseph Weltman, page 244.

personality who gives a personal assessment or philosophy of some of the wider implications of science. All these approaches have met with varying degrees of success. The programmes which resulted from them have at their best brought the viewer the excitement of scientific research and a greater understanding of scientific method, while at their worst these programmes have either been so superficial as to be largely devoid of any general interest, or have been so advanced as to be only suitable for science graduates.

In fact one of the main problems of science programmes is that of intellectual level. Scientific research is after all a highly specialized form of activity, on the other hand the television audience represents a wide spectrum of intelligence, education and interest. One way out of this dilemma has been to settle for a more specialized audience or at least one which is assumed to have a certain degree of sophistication. Actually there has been a growing tendency to plump for prestige programmes. Such programmes in general devote themselves to major fields of research. They usually have the big names of science, any number of facilities and generous budgets. And although these programmes may at times seem a trifle pompous, in good hands they can bring credit to the production teams and television organizations responsible for them. This is as it should be and no one would quarrel with it. In fact some of the best science programmes are in this category—programmes like the BBC's *Machines like Men.*

But science on television is not only a question of prestige programmes. There must be other programmes—perhaps not quite as spectacular—but which are aimed at the television audience as a whole, not just particular sections of it. During the past years there has been a great deal of talk about the vital need to expand scientific and technological education; scientists and technologists are being wooed from all sides; in fact science is very much in the public eye, while its impact will be increasingly felt in all sections of society. There is no reason therefore why this new spirit should not be reflected in television programmes in general.

What should be the starting point? Well, most people have an inborn curiosity about the things around them, about natural phenomena, about new materials and gadgets, about the working of their own bodies, about their aptitudes, skills and achievements and those of others. This inborn curiosity together with an existing fund of common experience and knowledge can form a jumping off point for science programmes of wide appeal—programmes which can give the average viewer some idea of the inter-relationships between different phenomena, in fact what science is and can achieve. It is this sort of thinking which has contributed so much to the success of the *You'd Never Believe It!* series (ABC-TV). The programme ostensibly investigates the scientific facts associated with sport and show business. It does this by starting from the familiar and the curious and then cutting across the traditional disciplines of science. What's more, specially designed, often somewhat unconventional experiments and demonstrations are used as illustration. The programme is in fact a sort of scientific entertainment. Yet at the same time the material is of sufficient interest to the scientists in the audience who are able to see scientific principles applied to subjects beyond their professional experience. In the past two years this method of presenting science on television has been further developed on the continent of Europe. That this approach has proved effective is borne out by the fact that, for example, in the Netherlands, these programmes are transmitted at peak hours on Saturday evenings. In fact audience research has shown these programmes to be among the three most popular on Dutch television. This then is a programme which appeals to all levels of the viewing public. A fairly obvious example of this multi-level appeal is of course the natural history programme where film or studio sequences showing the behaviour of some animal can interest not only the average viewer but also the professional zoologist as well as the psychologist. Even though the natural history programme is in a sense in a class by itself, it can have some things which other science programmes may often lack. The first is a sense of wonderment, a sense of personal discovery. The viewer can in fact see for himself the behaviour of plants, animals and insects. He is less talked at or preached to. The second is a pleasant absence of unnecessary jargon, or intellectual pretentiousness and pomposity. These can be a real barrier to communication because any successful science programme—or indeed any other programme—must be able to give the viewer the feeling of personal involvement. This personal involvement may even be extended to actual participation as was in fact done in *Science in the Making* series (BBC) some twelve years ago when viewers were asked to take part in mass experiments via television. There are of course limits to the extent to which audience participation can be used. Many topics do not lend themselves to this sort of treatment. Programmes dealing with some fields of science, especially those which are less familiar to the general public, require a great deal of very detailed preparation, if they are to be at all understood. This means a very careful attention to the logical development of the argument, and a due regard to the visual material to be used in illustrating the argument. Clarity and precision are of course of the utmost importance here. Clearly any form of simplification of the subject matter involves the risk of inaccuracies creeping in. A careful check by an expert is no guarantee. Anyway the risk will be with the producer until the end of transmission. A slip of the tongue on the part of the presenter, a faulty or inadequate lead up to an experiment or film, may cause head shakings among professional scientists. Even after everything's gone well and the care taken at every stage of the programme to make an initially complex subject understandable has paid off—are you then home and dry? Not by a long chalk! There will always be someone—generally a non-scientist—who will say that your programme was a bit too elementary. You can't win!

31 Programmes on Anthropology*

DAVID ATTENBOROUGH

THE image of the near-naked dancer, prancing to the beat of drums, is a travelogue cliché. Once it was fascinating—a glimpse of savagery and the unknowable primitive. Now, when it has been staled by repetition, that fascination in people with utterly different codes of behaviour can only be recaptured by an attempt to probe much more deeply into the anatomy of such alien societies. It can only be done, in fact, by explaining something of the findings of anthropology— and this is by no means easy.

The science of anthropology has a vast scope. Many of its branches impinge on older sciences—anatomy, archaeology, comparative technology. These aspects may be handled by modifications of techniques already employed in similar fields by scientific films and television programmes. However, it is social anthropology, the study of human relationships within a society, that has most relevance to our purpose. Little popularizing has been done in this crucial area and if it is to be achieved, new techniques and approaches must be developed.

Unhappily, social anthropology is burdened with a particularly heavy load of jargon. Furthermore, it deals with abstract principles that are difficult to translate into visual terms—kinship bonds, systems of beliefs, mechanisms of government, patterns of social change. Many of the theories that illuminate such concepts may seem

* SFTA Journal, Winter 1963.

abstruse to the layman. Sometimes, indeed, even their relevance may be difficult to recognize. To examine them in a television programme, ethnographic examples are essential and these can only be provided by film.

It is perhaps unreasonable to expect a passing traveller to produce the type of detailed, perceptive film that is required. Too often he has neither the time nor the knowledge to produce anything other than a superficial coverage, and he is seldom aware of the many subtle factors that are the mainspring and formative elements in a particular society. Indeed, the film we need can only be produced by someone with an insight into the findings of anthropology.

There are, however, several reasons why it is difficult for a practising anthropologist to provide such film, particularly if he is expected to do so in the process of his own research. Merely using a camera may hamper him. As an anthropologist he should be an inconspicuous observer whose presence does not disrupt or interfere in any way with the activities he is witnessing. But if he is to make a competent film of, for example, some ritual, he must obtain close-ups and wide-angle shots from several different viewpoints, and to do so may well disturb the participants in the activity he is recording. Worse, his value as a scientific observer may be considerably reduced, for instead of noting every action—and many may be going on simultaneously in widely separated places—his attention has to be distracted by the technicalities of handling his camera, and at crucial moments his eye, instead of being wide-ranging and alert for every detail, must be glued to his viewfinder.

This is not to say that the ciné camera has no place among the tools of the research anthropologist. The functions which it can perform, however, are both limited and specialized. It can, for example, be invaluable in analysing some complicated technique, such as weaving; it can record gestures and facial expressions at defined moments; it can produce a quick record of the identity of people involved in a ceremony and the manner in which they group themselves. But obviously film produced for purposes such as these is unlikely, by itself, to be of much value in a general exposition for the layman.

To produce the film we require an anthropologist must devote himself to the project for some considerable time and allow no other consideration to deflect him. He must be as expert in cinematic techniques and requirements as he is in his own discipline. He must already be familiar with the people he is studying and know precisely what he wishes his film to say before he begins filming. Few anthropologists would regard such work as being the most valuable way of spending their all too limited time in the field.

One or two workers, however, have done so. Jean Rouch has produced vivid and profoundly revealing records of ceremonials in West Africa, and John and Elizabeth Marshall of the Peabody Museum, Harvard University, have filmed many aspects of the life of a nomadic band of bushmen in the Kalahari Desert. These brilliant films are pointers to what can be achieved.

In the absence of such exceptional conjunctions of talents, expository anthropological film could be produced as a co-operative venture between an anthropologist in the field and a film team. Together they could hammer out a shooting script. The anthropologist could introduce the film-makers to the people and, as it were, sponsor them. In return, the film-makers might be able to document certain aspects of particular interest to the anthropologist's research. Such co-operation would necessitate sympathetic understanding of each other's requirements and objectives and would doubtless make heavy demands of patience and tact on both sides. But the results could be outstanding and invaluable.

The subjects tackled need not then be limited to the obviously bizarre elements in a tribal society, such as dances and rituals, which seem so picturesque and significant to the lay traveller. Instead, an attempt might be made to illustrate the much more diffuse but crucial factors such as kinship, economic organization, systems of government and so on, though here it is perhaps over-optimistic to hope that the complexities of these subjects could be conveyed entirely by location filming. Studio exposition, buttressed by the usual techniques of animated diagrams and so on, would be essential.

What is to be gained from such difficult work? It would certainly be possible to impart an understanding of societies organized on a totally different basis from our own. This is a need which is becoming increasingly urgent as the world contracts and as we sadly realize that racial misunderstanding—and its inevitable product, intolerance—remains more widespread and deeply-rooted than we often care to admit. In addition, by the comparative use of film shot in several areas among dissimilar people, we can begin to recognize the factors and compulsions, the necessities and inevitabilities, which operate within all societies of human beings. Thus we may be able to look back at ourselves with a degree of objectivity that can be achieved in no other way. By understanding other societies, we may at last begin to understand the tangled and mystifying workings of our own.

APPENDIX
THE ALLIED ARTS

The Designer's Requirements*

RICHARD LEVIN

JAMES MacTAGGART

DONALD WILSON

LEVIN: What we're all most conscious of is that production for television is governed by the time factor, and this can make conditions very hard for the creative team responsible for producing a play. Play production is increasingly a team job. Committees of people are in charge of the programmes, and it is for these groups that the writers, producers and designers work. At the BBC, the normal procedure is for a script to be put forward by the Script Department,

* *SFTA Journal, Summer 1962.*
Richard Levin, Head of BBC Design, discusses with writer Donald Wilson and producer James MacTaggart the extent to which the writer and the producer should take design into account when preparing plays for television.

Since 1962 there has been a clarification in Britain of the distinction between the terms "producer" and "director". Today the Producer is in the same position as a Film Producer. He is in charge of a single or a whole series of productions; the Director works with him, directs the actors in rehearsal and the cameras in the control gallery. In this discussion, therefore, for Producer we should read Director.

James MacTaggart writes: "The style of the productions for which I have been responsible over the past two years has changed radically. The introduction in the BBC Wednesday Play of a different approach to film (making it significantly cinematic instead of dreary 'telly' inserts) and its subsequent effect on studio camera work has made our discussion out of date. This runs so deeply that tinkering with the present text is pointless. On the other hand insofar as one talks about a play presented completely in the Studio, then I think the discussion absolutely valid. This all adds up to the fact that I can now clearly distinguish a television play which is all invention from a story on television which is based on observation. To the former the discussion is absolutely valid, but the latter now exists and raises a different set of problems."

and, once it has been accepted and becomes a definite project, for a
suitable producer to be assigned to it. It is at this stage that the
Design Department also learns of it; we are told what sort of play it
is and who is to produce it. We then allocate a particular designer
to the production who is likely to be in sympathy not only with the
subject, but with the producer who is to undertake it.

WILSON: From the writer's point of view, this question of design
raises the eternal problem of how far the writer should go towards
thinking of all the details of the final production on the screen. There
are many producers who expect writers to leave them complete
freedom to operate in so far as the details of presentation are concerned. And there are many writers, particularly those who are new,
or comparatively new, to television who have no adequate knowledge
of the complex operation of television production. Most of the
writers now come from outside television. They are in that sense
inexperienced. How can we expect writers in such a position to take
into account everything that's involved in presentation? Unless
you're a writer with actual experience of production, how can you do
more than set down what characters do, and what they say?

However, a trained writer's job, as I see it, is to make his intention absolutely clear to whoever is going to read his script. He must
state what we are to *see* happening, what we are to *hear* happening,
what the actors are to *say*. Beyond that, how much detail should he
provide? Well, I would suggest this should only go to the extent of
indicating what the *intention* is at each moment of the action, and
include those details which are specifically related to this intention.
For example, if a large poster appears in a play, the writer should
say what is to be lettered on it; and he should say precisely where it
is to be, if this is important to the action. Similarly, he should put
down any detail that affects what is happening in the course of the
action or reveals what a character is or does. And this is where the
writer may have to anticipate the nature of the set or some detail
connected with it. If he wants a sequence to be wholly visual, he
must specify what the pictures are to show, and any visual points
that reveal character. But this does not mean he must write elaborate
stage directions. Practical scripts are brief and revealing at the same
time. But if several sets are needed, the writer ought to be aware of
the particular difficulties that are involved in moving actors from one

set to another. Equally he should be aware of the opportunities that television offers, for example in terms of saving time. There is a considerable difference between television and theatrical time, as there is between film and theatrical time.

Once the practical script is written, the experts move in on it, including, of course, the designer.

LEVIN: In practice, the designer seldom comes into professional contact with the writer. He only gets the script after it's been mangled through the producer's mind!

MacTAGGART: Are you happy about that situation?

LEVIN: I think the designer can only deal with one person; he must be given a clear brief. He is concerned with practical things, with creating on a limited budget a series of sets which will make effective pictures on the television screen.

WILSON: Certainly I agree that someone has to make the final decision, and that this man is the producer, not the writer. Furthermore, I'm against a writer producing his own plays.

MacTAGGART: Well, I've a quarrel with this business of letting production procedure settle into a fixed and unalterable groove: script accepted, script adapted, producer appointed, designer appointed.

LEVIN: But surely before he goes to the designer with a script, the producer should have some firm images in his mind to pass over. If he hasn't got these images clear, then he should go to the writer, not the designer, in order to clarify them.

MacTAGGART: But I don't mean clarify, I mean *find* the image best suited to the author's purpose by a process of organic interaction and ideas—not an assembly line where cosmetics are applied to the corpse of the script after it has died. It should be living and changing until it reaches the screen. With the designer involved in this, the pictures have a chance of being essential and emotional, not arbitrary and dull. All right, so the organization collapses if we did this with every show. But if it could happen a few times, writers might be encouraged to get their ideas freed from the strait-jacket of what is believed to be normal television. A little work at the frontier and the centre of gravity might be induced away from plays written out of plays, which are arbitrarily shot in reverse-cutting two shots and the camera always points at the guy whose mouth happens to be open. Visual radio.

WILSON: What you're complaining of is in fact a *theatrical* legacy; it doesn't come primarily from radio. Let's face it, only ten years ago there was no television writing. None at all. The plays televised came almost entirely from the stage; it was these theatrical dramas that set the pace. The writers bred the television play out of the stage play, that is, a dialogue play. The writer for television, like the writer for film, has to free himself from the tyranny of dialogue. To win this freedom, he must be prepared to work with the producer in order to learn how to conceive and write from the start in visual terms.

MacTAGGART: The trouble with television at the moment is that we all tend to accept it as a writer's medium and leave it at that. The producers take their authority from the script. I think, for a while at least, it would be salutary to regard television as a producer's medium, if only to draw attention to the real possibilities that there are in it for the writer. So producers of the world unite; you've nothing to lose but the words!

WILSON: That's all very well. No one could carry out that ideal on the basis of realizing eight shows a year. Contrast a film-maker's schedule, with only one or two films a year, if that.

LEVIN: Don't forget that producers vary. Some work outwards from basic ideas that fascinate them; others are only happy working from the fullest kind of script.

WILSON: Of course there's always the danger in this free for all that the producer falls in love with himself and with the technical gimmicks he exploits at the expense of the writer. But naturally, writing for television isn't just producing words for actors or pictures for producers. Plays are primarily about people, their relationships and their crises, and the writer must use television's full potentialities to reveal this over and above providing the words. But when the producer and designer get together without the writer, the result can only too easily be a misinterpretation of the script. As I've said, the problem for the experienced writer always is: how much detail should he anticipate in his scripts of the kind that the producer and the designer inevitably have to invent themselves when they are landed with a writer inexperienced in television?

MacTAGGART: I want to see the whole thing done as a single creative act right from the start—the writer, producer and designer all working together on the basic idea.

LEVIN: Designers see things essentially in terms of pictures. Some producers are able to anticipate this; they too see their work in terms of pictures from the start. Others simply don't know how they're going to use a set until it's assembled there in the studio ready-made for them. They just aren't visually conscious, and they have to lean heavily on their designers in this respect.

MacTAGGART: But this is an appalling state of affairs. Why send a team of one-legged men to the Olympics? It makes design a kind of insurance policy to cover whatever the director may do with his cameras. Instead of providing backgrounds the designer should be defining space. The space in which the particular action *must* take place. To achieve this everyone must know what everyone else is up to.

WILSON: But we've already seen in the cinema how the original conception of a script can get completely lost through the gradual, corrosive intrusion of so many technical hands. We all know how efficiently experts can kill the writer's original idea, and it's always the basic idea which must be kept alive and fought for.

MacTAGGART: Of course. That's what I'm saying. It's a production team I'm after, who learn to work together and know each other's creative ways. In television, as it is organized at present, you're exceptionally lucky if you're allowed to go on working with the same people for any length of time.

LEVIN: Yes, I agree. Teams are the hub of good television. Team-building should be the ideal, at least for the most fully creative work. But teamwork of this kind would be utterly uneconomic if it were carried through the whole of television.

WILSON: But the best creative writers can't work as part of a team. In the case of adaptations from existing work, of course, it's different.

Everyone knows, roughly speaking, what they've got before they start.

MacTAGGART: To me the problems of the writer and the designer are similar. Since the show will end inside the camera it should begin there, conceived in terms of the axis of shots. If not, the cameras have to be an arbitrary after-thought. We need axial television, not peephole television.

WILSON: All right. I realize, of course, that the fault can lie in the writer producing intractable stuff for the producer. I know that good television can only come from good writing, and that for good writing in this medium it is essential for the writer to realize that what people do is just as important as what they say. If the writer doesn't do this, the producer has to start inventing action for himself, and the chances are he'll invent the wrong action. In any case, it's the action that gives the designer his cue.

LEVIN: Do you see any future for the designer as producer?

WILSON: I think his first difficulty would be handling actors and knowing how to get the most out of their performances. His job in any case would be to use his pictorial sense in order to add to the emotional impact of the drama.

MacTAGGART: Well, I'd like to see a man with a strong pictorial sense risking it as far as actors are concerned.

LEVIN: Let's put it another way. Is there room for a producer who stays down on the studio floor working together with a designer-director sitting up in the gallery, solely concerned with handling, along lines previously agreed, the pictorial presentation of the action through the cameras?

MacTAGGART: I think that's a most interesting idea with which we ought to experiment.

Design for Television*

JAN SCOTT

CHARLES LISANBY

JAN SCOTT

ONE of the most important characteristics in the art of television is movement—mobility of cameras in and around, even through, objects. Each of these camera movements gives to the viewer that magic feeling of being in an invisible cloak, so that he can follow the characters around when they refer to things and, while listening, go over and enquire into the object in question in the greatest of detail.

It is this quality of camera movement that makes designing for TV so very different from designing for the theatre. In the theatre you see everything from one fixed angle—and nothing in detail. The finest artists in the theatre are those who create impressions with big bold strokes; theatrical properties that "get across" the footlights are, when viewed close-to, coarse and unconvincing. But thirty feet away they are magnificent. As close-ups are the most important items in TV, designers spend much spare (?) time filling sketch books and photo files with records of all the little details they see in different locales, streets, etc.—that give them the key to the characters that inhabit those rooms and walk those streets.

The art of TV lies in the use of movement in light and shade simultaneously with light and shade in sound to create a dramatic effect upon the viewing audience. The chief difference between television and the stage is that TV possesses three major qualities unattainable in the theatre. Nor can these three qualities be imitated

* *Television Quarterly, Summer 1963.*

in any other art form, and in the use of them lies the secret of TV. They are:

(a) The possibility of making "close-up" of faces and objects in action in order to achieve emphasis.

(b) The controlled super-imposition of sound over action and vice versa.

(c) The possibility for one artist to control the entire dramatic action and *mise en scène*. When it has reached the perfection required by him, it is permanent. Herein lie the various endeavors of the scenic designer.

CHARLES LISANBY

To be a good designer you have to do things differently. Design is nothing but proportion. The proportions you set—the fact that you have labored with it—makes it yours. When you do what is natural to you—that's your style. And you have to recognize it as yours. It's a fragile creation. Someone says, "Why not cut this out?" But if you do that you lose the artistry, you lose the look. You lose the *style*.

We are always being confronted with the argument that TV design requires less talent than stage designing. The comparisons are always unfavorable—usually beginning when someone says, "Well, that's *television* design". I contend that it is more difficult to do good TV design. We must deal with the small, shifting frame, and yet must still do the same work required of the stage designer. We must create full stage sets as they do, and even the use of video tape doesn't make it less complex.

The designer fights the same battle all creative people must fight in TV. He seeks more recognition for his work. The movie designers long ago gave up their right to fame. Only rarely does one see proper credit for a film designer. He is buried somewhere in the credits with dozens of others. The respect a TV designer earns will, in the final analysis, depend not only on the quality of his work, but on the strength and intelligence of his producer. You have to find a way to fight a massive organization if you seek quality in design.

Styles in scenic design are as diversified and as confusing as a collection of railroad timetables in all languages. Style is an all-production element. Stylization demands consistency in all program phases, from writing to make-up. Much has been written on these phases, and the majority of persons in the TV profession know that these production conceptions are a carry-over from other entertainment media.

The aesthetic effect of a setting is more or less the special touch of the artist in the conception of a production, and in turn shows his peculiar stylistic traits in the execution of scenery. As a factor, it is almost intangible. The work of each designer is immediately identified by special qualities found in his finished settings.

Much of the information the designer needs must be painstakingly extracted from the script, as often the television writer has neither the literary inclination nor the time to write set descriptions. Here the producer, director and designer further unify the script for "business" involving scenery, transitions and other incidental information.

Television designers should not attempt to be too versatile; so many productions fall off because the designer attempted scenes about which he had insufficient knowledge. Although a designer or art director can satisfy most producers with a good design to suit any subject, it is better to get a reputation for being a specialist on certain subjects—there is the appreciation that good designers do not work as automated punch card machines.

Dance on Television*

VALERIE BETTIS

RALPH BEAUMONT

JOHN BUTLER

VALERIE BETTIS

*How well has television served you as a choreographer? What
kind of creative opportunity has it offered you?*

MY TV experience has been both exhilarating and frustrating.
The greatest freedom was afforded me, of course, in the early days of
TV when, with Paul Whiteman, we did 16 programs—on each of
which was offered almost a full 15-minute ballet. It was a musical
format. Because of Whiteman—and because we could get the best
music—it was an exciting experience. We didn't have to stage
around a specific singer or piece of music. I haven't had that much
creative freedom since! A dancer becomes unhappy when he feels
he is not being used properly, or when a producer or director has
some built-in thoughts about what dancers are trying to do. Then
you may get the old argument that "the audience won't understand".

But it's not all one-sided. Speaking as a choreographer, I feel
that most of the directors with whom I have worked are very much
aware of the relationship between what you are trying to do and how
they can help you. They are appreciative if the choreographer knows
something about how to employ the camera. The difficulty is that
there are too many choreographers who know nothing about the
"camera eye" and how distinct it is from the head-on proscenium
stage idea. The most vital experiences I've had in TV dance have
come when the director has had some knowledge and appreciation
of what we were attempting and used the camera in relationship
to that.

* *Television Quarterly, Summer 1965.*

Why, do you suppose, are there no regular weekly series presenting this material?

Primarily because of TV's economic structure. Dance, like musical comedy, requires production. We have all encountered the problem of the advertiser—who knows the present size of audience for the dance but cannot logically support the costs of production. The return would be too small. And there is such a large gap between what ETV and commercial TV can do. The ETV people haven't enough money to really do justice to the dance. It would be pleasant if there were some middle-ground between the extremes.

I may sound pessimistic, but I have never known any serious artist—in any of the performing arts—to get anywhere at all unless someone, whether from a network or elsewhere in the industry, who is really interested in advancing the art took hold of his ideas and saw that they got exposure. I don't believe an audience will suddenly materialize for dance on TV. There may be a growing awareness of dance in this country, but an audience will not simply come forward and say, "We must have dance on television". This situation will improve only if there is direction from the other end—when a sponsor or network or group of stations begins to make greater use of dance. Dance is a product that has to be sold. That's the law of mass media and it must be observed.

Let's turn, then, to the considerable amount of dance which does get on TV, ranging from work on Shindig, Hullabaloo, *and occasional works on such shows as Ed Sullivan's, and the more serious efforts on programs like* Camera Three *and the* Bell Telephone Hour. *Where can improvement be sought? What new ideas can be initiated?*

Choreographers are notoriously independent, but it might be well for them to seek more understanding of what the TV director faces. This is a technical as well as creative problem to be overcome. What is more necessary is that we strive for recognition of dance as a form of theater. There is, to me, a fantastic supply of American literature that can properly be handled only with dance and speech. Dance must be regarded as a form of poetry, and not just as spectacle or divertissement. This narrative form of dance might be the best way to develop the larger audience for the form. It has plot, story line, and a point of immediate focus and interest. Dancers have this kind of flexibility today—they are more total performers. If we look at the dance on the musical-comedy stage now, we can see that there is not a dancer around who does not do singing and speaking work. Even ballet people today are fine actors. If we try to work away from snips and cuts for background color or action, we may have a better chance of building a great TV audience for serious dance.

Is some of this being done now?

Of course, but as I pointed out earlier, this work is created out of older work. Even in ETV, most of the dance programs which are planned are of works already made. Since ETV has limited funds, it is to their advantage to record a work that is already choreographed—in some cases already fully mounted. Production work is thereby avoided. Original production comes only when you take a work already made and entirely rework it for the medium.

It is important that we start the process *fresh* in television. We think too much in the reverse order—just as when stage plays were taken before the early motion picture cameras with no thought of creating fresh for the film medium. And the fault is not all TV's. Often our finest choreographers fail to think about television as a distinct medium. They fail to consider how it can reshape "dance thinking".

Of course the ideal would be to have networks regard dance in the way they approach music, and create and support a dance company as they would orchestras or opera companies. The group itself would constitute the format, and while you could range over the established works you could also bring new, exciting choreography to the medium. I think the day will come when networks will begin to add this phase to their support of culture. They are getting into the theater, and the next step is into the other performing arts. All of it is available—the talent, the interest.

What you are suggesting, then, is that the industry enter into a subsidization of the dance as a worthy performing art until it can attract audiences on its own.

If we are to get new work and emerging forms, yes. The analogies already exist. Since opera became "respectable", ballet is being increasingly accepted. The contemporary dance is being given more attention in the community, even though interest in it was developed largely in the colleges. Touring companies cannot foster this kind of development. Most of the companies that go out today must be smaller (again economics!). They are limited to smaller works. Even Martha Graham cannot afford to tour with big productions. All of the companies can tour around the world if they get support from Government, but until we finally accept the idea that you can't always judge the product by how much money it makes we will not expand the art.

That's where TV could do wonders. TV can bring about a state of national familiarity with dance and its serious purposes better than any other medium. If music had not profited from recording, that whole booming development within our culture would have been slowed to a standstill. Dance must exist visually—on a stage, or in films and on TV, but it is primarily TV that can change the American attitude toward dance.

And you feel this cannot happen in existing circumstances?

Not easily. We are still seeking the new, the serious and the experimental, but the need for audience is difficult to ignore. I recall being asked to dance to Duke Ellington. This is great in its way, but there is no Ellington, including even Duke's largest symphonic works, that I want to dance to. As a dancer I would be neither one thing nor another—not creating something fresh or serious and also not creating just entertainment. That is frustrating. I was expected to make into something popular a phenomenon which doesn't lend itself to that approach.

Perhaps what I am saying is that television owes the dancer—as a serious performing artist—the best possible conditions for creative expression. All that is being done is good, and we are grateful for it, but like all artists we need more outlet, more room to let people sense our contribution.

JOHN BUTLER

Has TV fairly presented and represented dance as a performing art?

UNFORTUNATELY, the calibre of dance exposed on TV is not always what it might be. This is a serious fault, but the graver fault is the way in which time and talent are wasted in bad viewing hours. There have been works that used a full company of dancers, a full symphony orchestra, and earned plaudits from some fine critics, but were seen by almost nobody. They were put on from 10.00 to 11.00 on Sunday morning, and no one saw them, even though they were serious and exciting projects. I know some good things do get into choice viewing times, but they are not commissioned works. One of the few evening programs that does try to do serious material is *Bell Telephone Hour*, but it has been pointed out that this is not work commissioned for television. It is stage presentation brought before the cameras. And I think it is nearly impossible to take a large scale piece and make it work for camera unless you re-choreograph from the outset.

I am pessimistic about the future of serious dance as a major factor in TV programming. I used to have the conviction that an audience's appetite for good dance would begin to grow and that TV would feed it. Only a few years ago—when we first did *Amahl*—such things were an instant public success. Things like *Omnibus* and *The Seven Lively Arts* were around to feed a taste—but over the years, one by one, they have disappeared. It's not right, because there have been remarkable talents and great productions. The history of the Sunday morning shows makes it obvious that you can get any artist to work for you if he respects the program. Once you give someone a completely unrestricted commission you can get the best to work for you—and for little pay. It isn't snobbery that causes so many to turn away from the medium. Everyone has changed his mind about appearing on TV. It is just that the prime-time dilemma scares so many of them. They feel lost and unable to use their full creative powers. They want to do more than they are asked to do.

How do you react to TV as compared to stage or film?

Perhaps I speak for most dancers and choreographers when I

say that TV is sometimes incomprehensible to us. I am excited about the medium or I wouldn't have stayed with it so long. Even if I didn't like it, I suppose I would go on doing entertainment shows to earn my rent money, and shut up. But I still do the Sunday morning kind of show. I still accept original commissions—and I stay enthusiastic. But all of us are lost in a business world, I think. Except in our craft, we are not disciplined people, and we do ourselves great harm by each going off on his own private tangent and complaining and wailing about things we do not understand. The best thing for all of us is to keep at our work, and hope for the best.

RALPH BEAUMONT

In what ways could dance on TV be improved in technique?

I THINK the dance would be more understandable, and more satisfying, if choreographers were able to call camera shots themselves. If they are working with someone who knows what to do, it's a great help. But this is not always enough. When I choreograph for television I become the camera. I know what the shots are, where the camera is, and where it will be next. Too often you'll find a director with his own ideas, and he may miss the point of the action completely. Some will sit across the studio and never study the action closely. I have had directors, particularly overseas, who can bring life to numbers that would otherwise be boring with tricky camera work, but they can also destroy some very fine things. The choreographer should know what he wants and try to get it.

When I choreographed for Italian TV I saw a lot of experimentation with the camera. But it began to become corny—just a phase. Some of the shots were interesting, when used well and with taste. Putting the camera in the pit, for example—right at the dancer's feet—creates interesting effects. In one case a back-stage camera was used, and you saw dancers rushing from the wings to get into position. It gave the program a kind of "backstage at the *Folies Bergère*" flavor. You saw people rushing up and down the stairs, taking up position on the floor, and so forth. Sometimes I think Italians are overly conscious of women's backsides, but except for some doubtful shots, this camera work did add a dimension to the show.

I'm looking forward to the possibilities of dance in color on American TV. If a number is considered great in a studio it will come out brilliant in color. Color increases depth, which is vital in a space art like the dance. Life is color. The theater is color, and that's as it should be. All dance numbers should be seen in color.

But I ought to qualify my enthusiasm for techniques generally. Certainly TV can allow a kind of presentation the proscenium cannot. You can go to four sides instead of one. You can take a camera in a circle around action—all around it, under it, and above it. But I am not really inclined to admit that TV has advanced the form of dance. I've seen little that is different from musical shows. I can't think of an instance when I've seen any dance on TV that has not previously been seen on the stage or in night clubs. Perhaps the dances of ethnic groups might be an exception, but that applies only to audiences outside New York. My family sees very little dance except what TV brings to them, and consequently they are impressed with the June Taylor dancers. They would also be impressed with Radio City Music Hall dance. But the New Yorker would find that hardly novel. The camera makes new technique possible. It makes it easy to put over a small piece of business. It aids in giving dance a narrative thread. It can give dance a flow that the movies cannot provide—but I don't think it has really introduced new forms at all.

Of the media, then, you would not choose TV as best for your work?

I prefer the theater. Television has given me good training—and taught me how to work fast. I would like to do occasional work on TV, but the thought of 26 weeks is like a sentence to Sing Sing. Perhaps it's the restriction in time that's placed upon you in TV. In Italy, for example, neither time nor money seemed to be a problem. I was able to use 35 dancers for a show there, and that number of dancers is unheard of here. I could say to the set department: "I want 18 columns and a 40-foot staircase for this number", and get it. In America you must think of cost probabilities before you even begin to plan a number.

I am a union member, but I think we have begun to throttle the creative purpose. I think some unions must begin to backtrack, and re-evaluate their importance. American dancers are the best trained I have seen, but so many other unions have beat them to the punch that they earn nowhere near their worth. It has become a habit, after everyone has gotten in his claims upon the people doing the show, to reduce the number of dancers. There must be so many stage-hands, so many electricians, so many musicians—but no one who speaks for the dancer says, "You must have 20 dancers". I am in favor of everyone making a living, but I think it has gotten out of hand. Before I became a choreographer, I often thought that even dancers were asking for the wrong things. Something has been lost sight of.

The Forgotten Art: Music for Television*

PAUL WESTON

THE move from the motion picture or recording field into television can be a depressing experience for a composer, director, or arranger. He has come to expect an effective set-up, whereby the orchestra is properly spread out for good balance, but discovers in television that the musicians are huddled into an incredibly small corner of the studio. The trombone player must exercise reasonable care each time he extends his slide. Violinists are packed together like musical sardines, and a wandering bow can easily cause a permanent eye injury. If the conductor is particularly aggressive—or if musical stars happen to have some concern about how they sound, then a half-hour may grudgingly be allowed for purposes of gaining audio balance. If the time cannot be spared, the audio man (who is huddled in a booth of woefully inadequate size) fights the battle alone, hoping that orchestrations will not be too thick and that the singer will project sufficiently to prevent orchestral spill into the boom microphone. The show goes on, and if the sound has even half the quality a hi-fi listener might demand of his own phonograph, an enormous victory has been won.

Any conductor who shies away from the television medium for these reasons is depriving himself of a rich experience to be found nowhere else in show-business. The conductor who has spent much time in television soon finds recording and motion pictures rather

* Television Quarterly, Spring 1962.

tame and unexciting by comparison. As in so many other facets of television creation, the fight is rough, but the victory offers twice the sense of accomplishment and satisfaction that might be gotten in the clean, well-ordered recording studio. Further, the leisurely pace of the motion picture industry provides nothing comparable to the challenge of the TV "special", where the music must be arranged in three days, rehearsed in three hours, and balanced in three minutes.

But challenge of itself has no virtue unless there is a sense of accomplishment—a feeling that real progress has been made in the difficult task of bringing order out of chaos and quality out of the conditions that prevail. Television music has had a long history, and the significant strides which have been made ought to be catalogued here.

Since the earliest days of network television, many musical directors have tried to introduce some of those techniques which were successfully used in motion pictures and in recording studios. Their job has been made more difficult as a result of the "nobody-cares-what-it-sounds-like-as-long-as-the-picture-is-good" syndrome which has taken hold of so many industry people. Yet, many of the techniques which were ridiculed in 1952 are considered standard procedure today.

Pre-recording is perhaps the most important musical technique which has evolved in television. The artist or group records the musical number in advance of the program and then mouths the words while the recording is played during the actual airing of the show. Although this is customary procedure in motion pictures, many performers in television resisted it for a variety of reasons. Some performers were simply unable to synchronize their actions with their pre-recorded voice track. Others lacked the patience required to listen to the recording long enough to remember what had been done. A few probably honestly believed that the *immediacy* of "live" performance was more important than good sound.

No one would deny that for a slow ballad, which can be shot in close and thus permit the boom microphone to be kept fairly near the artist's head, a live rendition is to be desired. The singer is free, and with proper orchestration the sound will be perfectly adequate. Trouble will normally occur in rhythm and production numbers; the artists must move freely, and the rhythm is naturally heavier. It is then that the band sounds may spill into the performer's microphone and drown out the singer. The most unpleasant effect comes when the listener can actually hear two drum and two bass beats—one coming directly into the orchestra microphones and the other coming a fifth of a second later, after it has crossed the stage and been picked up in the performing area. No matter how good the picture may be in this case, the listener will feel uneasy about what he is *hearing*, and the situation must be made right at the outset.

An additional technique has been developed over the years, despite its taxing effect upon the conductor's emotional system. This technique involves putting the orchestra in a different studio and having the singer's voice piped through earphones to the conductor while the orchestra is piped through speakers into the studio. If the singer can get used to working with speakers, which can be brought much closer to him than the orchestra itself, the effect will be excellent. There are no lags in sound, and no double bass and drum beats to worry about.

It is naturally safer to have two TV monitors and two headsets (both on separate circuits) at the conductor's desk, for if either a monitor or a headset fails to work during the show, panic and disaster will set in quite readily. This is one of the hard lessons those in TV music have learned over the years.

There is still another technique for improving quality. If the artist does not wish to pre-record a rhythm tune or a production number, the orchestra track *only* may be pre-recorded for playing in the studio while the performer sings live to this accompaniment. This procedure obviates concern about muddled sound or double orchestra pick-up.

One of the more exciting technical advances has come in the use of the radio microphone. Microphones concealed on the person of the singer broadcast a signal to be picked up in the control room. The problems of the boom microphone are thus eliminated. When radio microphones first came into use, there were a few exciting and confusing moments, as when a police call might suddenly join the singer's voice on the air. Now that equipment has been refined, these accidents no longer occur.

Technical achievements notwithstanding, the best sound can still be obtained by placing the microphone in full view of the audience, right in front of the singer. This is good old fashioned radio-style balance. For a long time it was considered very bad form to permit the microphone to be seen, but this taboo has been relaxed somewhat lately as a result, perhaps, of the very effective Perry Como medleys, which gave clear indication that the best sound treatment in television may lie somewhere between radio and motion picture approaches. Naturally, if a boy is singing a love song to a girl, the visible microphone would be distracting, but the "visible mike" taboo should be relaxed in other areas as time goes on.

Technical problems are frequently less trying than human problems. Of all those artists who make the television conductor's life a merry one, the "bar-skipper" is the worst. This peculiar breed of performer may simply skip a bar or a few beats without notice, leaving the conductor and a very confused orchestra behind. The situation must be caught immediately to prevent complete collapse.

The simplest and most effective solution to this problem may be to force the performer's retirement from show business, but the impracticality of this solution is apparent, for some of the biggest singers in the business are "bar-skippers". A more practical solution is to provide the pianist with a set of earphones. Then, when the "bar-skipper" goes into his act, the conductor can wave out the band, have the pianist "radar in" on the errant vocalist, and let the band come in when the pianist and the singer are flying together. Since most of the "bar-skippers" are well known to the musical fraternity, fore-warned is fore-armed.

Beyond the technical proficiency that has been accumulated over the years, what genuine accomplishments can television music point to, and what future achievements can it expect to attain?

Music for television has had a difficult time in holding its own. Under the tyranny of ratings, a musical show can have an audience of fifteen million people and still be judged a failure. Glowing reviews do not often help. Producers of musical and musical-variety programs often are forced to design shows of studied mediocrity, with the hope of creating a large enough segment of the viewing audience. Frequently this effort to boost ratings brings into musical programs singers and dancers who would provoke catcalls in any high school production, if they were to be judged only by their musical talent. So long as such performers deliver ratings, the quality of their performance is never questioned; this condition alone has wrecked more "specials" than any other single factor.

But it would be unfair to say that there have not been distinguished contributions in the field of musical television. Among the triumphs are the Leonard Bernstein music lectures *in toto*, the songs which Cahn and Van Heusen wrote for the Frank Sinatra production of *Our Town*, and the Henry Mancini scoring for *Peter Gunn*. It was the latter which really drew our attention to television scoring and which led to a decided improvement in the quality of most subsequent scoring of background music for the medium. The same Mancini *Peter Gunn* scoring heralded the first important use of jazz in television backgrounds.

Although jazz has been our only real American art form, it has yet to enjoy the kind of presentation on television which it enjoyed in recordings and radio. On those rare occasions when television has offered jazz, the success has been instantaneous. It is impossible to estimate the contribution made to the first Fred Astaire program by David Rose's jazz backgrounds and the carefully developed audio balance, but many of those who happily tapped their feet—and later voiced noisy approval—were aware that they had witnessed not only an incomparable performer, but had been treated to the proper use of music on television.

In the late '30s and early '40s, when the era of big bands gave us a pronounced quality of jazz in popular music, American popular music prospered. This era gave to the world the great standard songs which are being recorded over and over again in albums today. The current shocking state of our popular music should be a source of concern to everyone involved in any entertainment medium, whether it be radio, motion pictures, recordings, or television. The quality of this music can be improved only when we recognize the moral responsibility involved and work together for improvement.

In the days of radio's greatness the task was easier; cost factors were not so dominant then. A radio network could carry sustaining shows featuring fine music and good instrumentalists, but a television network could hardly be asked to devote hours of prime time in order to raise single-handedly the standards of American music. Nevertheless, an industry-wide effort is needed to do something about the state and condition of popular music. Television, because of its enormous impact on our culture, could provide the means whereby some improvement is made.

To be sure, we should not expect the average television viewer to exclaim aloud, "Listen to that wonderful balance!" or "Boy, is that jazz band ever swingin'!" Still, there can be no doubt that these elements make a major contribution to an effective television program; the viewer has just as much right to expect them as he has to expect lavish sets, beautiful costumes, and well-rehearsed choreography. Only when the producer budgets money for time-consuming audio balance with the same degree of attention that he gives to non-musical items, will the viewer be given the rare opportunity to see and hear how great a musical show can be.

Those who have some responsibility for the future development of the television arts can make major contributions in two areas. First, they should look into the state of our popular music and see what efforts can be made to improve its quality and impact upon our own nation and upon the world at large. Next, they can give greater recognition to the fact that television requires the use of two senses, both sight *and* hearing, and insist that the latter be given proper attention, if only for the sake of the audience.

The American public's appreciation of hi-fi and stereo sound recordings is a certain indicator that listeners have become accustomed to better sound reproduction. Television can no longer expect its proper share of entertainment time, attention, and money from this public unless it is willing to take a long, hard look at the way in which TV music is presented.

Biographical Notes

Contributors:

THE JOURNAL OF THE SOCIETY
OF FILM AND TELEVISION ARTS

David Attenborough

Born London, 8th May 1926.

Educated Cambridge: Natural Sciences Tripos. Joined BBC as trainee producer 1952. Responsible for travel and exploration programmes 1955–64. Controller BBC-2 1965.

Programmes include: *Animal Vegetable Mineral*, *The Crossing of Antarctica*, *Travellers Tales*, *Adventure* (producer), *Zoo Quest* (production and appearance).

Cyril Bennett

Born London, 23rd April 1928.

Former newspaperman. Joined Rediffusion Television as writer/producer 1956. Producer *This Week* 1961. Executive Producer (Public Affairs and Documentary) 1963. Director of Programmes 1965.

Richard Cawston

Born Weybridge, Surrey, 31st May 1923.

Educated Oxford. Joined BBC Television 1947 as film editor. From 1950–54 Producer of Television Newsreel. Since 1955 has specialized in producing documentary films. In June 1965 appointed Head of Documentary Programmes, BBC Television.

Programmes include: *This is the BBC, On Call to a Nation, The Lawyers, Television and the World, The Schools, The Pilots, Born Chinese.*

Tom Courtenay

Born Hull, 25th February 1937.

Actor.

Films include: *The Loneliness of the Long Distance Runner, Private Potter, Billy Liar, King and Country, Operation Crossbow, King Rat, Dr. Zhivago.*

Sir Geoffrey Cox

Born Palmerston North, New Zealand.

Educated Olago University, New Zealand and Oxford. Entered television industry in 1956. Editor of Independent Television News, London. Knighted 1966. General Election programmes 1959, '64, '66.

Rosalie Crutchley

Born London, 1921.

Actress.

Films include: *Sons and Lovers, No Love for Johnnie, Greyfriars Bobby, Girl in the Headlines, The Haunting.* Television includes: *A Winter's Tale, The Franchise Affair, Cradle Song, Galileo, The Count of Monte Cristo, The Executioner* (1966).

Robin Day

Born London, 24th October 1923.

Educated Oxford. President of the Oxford Union Society 1950. Barrister, Middle Temple 1952. BBC radio producer 1955. Independent Television News 1955–59 as Newscaster, Interviewer and Parliamentary Correspondent. BBC Television since 1959 as commentator and political interviewer.

Programmes include: *Panorama* (BBC TV) and numerous political and topical programmes, e.g., *Gallery, People to Watch*, 24 *Hours, Election Forums* 1964 and 1966, and many special programmes.

John Elliot

Born Reading, England, 1918.

Educated University of London (King's College). Wrote and directed documentary films 1945–49. Staff of BBC TV 1949–64. Film, documentary and drama writer and producer. Seconded to staff of United Nations 1955–56. Since 1964 free-lance writer.

Programmes include: *War in the Air* series 1954–55, *The Golden Egg* 1958, *High Fidelity* 1958, *A for Andromeda* 1960, *Andromeda Breakthrough* 1961. Producer *Sunday Play* and *First Night* 1962–64, *Hunt the Man* and *The Truth Game* 1964, *Mogul* 1965, *The Troubleshooters* 1966.

Kenneth Fawdry

Born Clifton, Bristol, 8th March 1914.

Educated King's College, Cambridge. Teacher in Classics and Modern Languages at Christ's Hospital, Malvern College, St. Marylebone Grammar School 1937–48. Assistant Lecturer, London University Institute of Education 1946–48. Senior Education Officer, Schools Broadcasting Council for the U.K. 1950–59. Head of Schools Television, BBC 1959 to date.

Paul Fox

Born 27th October 1925.

Via Newspapers and Newsreels to BBC Television in 1950. Television Newsreel, Editor *Sportsview* 1954, and other sports programmes, Editor *Panorama* 1961, Head of Public Affairs Programmes 1963, Head of Current Affairs Group, BBC TV 1965.

Programmes include: First *Sportsview* 1954, *Sports Special, Grandstand, Panorama* (1961–63), *Olympic Games* 1960, various current affairs special programmes, including first television broadcast from Moscow, first "Telstar" broadcast from New York and first "Early Bird" broadcast between Europe and North America. Co-Editor General Election Results Programmes 1964 and 1966.

Lewis Greifer

Born London, 19th December 1915.

Writer. Entered industry in 1954.

Films include: *The Man Who Finally Died, The Ruffians, The Gold Inside*. Television includes: *Ghost Squad* (Story Editor), adaptation *The Pinedus Affair*, individual episodes *Ghost Squad*, etc.

John Grist

Born Southampton 1924.

Formerly editor of *Gallery*, now Chief Assistant, Current Affairs programmes, BBC Television.

Dilys Hamlett

Born Hampshire.

Educated Old Vic Theatre School. Actress. Played Miss Julie in Edinburgh 1953, two seasons with the Stratford Memorial Theatre Company, West End in *Passage to India, The Miracle Worker, Peer*

Gynt and *Measure for Measure* at the Old Vic. Television appearances include: *A Question of Guilt, Women of Troy, The Assassins, Hedda Gabler.*

Antony Kearey

Executive Producer and Head of Plays, Rediffusion Television 1965. Previously Executive Producer/Director for ATV Drama. Entered industry on television side as drama director on the High Definition System.

Richard Levin

Born London, 31st December 1910.

Educated London University College. Industrial Designer. Designer, Festival of Britain Travelling Exhibition. Head of Design, BBC TV 1953 to date.

James MacTaggart

Born Glasgow, 25th April 1928.

Educated Glasgow University (M.A.). Forces Broadcasting 1948–49. Actor 1950–56. Producer Sound Radio 1956–57. P.A. BBC TV Glasgow 1957–59. Director BBC TV since 1960 including two years as Producer, culminating in *Wednesday Play* series 1965. Now directing again. Some writing. Director: *Storyboard* 1961, *Studio* 4 1962 and many other singles, *The Boneyard, The Portsmouth Defence* 1966. Producer: *Teletale* 1963, *Wednesday Play* 1965.

James McCloy, D.F.C.

Born Liverpool, 11th April 1914.

Educated Liverpool University (B.Sc.Hons.). After RAF Bomber

Command became more interested in the communication of science than in research. Became producer in sound radio 1948. Television science producer Talks Department BBC TV 1954. Now senior producer in the new department of Further Education Television.

Frontiers of Science series 1954–57, *Inventors Club* 1955, *Science Review* 1954–56, *A Question of Science* (magazine programme) 1957, *Science is News* 1959, 500 *Million Years* 1958, *Life Before Birth* 1960, *Man in the Making* 1960, *The Science of Man* (50 programmes 1963–65).

Robert McKenzie

Born Vancouver, Canada, 11th September 1917.

Educated University of British Columbia (B.A.), University of London (Ph.D.). Teacher of Political Sociology at London School of Economics 1949 to date, and Broadcaster on Current Political Subjects for BBC since same date. Currently with BBC TV 24 *Hours*, General Election broadcasts, *Gallery* 1960–65, etc.

David Mercer

Born Wakefield, Yorkshire, 27th June 1928.

Educated Durham University (B.A.Hons.). Teacher 1956–63. Writer. Programmes include: *Where the Difference Begins* 1961, *The Buried Man* 1962, *A Climate of Fear* 1962, *A Suitable Case for Treatment* 1962, *A Way of Living* 1963, *The Birth of a Private Man* 1963, *For Tea on Sunday* 1963, *And Did Those Feet* 1965.

Andrew Miller Jones

Born London, 1910.

Educated Oxford (M.A.). Since November 1957 in charge of the Television Section of BBC Staff Training Department and responsible for courses in all aspects of television production, including the producers' use of film. Devised and launched *Panorama* in 1953. Produced and edited the programme until 1955.

Christopher Morahan

Born London, 9th July 1929.

Educated Old Vic Theatre School. Worked in theatre before going into TV in 1955. Director for ATV 1957–62. Free-lance since then— worked for BBC and ABC TV, and has largely been associated with Drama on BBC-2 since 1965.

Programmes include: *Emergency-Ward 10* 1957–59, *Probation Officer* 1959–60, and numerous plays including *John Gabriel Borkman* (ATV), *The Devil on Sunday*, *The Man*, *The Long Distance Blue*, *Rosemary*, *The Slaughtermen*, *The Hooded Terror*, *The Orwell Trilogy* on BBC-2, *Progress to the Park*, *A Game Like—Only a Game*, *A Month in the Country*, *Z Cars*.

Peter Morley

Born 1929.

Joined Rediffusion Television in 1956 after eight years of documentary film-making as film editor, writer and director. Producer of *This Week* from 1961–63. Now senior producer and director for Rediffusion Television.

Programmes (full-length documentaries) include: *The Two Faces of Japan, Tyranny—the Years of Adolf Hitler, Israel Rises—a Nation in the Making, Heartbeat of France, Defeat in the West, A Son of Liberty, Black Marries White—the last Barrier, LSO—The Music Men*. On behalf of Independent Television the five-hour outside broadcast programme of The State Funeral of Sir Winston Churchill. Presently producing a 13-part documentary series on the Life and Times of Lord Mountbatten.

Sydney Newman

Born Toronto, Canada, 1st April 1917.

Commercial and Fine Artist, Documentary film-making for National Film Board of Canada under John Grierson—credits on over 350 films, Canadian Broadcasting Corporation 1952, as OB Director then

Head of Drama in 1954—General Motors Theatre, On Camera, etc. ABC Television England as Head of Drama and Producer of *Armchair Theatre* 1958. BBC TV as Head of Drama Group 1962.

George Noordhof

Born Bloemendaal, Netherlands, 19th February 1922.

Graduated in Metallurgy at Imperial College of Science, carried out postgraduate research in Physical Chemistry at Cambridge. Producer Science television programmes BBC 1951–55, TV Consultant to Shell International Petroleum Co., Scientific Film Department National Film Board of Canada, Free-lance CBC/TV, returned to Britain 1959 and free-lanced for ABC TV, Rediffusion, Granada, Anglia TV, Tyne Tees TV, as writer-producer-presenter of programmes. Recently producer-director-writer-presenter for Dutch TV programmes.

Inventors Club, Science Review, Science in the Making 1951–55, *Tomorrow is Now* 1957–59, *Story of Industry, Story of Medicine, Science and Understanding, You'd Never Believe It, Round About 6.15, Dawn University* 1959–63.

David Robinson

Born Lincoln, 6th August 1930.

Educated King's College, Cambridge. First job as assistant to Basil Wright. Subsequently journalist—at various times assistant and later associate editor *Sight and Sound*, Editor *Contrast* (now defunct). Currently film critic *Financial Times*. Works frequently both for radio and television.

Norman Swallow

Born Eccles, Lancashire, 17th February 1921.

Educated Keble College, Oxford. Features producer BBC Radio 1946–50. Documentary writer-producer BBC TV 1950–57, Assistant

Head of films BBC TV 1957–60, Assistant Editor *Panorama* 1960–63, free-lance writer-producer-director since 1963.

Programmes include: *An American Looks at Britain* (series) 1951, *Places with Problems* (series) 1952, *Special Enquiry* (series) 1952–57, *The World is Ours* (series) 1954–56, *Panorama* 1960–63, *A Wedding on Saturday* 1964, *The End of a Street* 1964, *This England* (series) 1965–66.

Arthur Swinson

Born St. Albans, Hertfordshire, 11th May 1915.

After war service, mostly in the Far East, began writing for the theatre. After production of a comedy *The Bridge of Estaban* in 1949 invited to join BBC as writer and producer. Stayed for 12 years, working first in radio and then in television. Has some 140 credits in each medium. Resigned in 1961 to free-lance. Since then has written plays, features, documentaries and series episodes for both radio and television. Has also written nine books—three of them on television, three in the field of military history and two on medical subjects. Has just finished a history of the North-West Frontier of India.

Aubrey Singer

Born Bradford, Yorkshire, 21st January 1927.

BBC TV Producer since 1949—some 100 programmes. Worked in BBC New York office 1953–56. Became interested in science programmes in 1957. Now Head of Science and Features, BBC TV.

Don Taylor

Born London, 1936.

Educated Oxford. In television 1960–65, then free-lance to concentrate on stage work.

Programmes include: *The Generation* (trilogy) 1960–62, *A Suitable Case for Treatment* 1962, *For Tea on Sunday* 1963, *And Did Those Feet* 1965 (all written by David Mercer), *The Train Set* 1960, *Summer, Autumn, Winter, Spring* 1961, *The Winter's Tale* 1962 (all BBC). Latest stage work: *Fanny's First Play* 1965, *The Philanderer* 1966.

Ken Taylor

Born Bolton, Lancashire, 10th November 1922.

Educated Old Vic Theatre School. Work in theatre management. Began full-time writing in 1956 for television and films. Now writing new TV trilogy, *The Magicians* for BBC-2.

Programmes include: *One of Us* 1957, *China Doll* 1960, *The Long Distance Blue* 1961, *The Slaughtermen, Parkin's Primitives* 1962, *Into the Dark, The Tin Whistle Man* 1963, *The Devil and John Brown* 1964, *The Seekers* (trilogy) 1965.

Joseph Weltman

Born Manchester, 19th October 1910.

Educated Cambridge and Tubingen. Teaching 1933–40. RAF 1940–46, BBC 1947–60, Granada Television 1961–63, ITA 1963 to date.

Donald Wilson

Born Dunblane, Scotland, 11th September 1910.

Educated Glasgow School of Art. Journalist, film script-writer, film production manager, Army (1939–45), film director and producer, television writer. Head of Script Department BBC TV 1955–63. Head of Serials 1963–65. Senior Producer 1966.

Programmes include: *The Six Proud Walkers* 1954, *Dead Easy* 1957, *Flight of the Dove* 1958, *No Wreath for the General* 1960, *The Royalty* 1957, *The Intervener* 1961, *Hornblower* 1963, *Rupert of Hentzau* 1964, etc.

Contributors:

TELEVISION QUARTERLY,

THE JOURNAL OF THE NATIONAL
ACADEMY OF
TELEVISION ARTS AND SCIENCES

Minna K. Barnett

Teacher in the Secondary Schools, New York City. Assigned by New York City Board of Education to New York State Regents Educational Television Project 1960–61. Former John Hay Fellow, Columbia University.

Ralph Beaumont

Born Pocatello, Idaho, 5th March 1926.

Dancer and choreographer. Choreographed stage productions in New York, London and Italy. Arranged productions at Brussels World's Fair (1958) and New York World's Fair 1964–65. Danced in many motion pictures and major TV variety shows.

Jules Bergman

Born 21st March 1929.

Began news career in 1948 with *Time* magazine, writing in fields of medicine, science, religion. Is presently Science Editor, ABC TV, responsible for coverage of major space shots and science program production.

Programs include: *How Safe is Flying?*, 60 *Hours to the Moon, The Big Bomber Battle.* Books authored include: 90 *Seconds to Space* and *Two for the Sky.*

Valerie Bettis

Born Houston, Texas.

Dancer and choreographer. Has appeared in television, motion pictures, Broadway and off-Broadway productions. Ballets, dance-theatre works and concert tours. Honors include citation for "Best Choreography on Television" and Two Donaldson Awards.

Ray Bradbury

Born Waukegan, Illinois, 22nd August 1920.

Writer. Best known for such science-fiction novels as *The Golden Apples of the Sun* and *Fahrenheit* 451. Among screenplays are *Moby Dick*, in collaboration with director John Huston. Among series for which he has television script credits are *Alfred Hitchcock*, *Twilight Zone* and *Alcoa Premiere*.

John Butler

Born Memphis, Tennessee, 29th September 1920.

Director, choreographer and dancer. Actively involved in TV choreography since the early 1950s. Has choreographed and danced in productions throughout United States and Europe.

David Chandler

Writer. Has published three novels and written several screenplays. Television scripts produced on *Zane Grey Theatre*, *The Third Man*, *Convoy* and *Hogan's Heroes*.

Fielder Cook

Born Atlanta, Georgia, 9th March 1923.

Producer and director. Associated with Franklin Schaffner in the

Directors Company, which produced dramas for *DuPont Show of the Week* (NBC TV). Directed feature-length film, *A Big Hand for the Little Lady*, for Warner Brothers. Produced and directed film, *Flight and Pursuit*, for National General Productions.

Hugh Downs

Born Akron, Ohio, 14th February 1921.

Television personality and program host. Began TV career as host of the Arlene Francis *Home Show* (NBC TV) in 1954 and was announcer for *Caesar's Hour*. Appeared with Jack Paar's *Tonight Show* from 1957 to 1962, when he became anchor man on NBC TV *Today Show*.

Rowland Evans, Jr.

Born White Marsh, Pennsylvania, 28th April 1921.

Newspaper reporter and columnist. Worked for New York *Herald-Tribune* and Associated Press before becoming a syndicated columnist in 1963.

Reuven Frank

Born Montreal, Quebec, 7th December 1920.

Television journalist. Named Vice-President, NBC News in 1966. Prior to association with NBC in 1950, he was Night City Editor of Newark *Evening News*. News Editor of *Camel News Caravan* 1950–55. Producer, *Background* 1955. Executive Producer, *The Huntley-Brinkley Report* 1956–65. Also produced NBC News television coverage of 1956, 1960 and 1964 Political Conventions and Elections, as well as *The Chet Huntley Reporting* series.

Lewis Freedman

Born New York City, 13th February 1926.

Producer, director, program executive. Producer of *Camera Three* (CBS TV) 1956–57. Produced over 40 *Play of the Week* productions and 13 dramas for *DuPont Show of the Week*. Named Director of Programming New York's Educational TV Station, WNDT, in 1965.

Lou Hazam

Born Norwich, Connecticut, 3rd January 1911.

Documentary writer and producer. Began career as radio free-lance writer. Joined NBC as writer of *Home is What You Make It* and *Living* series. TV writing-production credits (all for NBC TV) include *The March of Medicine* series; individual productions: *The Way of the Cross, The River Nile, Shakespeare: Soul of an Age, U.S. #1: American Profile, Greece: The Golden Age, John F. Kennedy Remembered, The Capitol: Chronicle of Freedom,* and *Michelangelo: The Last Giant.*

Don Hewitt

Born New York City, 14th December 1922.

Former newspaper editor and war correspondent. Joined CBS TV in 1948. Has served since as producer and director for CBS TV daily evening news programs. Was Senior Producer for coverage of the National political conventions. Produced, for all three networks, the first Kennedy-Nixon Debate. Is currently Executive producer for CBS News.

Gordon Hyatt

Born Springfield, Massachusetts, 12th November 1934.

Documentary Producer. Joined staff of WCBS TV in New York City in 1961. Is currently Senior Staff Producer for the station's documentary unit. Among programs written and produced are various documentaries devoted to architecture and planning. Titles: *La Vie Elegante*, *A Question of Values*, and *The Responsive Eye*.

Sheldon Leonard

Born New York City, 22nd February 1907.

Producer, Production Executive. Began career on Broadway as an actor. Performed on major radio network comedy series. Joined the Danny Thomas Television program as director in 1953, and was later named Producer-Director. Formed T. & L. Productions with Thomas and became Executive Producer of *The Andy Griffith Show*, *Gomer Pyle, USMC*, *The Dick Van Dyke Show* and *I Spy*.

Charles Lisanby

Born Princeton, Kentucky.

Designer. Has designed settings for major TV programs. Created scenery, costumes and lighting for both Broadway and off-Broadway productions.

E. G. Marshall

Born Owatonna, Minnesota, 18th June 1910.

Actor. Began career with a Shakespearian Company in early 1930s. On Broadway, he appeared in such plays as *The Iceman Cometh*, *Waiting for Godot* and *The Crucible*. Motion picture credits include *The Caine Mutiny* and *Compulsion*. Has appeared in several TV productions, and was co-star of *The Defenders*.

Paul Monash

Born 14th June 1917.

Writer and producer. Numerous TV and motion writing-production picture credits. Executive producer of *Cain's Hundred*. Adapted *Peyton Place* into a continuing series, and became Executive Producer when series was first aired in 1965. Has written two novels.

P. Kenneth O'Donnell

Born Worcester, Massachusetts, 4th March 1924.

Public servant. Was Assistant Counsel, U.S. Senate select committee on labor-management relations 1957–59. Appointed a special assistant to President Kennedy 1961.

Carl Reiner

Born New York City, 20th March 1923.

Actor, writer, director. Began career during World War II, touring Pacific in GI revues. Appeared in Broadway musicals in post-war years. Joined Sid Caesar in *Your Show of Shows* 1950. Most recently writer and director-producer with *The Dick Van Dyke Show*.

George Schaefer

Born Wallingford, Connecticut, 16th December 1920.

Drama director and producer. Broadway credits include *Write Me a Murder* (producer-director) and *Teahouse of the August Moon* (co-producer). Formed Compass Productions in the 1950s to produce *Hallmark Hall of Fame*. Responsible for production of over fifty major dramatic works for television.

Franklin Schaffner

Born Tokyo, Japan, 20th May 1920.

Director. Associated with Fielder Cook and Jacqueline Babbin in The Directors Company. Directed original dramas for *DuPont Show of the Week* (NBC TV), including *Big Deal at Laredo*, *The Shadowed Affair* and *Two Faces of Treason*. Directed *The Stripper*—a feature motion picture for Twentieth Century-Fox.

George C. Scott

Born Wise, Virginia, 18th October 1927.

Actor. Began professional career in roles for the New York City Shakespeare Festival and off-Broadway Productions. Among motion picture credits are *Anatomy of a Murder* and *The Hustler*. Has appeared in such TV productions as *The Power and the Glory*, *The Picture of Dorian Gray* and the CBS TV series, *East Side/West Side*.

Jan Scott

Born Chicago, Illinois.

Scenic designer. Began TV work in Chicago, designing for such programs as *Garroway at Large* and *Kukla, Fran and Ollie*. Joined NBC TV in 1954. Network credits include *Peter Pan*, *Big Deal at Laredo*, several *Hallmark Hall of Fame* productions.

Barry Trivers

Writer. Has written nearly 40 screen plays and almost 100 TV scripts, for such series as *Naked City* and *Slattery's People*. Is president, TV-Radio branch, Writers Guild of America.

Mike Wallace

Born Brookline, Massachusetts, 9th May 1918.

Television journalist. Began *Nightbeat*, a nationally televised interview series, in 1956. Has covered national political conventions, built news staffs for New York TV stations. Is presently anchor man for daily *CBS TV Morning News with Mike Wallace.*

Paul Weston

Musical composer, arranger, conductor. Has released more than 20 orchestral albums. Popular compositions include *Day by Day, Shrimp Boats, I Should Care.* Among serious compositions are *Crescent City, The Bells of Santa Ynez* and *Mass for Three Voices.* Was founder and first president of The National Academy of Recording Arts and Sciences.

Tom Wicker

Born Hamlet, North Carolina, 18th June 1926.

Journalist. Former Nieman Fellow. Worked for the Winston-Salem *Journal*, Nashville, *Tennessean.* Joined Washington Bureau of *New York Times* in 1960, and is now Bureau Chief. Has authored novels and books of non-fiction.

Subject Index

Name and Programme Title Index

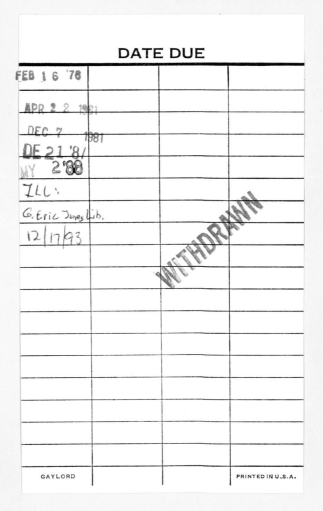